Dr. Gerd Heuschmann
BALANCING ACT

—— The Horse in Sport ——
An Irreconcilable Conflict?

Translated by Coralie Hughes

TRAFALGAR SQUARE
North Pomfret, Vermont

First published in the United States of America in 2012 by
Trafalgar Square Books
North Pomfret, Vermont 05053

Printed in China

Originally published in the German-language as *Balanceakt: in dubio pro equo* by Wu Wei Verlag, 86938 Schondorf, Germany, 2011

Disclaimer of Liability
The author and publisher shall have neither liability nor responsibility to any person or entity with respect to any loss or damage caused or alleged to be caused directly or indirectly by the information contained in this book. While the book is as accurate as the author can make it, there may be errors, omissions, and inaccuracies.

Trafalgar Square Books encourages the use of approved riding helmets in all equestrian sports and activities.

ISBN: 978-1-57076-529-2

Library of Congress Control Number: 2012936951

Photos: pp. iii, xiii, 25, 51 *right and left*, 55 *middle*, 56, 61 *left*, 74, 104, 105, 178, 181 (Christina Wunderlich); p. 97 (Barbara Ebner); p. xviii (Manfred Leitgeb); pp. 2, 10, 31, 32, 40, 62, 63, 81, 84 *left*, 99, 130, 132, 184, 188 (Private Archive Heuschmann-Lütgendorf); pp. 3, 4, 12, 17 *above right and below*, 18, 19 *middle below and right*, 20, 38, 60, 61 *right* , 67 *right*, 77, 93, 97, 103, 126, 139, 191, 193 (Maximilian Schreiner); p. 5 (CP Pferdefotografie); p. 9 *Kseniya Abramova*, 113 and 174 *montego6*, 195 *Anita Zander*, 206 *Foto LS* (fotolia); pp. 7 and 90 *Michael Brandl*, 15, 17 *above left and middle*, 39 *Marck Rühl*, 46 *Horst Streitferd*, 48, 170 *middle*, 200 *Julia Wentscher*, 90 *Holger Schupp* (Horses In Media); pp. 21, 111 (Candida von Braun); pp. 23, 41 (Julia Petersen); p. 26 (Gabrielle Boiselle); pp. 30, 86, 96, 207 (Barbara Schnell); pp. 33, 35, 42, 49, 50, 52, 53, 58, 73, 80, 84 *right*, 129, 145, 154, 171, 176, 210 (Kathrin Hester); pp. 37, 56, 75, 79, 82, 117, 138, 146, 151, 185, 187, 202 (Anke Panzner); p. 45 (Gerald Gattinger); pp. 55, 67 *left*, 166, 170 *left*, 203 (Valentina Goeck); pp. 71, 87, 144, 201 *above* (Ernst W.); pp. 128, 149 (Eva Potocnik); pp. 156, 159, 167, 169, 196 (Gabi Schürmann); p. 36 (from the film *If Horses Could Speak* by Dr. Gerd Heuschmann); p. 180 (Sibylle Wiemer); p. 227 (Horst Becker); p. 224 (Dr. Fritz-Endoskope u. Videosysteme—www.dr-fritz.com Swissvet/USA); p. 218 (U. Helkenberg); p. 208 (Tanja Richter from *Illusion Pferdeosteopathie*, Wu Wei Verlag); p. 198 (Info Jelinski); p. 112 (Archive Spanische Hofretschule); pp. 55, 170, 177, 183, 190, 193 *(every effort was made to locate the photographer, who will be credited in a future edition of this book should he make himself known to the publisher)*

Illustrations: pp. 81, 109 *below left*, 186, 200 (Kaja Möbius); pp. 64, 70, 107, 109 *above right*, 116 *above*, 117 *below right*, 118, 119, 123 *below right*, 124, 125, 134, 141, 142, 152, 161, 142 *above right* (Sue Harris); p. 123 *below left*, 175 (Dr. Gerd Heuschmann); p. 122 (Pixomondo, Wu Wei Verlag); pp. 116 *below*, 123 *above*, 130, 162 (from *Große Teieranatomie* by Gottfried Bammes, Wu Wei Verlag); p. 174 (Stefan Stammer); p. 215 (from *Richtlinien* Book 1, FN Verlag); p. 213 (from *Marginalien für Pferd und Reiter* by Waldemar Seunig, Wu Wei Verlag); p. 211 (Deutsches Pferdemuseum, Verden); pp. 113, 174, 201 (variation of the figure by Michael Strick in *Denksport Reiten,* FN Verlag)

Interior design by Christine Orterer
Cover design by RM Didier

10 9 8 7 6 5 4 3 2 1

DEDICATION

Dedicated to all those who like me—or not!

My wife Johanna Heuschmann LÐtgendorf, Her Royal Highness Princess Haya Bint Al Hussein, Isabella Sonntag, Hardy Martins, Thies Kaspareit, Dr. Klaus Miesner, Anky van Grunsven, Sjef Janssen, Isabell Werth, Klaus Balkenhol, Michael Putz, Dr. Astrid von Velsen Zerweck, David de Wispelaere, Peter Krein¬berg, Frédéric Pignon, Christine Felsinger, Gabriele Pochhammer, Siegmund Friedrich, Christine StÐckelberger, Dr. Werner Schade, Hannes MÐller, Melanie Tschöpe, Markus Waterhues, Caroline Hat¬lapa, JÐrgen Kemmler, Christina Wunderlich, Sandra BÐrgel, Johann Riegler, Kathrin Roida, Alexandra Kuehs, Siegrid Leichtl, Susanne Til-kowski, Karin Wiesner, Gabi SchÐrmann, Arthur Kottas Heldenberg, Dr. Robert Stodulka, Prof. Dr. Christine Aurich, Prof. Dr. Jörg Aurich, Corinna Lehmann, Michael Geitner, Dr. Thomas Ritter, Peter Pfister, Hans Peter Schmidt, Roland Moore, Vera Protzen, Anja Beran, Steffi Martens, Hans Heinrich Isenbart, Dominique Barbier, Luis Valenca, Dr. Filipe Graciosa, Bernd Richter, Dr. Ludwig Christmann, Dr. Friedrich Marahrenz, Dr. Michael DÐe, Susanne Schmitt Rimkus, Anabel Balken¬hol, Ulla Salzgeber, Matthias Alexander Rath, Christoph Koschel, Nadine Capellmann, Carola Koppelmann, Helen Langehanenberg, Anna Katharina LÐttgen, Anja Plönzke, Dorothee Schneider, Ellen Schulten Baumer, Gina Capellmann LÐtkemeier, Kristina Sprehe, Brigitte Wittig, Sabrina Finke, Anja Bornhöft, Annabel Frenzen, Kathleen Keller, Louisa LÐtt¬gen, Carolin Nowag, Guido With, Eckart Mey¬ners, Petra Hachmeister, Tatjana Klein, Ute Grindl, Petra and Reinhard Römer, Melanie Marek, Svenja Peper, Katja SÐß, Prof. Hans JÐrgen FlÐgel, Sanneke Rothenberger, Katalin Garrn, Florine Kienbaum, Jonas Schmitz Heinen, Lena SchÐtte, Dr. Evi Eisenhardt, Uwe Mechlem, Dr. Volker Moritz, Dr. Dieter SchÐle, Götz Weber Stephan, Rolf Beutler Bath, Angelika Frömming, Walter GÐnther, Volker Hahn, Dieter Krönert, Heinz Lem¬mermann, Dr. Josef Knipp, Friedrich Hermecke, Franz Karl Peiß, Gott¬hilf Riexinger, Katrina WÐst, Uwe Spenlen, Dr. Heinrich Zapp, Hans Joachim Eitel, Peter Engel, Dr. Rudolf Fuchs, Martin Richenhagen, Holger Schmezer, Reinhard Seim, Gert Stumme, Peter Holler, Dr. Dietrich Plewa, Klaus Ridder, Richard Hinrichs, Ilja van de Kasteele, Eva Maria Recker, Aline MÐller, Julia Schay Beneke, Annegret Strehle, Volker Camehn, Hans MÐller, Jörn Dwehus, Amos Kotte, Dr. Heiko Meinardus, Wolfgang Burkhardt, Klaus Peter Grunert, Monika Schaaf, Alexa Dormeier, Thorn Twer, Susanne Posch, Frank Horns,

Ulrike Bletzer, Katharina Schön, Petra Lahnstein, Walterpeter Twer, Christopher Pilger, HSM a.D. Karl Freye, Judith Balkenhol, Breido Graf zu Rantzau, Dieter Graf Landsberg Velen, Theodor Leuchten, Gustav Meyer zu Hartum, Rudolph Erbprinz von Croy, Peter Hofmann, JÐrgen Laue, Thomas Hartwig, Christoph Hess, Gerlinde Hoffmann, Georg Ettwig, Friedrich Otto Erley, Dr. Nikolai von Bre¬vern, Rainer Reisloh, Thomas Ungruhe, Dr. Joachim Wann, Reinhard Wendt, Carsten Rothermund, Frank Ostholt, Antonio Moreno CalderÐn, Manuel Méndez Parejo, Antonio Diosdado Galán, Manuel Vidrié GÐmez, Francisco Javier García, Alvaro Domecq Romero, Elisabeth GÐrtler, Mag. Erwin Klissenbauer, Fabian Scholz, Dr. Dirk Remmler, Dr. Augusto Fernandez, Peter Breitner, Brigitte Hofmann, Marie Luise von der Sode, Dieter Hölscher, Uwe Kröll, Wolfgang Kutting, Susanne Ridderbusch, Karin LÐhrs, Ursula Scholtz, Andreas Werft, Renate Elberich, Christina Barofke, Johannes Beck Broich¬sitter, Georg W. Fink, Martin Fink, Alfons Friedberger, Christiane Horstmann, Friedhelm Petry, Holger Schulze, Dieter Spiess, Hans Tegelmann, Kurt Albrecht von Ziegner, Dr. Doris Wendt, Dr. Peter Guyot, Bruno Vogel, Sigrun Stark, Agnes KÐh¬lechner, Gerhard Ziegler, Christian Abel, Michael Hohlmeier, Dr. Peter Danckert, Nicole Schwarz, Walter Kind, Renate Schmolze, Franz Peter Bockholt, Klaus Martin Rath, Ro¬bert Kuypers, Dr. Burkhard Dittmann, Hans-¬Joachim Begall, Albrecht Hertz Eichenrode, Erika Putensen, Jörg Maier, Ilja Waßenhoven, Hanno Vreden, Klaus Blässing, Karl Heinz Groß, Andreas Lorenz, Erika Ihlau, JÐrgen Laue, Heidi Hame, Matthias Karstensen, Wolfgang Brinkmann, Hans JÐrgen Meyer, Eckhard Wemhöner, Joachim Geilfus, Elke Miemietz, Miriam Abel, Karl Zingsheim, Thomas Schiller, Dr. Juliette Mallison, Michaela Lenartz, Dr. Jan Holger Holtschmit, Ina el Kobbia, Friedrich Steisslinger, Kurt Pfannkuche, Jochen Schu¬macher, Manfred Raichle, Jacqueline Schmieder, Monika Hohlmeier, Helmut Kannengießer, Peter Fröhlich, Dietmar Dude, Kai Haase, Klaus Oetjen, Klaus Peter Zahn, Dr. Klaus Lemcke, Friedrich Witte, Rolf Peter Fuß, Dr. Peter Ritter, Ernst Ehrmanntraut, Klaus Altmeyer, Ralph Hartung, Reinhard Brähne, Dieter Medow, Matthias Karstens, Erlfried Hennig, Marion Irmer, Claus Bergjohann, Jörg Maier, Dieter Doll, Franz Lauster, Manfred Weber, Georg Ochs, Dr. Hartwig Tewes, Wolfgang Jung, Horst von Langermann, Dr. Ingo Nörenberg, Manfred Schäfer, Dr. Thomas Nissen, Dr. Manfred Köhler, Uwe Witt, Wilhelm Weerda, Heiner Kanowski, Dr. Wolfgang

DEDICATION

Schulze Schlep¬pinghoff, Paul Schockemöhle, Ulrich Kasselmann, Martin Spoo, Karl Heinz Bange, Hans Willy Kusserow, Wolf Lahr, Norbert Freistedt, Dr. Matthias Karwath, Uwe Mieck, Petra Wilm, Lars Gehrmann, Dr. Peter Allhoff, Ulrike Struck, Diether von Kleist, Ahmed Al Sam¬arraie, Peter Pracht, Klaus Vössing, Ulrich Seuser, Dr. Georg Oeppert, Dieter Bösche, Dr. Uwe Clar, Hans Heinrich Stien, Dr. Elisabeth Jensen, Dr. Kai C. Otte, Claudia Sirzisko, Joachim Völksen, Volker Hofmeister, Kurt HillnhÐtter, Klaus Biedenkopf, Florian Solle, Egon Wichmann, Mareile Oellrich Overesch, Eckart Ohnweiler, Hans Britze, Hans JÐrgen Förster, Dr. Hinni LÐhrs Behnke, Ruth Klimke, Dr. Hanno Dohn, Dieter Stut, Gabriele Heydenreich, Renate Herzog, Dr. Wilma Ubbens, Klaus Harms, Dr. Andreas Meyer Landrut, Dr. Hanfried Haring, Soenke Lauterbach, Hans JÐrgen Armbrust, Dr. Jan Hein Swagemakers, Heinrich Hermann Engemann, Klaus Roeser, Jonny Hilberath, Dr. Cordula Gather, Uta Helkenberg, Adel¬heid Borchardt, Dr. Dennis Peiler, Carsten Rohde, Dr. Lutz Körner, Dr. Matthias Gräber, Maria Schierhölter Otte, Hans Heinrich Meyer zu Strohen, Dr. Alexander Merz, Dr. Michael Dahlkamp, Heidi van Thiel, Lars Meyer zu Bexten, Dr. Thomas Januszewski, Dietmar Gugler, Dr. Matthias Niederhofer, RÐdiger Schwarz, Wolfgang Leistner, Dr. Hilde Skowronek, Sabine Abt Achtert, Rosina Jennissen, Dagmar Sauer, Susanne Bösche, Hugo Matthaes, Ulrich Wulf, Friederike Fritz, Thomas Sagkob, Lutz Rensch, Heinrich Ohlig, Meike Jakobi, Mareike Roszinsky, Almut Frank, Ernst Bachinger, Bettina Treiber, Gabriele Kaczmarek, Simone Hahmeier, Jean Claude Dysli, Heide Kröber, Dr. Anita Schade, Familie Max Theurer, Gerhard and Inge Heuschmann, Rainer and Heidi Heuschmann, Anna, Lisa and Christian Heuschmann, Andrea and Victor Baltus, Dominique, Melissa and Florian Baltus, Katja Jordan, Fabian Heuschmann, Erika and Otto Kolb, Peter Heer, Jutta Klewitz, Prof. Kurt Mrkwicka, Diana WÐnschek, Michael Seletzky, Mag. Nora Poschalko, Mag. Marina Kronaus, Johanna LÐtgendorf, Philipp LÐtgendorf, Prof. Dr. Dr. Ro-bert Prantner, Dr. Johanna Prantner, Alexandra LÐtgendorf, Philipp Percig, Thomas Prantner, Mag. Petra Mödlhammer Prantner, Moritz Prantner, Michael Ripploh, Fran Ripploh, Patrick Kittel, Andreas Helgstrand, Catharina Lippert, Edith Großekosmann, Do¬rothee Fernandez, Heiwi Reckhorn, Marion and Peter Jennissen, Martin Plewa, Ingrid Klimke, Paul Stecken, Hubertus Schmidt, Sandra Bartels, Inken SchlÐter, Dr. Werner Jahn, Dr. Eberhard SchÐle, Annette von Hartmann, Sandy Mooney, Ginny Elder, Linda Hoover, Nicola Stauder, Jana Steffen, Steffen Peters, Jennifer Conour, Andrea Jähnisch, GÐnter Seidl, Thomas Haag, Sebastian Frisch, Teresa Dornbusch, Antje Kerber, Barbara Schulze Rieping, Bettina Anhut, Moni Meiners Pils, Marianna Castro, Peggy Cummings, Melissa Sims, Davi Carrano, Carla Omura, Charlotte Bottermann, Dirk Weber, Elmar Lesch, Josef Kirchbeck, Annegret Kirchbeck, Dr. Heinrich Bottermann, Emily Baker, Nic and Ali Cooksen, Gillian and Shirley Higgins, Frank Gerding, Florentina Mortsch, Frank Wohl¬horn, Frank Peters, Helmut Korte, Marc Schaffetter, Petra Herrmann, Hermann Vollmers, Hubert Brinkmann, Cord Meiners, Dr. Albrecht Fenner, Daniela Grönke, Alexandra Mellert, Kai and Ulrike Keller, Andrea Andrighetto, Jana Mahrer, Katrin Weisgerber, Maria Mevert, Martin Kramer, Dr. Michael Nowak, Nils Kjaergaard, Nicole KÐnzel, Hans GÐnter Winkler, Debby Winkler, Pamela Belitz, Dr. Ulrich Wendelberger, Susanne Bucher, Michael Puhl, Rosita Dangmann, Sita Jenkner, Sophie, Jenkner, Silvia and Reinhard Voll, Iris Kleber, Saskia Schmitt Schillig, Thomas Kischlat, Frank Große Venhaus, Ursi Kaelin, Uwe Wessendorf, Daniel Hofstatt, Willy KrÐmpel, Dr. Marlene Zähner, Dagmar Orio, Prof. Heinz Meyer, Andrea Neven, Andrew Murphy, Dr. Annette Wyrwoll, Angela Paltram, Anna Millne, Anne Schmatelka, Heinrich Wilhelm Johannsmann, Fritz Johannsmann, Arlyn Desico, Prof. Arthur Grabner, August Deitermann, August GrÐndker, Dr. Werner Baakmann, Beatrix Schulte Wien, Birgit Beck-¬Broichsitter, Kirstin Becker, Monika Behrens, Ann Kathrin Linsenhoff, Beth Boumer, Dr. Kalle Blobel, Roland Blum, Carsten Bollert, Stefan Borgmann, Joris Naumann, Jens Brockmann, Dr. Axel Brockmann, Jochen Schleese, Dr. Sascha BrÐckner, Clemens BrÐggemann, Heinz BrÐggemann, Christian Carde, Marek Buck, Caroline Larrouille, Christian Först, Linda Christie, Clemens Heider, Conny Enders, Christina Drangel, Greg Eliel, Dr. Elke and Dr. Wolfgang Pschorer, Fam. Ziegelwallner, Fatma Ormeloh, Frida Hess, Knut Giersemehl, Gil Merik, Gonzales Soares, Silvia GrÐnewald, Eberhard Schneider, Helle Kleven, Jean Bemelmans, Joana Fisher, Johannes LÐckmann, Regina Johannsen, Dr. Josef Kastner, Julie Taylor, Kaja Möbius, Karen Ososki, Karen Link, Katrin Meyer, Kristin Oschee, Arno Lindner, Manolo Mendez, Manuel Parache, Maureen Rogers, Hans Melzer, George Morris, Fa. Neumeister, Nina Stadlinger, Jörg Oeppert, Pam Lane, Peer Waaler, Burkhard Wahler, Birgit Popp, Prof. Willeke, Rika Schneider, Prof. Sabine Kliesch, Dr. Eberhard Senckenberg, Ebbi Seemann, Dr. Isabell Fiebiger Heuschmann, Stefan Stammer, Stefan Remmel, Steffi Strobel, Elke Stegemann, Prof. Sue Dyson, Sue Harris, Dr. Sybill Moffat, Sybille Wiemer, Sylvia Loch, Tom BÐttner, Tomek Twardowski, Tony Haßmann, Angelika Trabert, Susanne Trantow, Uli Bäcker, Uwe Lukas, Wilhelm van Gunst, Dr. Veronika Wiedemann Stahl, Peter von Eckhard, Waltraud Weingarten, Linda Weritz, Dr. Wolfgang Matzner, Wolfgang Eder, Andreas Hausberger, Herwig Radnetter, Harald Bauer, Jochen Rothleitner, Rudolf Rostek, Christian Bachinger, Herbert Seiberl, Marcus Nowotny, Marius Schreiner, Florian Zimmermann, Helmut Oberhauser, Florian Bacher, Phillip Burg, Florian E. Zimmer¬mann, Hannah Zeitlhofer, Christopher Egger, Mathias Krenmayr, Agnes St. George, Kevin Staut, Meredith Michaels Beerbaum, Rodrigo Pessoa, Rolf Göran Bengtsson, Billy Twomey, Ludger Beerbaum, Ser¬gio Álvarez Moya, Jeroen Dubbeldam, Malin Baryard Johnsson, Simon Delestre, Philipp Weishaupt, Edwina Alexander, Christian Ahlmann, Luciana Diniz, Denis Lynch, Lars Nieberg, Harrie Smolders, Pius Schwizer, Simone Deitermann, Andreas Dibowski, Michael Jung, Andreas Ostholt, Kai RÐder, Anna Warnecke, Sandra Auffahrt, Marina Köhncke, Julia Krajewski, Kai Steffen Meier, Julia Mestern, Dirk Schrade, Anna Siemer, Peter Thomsen, Benjamin Winter, Bettina Hoy, Beeke Kaack, Robert Sirch, Ina Tapken, Sabine Deperade, Freya FÐllgraebe, Franka LÐdeke, Jana Weyers, Henning WÐrz, Bea Borelle.

CONTENTS

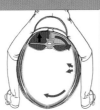

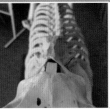
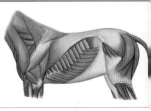

 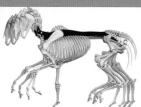  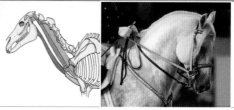 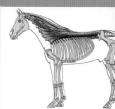

FOREWORD
by Sabine Neumann

Books can't change the world, but they can demonstrate where abuse is happening and inspire new ways of thinking. That is what Dr. Gerd Heuschmann accomplished with his highly regarded first book *Tug of War* (Trafalgar Square Books, 2007). A veterinarian, Dr. Heuschmann first completed professional horsemanship training (*Pferdewirt*), then received the Stensbeck medal. For many years he has devoted himself to horse-friendly training methods and has pleaded for a dialogue with advocates of other ways of riding. As the leading opponent of forceful methods, he crusaded against "Rollkur" and criticized the leaders of equestrian sport. He wrote open letters to the FEI (Fédération Equestre Internationale), the German Equestrian Federation (Deutsche Reiterliche Vereinigung), and the German Association of Judges (Deutsche Richtervereinigung). In February of 2010, he traveled to Lausanne with about 41,000 signatures against Rollkur. The FEI meeting passed a resolution disapproving aggressive training methods.

Above all, Dr. Heuschmann has made a name for himself as an expert in the field of biomechanics. For some time this veterinarian has offered practical seminars for horse-and-rider pairs with problems. He has been criticized for some of these: There is disagreement as to whether it makes sense to sit on a horse needing retraining in public; anyone who does so runs the risk of looking bad on resistant horses. Experienced riders and trainers know that a 20-minute demonstration will not alleviate training deficiencies and the consequences of poor riding. But one can take the first step in the right direction.

Dr. Heuschmann succeeds in demonstrating solutions focusing on how a horse can be encouraged into a horizontal balance and how the rider can find rhythm, suppleness, and contact with his horse. Although his manner of riding appears unconventional at first sight, it is about basic work. And in that context, it makes absolute sense. Only when the basics are present can harmony develop, which we riders all cherish as the feeling of happiness on horseback.

In reality, it is precisely the basic training that is frequently neglected. It is common practice for training barns to ride horses in side reins and experiment with various and sometimes very sharp bits to "put on the brakes." Also sharp spurs and long whips are part of the daily "weaponry" of many riders in order to renew the horse's desire to go forward—the desire he has lost. Many riders never experience having a horse in front of the leg, to have the impulsion come through his body to their hand, with the horse reacting sensitively to a shift in weight and connecting with them through the seat. The beautiful dream of happiness on the horse's back remains an illusion.

On the other hand, there are times when many riders come to the conclusion that they have a completely stiff and tight horse. Perhaps even a horse that is no longer willing, or even strongly resists and is uncontrollable. Even more discouraged are those whose horse has a lameness that can't be helped by any veterinarian or therapist and for which there is no apparent cause on either ultrasound or radiographs. As a consequence, many riders sell their horse and get a new one. Others turn their four-legged partner out to pasture and stop riding. Still others make the pilgrimage from veterinarian to veterinarian, from physiotherapist to physiotherapist, from riding teacher to riding teacher, from saddler to saddler, from farrier to farrier, from stable to stable—always in hope that someday he will be better. Many of these horse owners land in Dr. Heuschmann's seminars or in his veterinary practice.

In our highly technical and industrialized world, there is a merciless competitive drive. On one hand, our life is marked by the thoughtless treatment of ourselves and the resources of the earth. On the other hand, outdoor sports, wellness, and "biofoods" are booming. Perhaps the longing for nature, balance, and "authenticity" lead more people to horses and to riding. Nevertheless, the riding world is no island of the blessed, but rather a mirror of our society and its difficulties. At the extremes, our horse sport shifts between the hunt for medals and being a petting zoo. On one hand, horses are treated as a piece of sporting equipment or merchandise. On the other, they are personified and molly-coddled. In the process, the horse himself gets lost.

This book doesn't deal with training alone, but also with horsemanship and horse welfare. Dr. Heuschmann leaves no doubt that the good of the horse must always be the primary focus when handling and riding horses. It is not only a balancing act to stay physically balanced on the horse's back, it is a much larger balancing act to attempt to do justice to the nature of the horse as a flight and herd animal while requiring performance from him. Dr. Heuschmann's critical reflections on competitive and pleasure riding are an important contribution to steer us away from negative developments in both realms. Controversial discussions are not only allowed in a democracy, they are necessary in order to move in a positive new direction. I hope that this book is successful in encouraging new ways of thinking.

Sabine Neumann

INTRODUCTION:
THE H.DV.12 TURNS 100
by Kurd Albrecht von Ziegner

I read with interest the first German edition of *Balancing Act* by Dr. Gerd Heuschmann. After his bestseller *Tug of War*, it was to be expected that this book, too, would sell well and quickly. And now, the timing of the second edition couldn't be better, because the *H.Dv.12*, the book that has served as a foundation for German equestrian training, is 100 years old!

In his capacity as the King of Prussia, Kaiser Wilhelm II enacted these equestrian regulations in 1912, which had full legal force in the army. Today's *Richtlinien für Reiten und Fahren* [Guidelines for riding and driving] of the German Equestrian Association (FN) are anchored in these regulations.

Kurd Albrecht von Ziegner

Excerpts from the Order of the Cabinet from June 29, 1912, read as follows: "Deviation from the regulations and equestrian principles is forbidden." They were strictly followed even after the Second World War. The FN's "Guidelines" were written by inserting some expansion on the text and a few clarifying additions—without casting doubt on the fundamentals.

The *H.Dv.12* was the first binding equestrian instruction, which brought together the knowledge and experience of the old masters in military form "as short as possible, but as clear as necessary." The suppleness and relaxation (*Losgelassenheit*) of horse and rider is the foundation of all training and is prioritized above all other elements.

The requirement of a "secure, calm and relaxed (not forced) seat" is timeless. Only "from a correct seat can correct aids be given." "Moderation in demands" in training is stressed many times in order "to not damage the animal."

With *Balancing Act*, Dr. Heuschmann has once again put himself in the middle of the tension between those of us trained in the German classical riding tradition and those who are focused on competition. He speaks freely and clearly so that the reader knows exactly where he comes from: in defense of classical teaching against the ever-growing manipulation of horse sports for the purpose of spectacle, television ratings, and profit, often to the detriment of the horse's health.

The author correctly bases his often critical comments on the above-mentioned "Guidelines," which are, in turn, based on the *H.Dv.12*. As he takes a position against questionable training methods in vogue today, Dr. Heuschmann consistently references the Guidelines, especially the Training Scale, as the foundation for his sometimes harsh criticism. He also substantially undergirds his thesis with citations from the old masters.

As a veterinarian, Dr. Heuschmann is a highly qualified horseman. His expansive knowledge of the horse and especially the biomechanics of the gaits make him well suited to be a passionate supporter of the classical riding culture. The health and well-being of the horse at work is always his primary concern. He refers to the "Ethical Principles of Horsemanship" and the "Basic Rules of Conduct," which were established by the FN (see pp. 9 and 231). He also points out the deviations from these fundamental principles, which are unfortunately seen in many barns. Exemplary riding instruction is rare.

An apparent and expanding insecurity about the right way to train has inevitably led to methods that have nothing to do with classical teaching. Even the Fédération Equestre Internationale (FEI), the highest authority in horse sport, has recently accepted "LDR" (low, deep, round) as an acceptable new method—a dangerous watering down of the detestable "Rollkur," which I have previously referred to as a "straightjacket." This has caused many riders to lessen their adherence to the foundation of classical teaching, without concern that the responsible leadership organization would or could do anything about it. How else could it be in our freedom-oriented society? I don't have an easy answer for this, either.

This brings to mind the year 1936, when I experienced the Olympic Games in Berlin as an 18-year-old. German riders with German horses won all six gold medals in the six events. That seems incredible when you reflect on the state of training today. How was that possible? This success was the logical result of a training system, the *H.Dv.12*, that was practiced with enforced discipline. It was no accident—something to think about!

We officers of the cavalry were required to almost memorize the *H.Dv.12*. In our studies, one sentence—printed in bold—was hammered into us: "Relaxation and Suppleness (*Losgelassenheit*) in the horse is the first requirement for success of all dressage (training)." Elsewhere it states: "Relaxation and suppleness of rider and horse stands as the priority in all work; only when this is achieved can collection exercises begin."

This emphasis of classical teaching seems to be forgotten today. It doesn't seem to matter to many trainers that the quality of Rhythm, Straightness, and Impulsion is dependent on the degree of suppleness. It takes time.

Nevertheless, I noticed in the last show season that the public can tell very well whether a horse in the dressage arena struggles under excessive tension to fulfill his job, or if he performs almost "by himself" in willing obedience and relaxed lightness. The judge has the unique opportunity and duty to clearly indicate through his marks a preference for correct training according to classical teaching.

In the early years of my training in the United States, I saw even in the FEI tests only tense, crooked horses, forced into a "straightjacket," suffering while hanging on the curb.

To counteract this, I developed the Prix St. James, a dressage test in two parts:

Part 1 was an exercise at a lower level (snaffle bit, standard jacket), which included allowing the reins to be "chewed out of the hands" at the trot. Riders who didn't achieve 60 percent in Part 1 were not allowed in Part 2, the Prix St. George. Placing was determined by the addition of the scores from Part 1 and Part 2. The judges were impressed in that there was a distinct difference the next year. Many "leg movers" had developed into "back movers" (see p. 66).

Certainly we can't proceed in this way with these two Parts, but perhaps there is an idea here of how we can put more weight onto the foundational principles of training (the Scale) in judging dressage.

We should be thankful that Dr. Heuschmann has taken the trouble to "stir the pot" once again in order to make it clear what is happening, not just for the benefit of the horses, which have served humans for thousands of years with their blood and sweat. They have earned being treated with respect and fairness. We should keep watch that their health and well-being always stands ahead of other considerations—both in daily work and at the competition grounds. And let us step forward without hesitation when we witness pain inflicted or unfairness...of any kind.

Riding doesn't need to be reinvented. Let's take the one-hundredth anniversary of the *H.Dv.12* as an opportunity to once again embrace the proven principles of the old masters as the foundation of our training of horse and rider.

May this book gain the attention of all those who find joy in riding, and may it strengthen those accountable for leading our incomparable sport as they struggle to maintain and assert the classical teachings despite troubling headwinds.

Kurd Albrecht von Ziegner

ABOUT THE BOOK AND THE AUTHOR

by Dr. Heinrich Bottermann

Dr. Gerd Heuschmann

A long time ago, our relationship with horses changed from that of caring for a work animal to that of caring for a pleasure and sport partner. For the considerable number of people who choose interaction with animals as a preferred leisure activity, horses have become an important part of their lives. Compared to other sports, the relationship with a living animal presents the human with a special challenge: She must work on and improve herself in order to one day attain partnership with the horse.

Those people who deal with animals in their free time obviously have a higher interest in questions concerning the ethical treatment of animals. Ethical animal protection is also a societal good that has even been promulgated in the laws of many countries where animal protection is a federal goal and basic conditions to protect animals are spelled out by regulations. There are rules concerning the care and living conditions and also the use of animals, including to what extent an animal can be raised strictly for human purposes. Pleasure and sport activities are less about daily survival and more about an improved lifestyle.

Against this backdrop, there needs to be a critical way of looking at how horses are used for pleasure and sport purposes. Is the intended use aligned with the natural capabilities of the animal? Are the training methods appropriate for the animal or do the training methods fulfill other purposes? Discussions on the horse scene have been focusing on these questions for many years. Disagreements between the different viewpoints have never been fully resolved.

The correct training of horses is an important starting point for horse-friendly care that aligns with animal protection. From my observation over the past several years, it should not be taken for granted that one can enter a riding arena and actually see riding that is appropriate for the horse.

With the publication of *Tug of War*, Dr. Gerd Heuschmann denounced the abuses observed in both sport and pleasure riding and provided the biomechanical foundation for horse training. Now, with this new book *Balancing Act*, Dr. Heuschmann attempts to further sensitize his readers and to provide them with a horse-friendly training method. He has succeeded! A well-trained horse, whose individual physical performance capabilities are considered and whose mental state is respected, is capable of being a partner for sport and pleasure (that is, when there are no health limitations). This is practical animal protection, and exactly what should be the maxim of every person who interacts with horses.

HIGH POINTS IN THE AUTHOR'S LIFE

1959	Born in Marktredwitz, Oberfranken, Germany.
1979–1980	After the *Abitur* (high school), studied to be a *Pferdewirt* (a combination professional rider, trainer, and farm manager) under Martin Zorn, and achieved a major in riding at the training center (*Landesleistungszentrum*) in Ansbach.
1980–1981	Continued *Pferdewirt* training with a major in riding at the German riding school in Warendorf under Dr. Wolfgang Holzl. Awarded the Stensbeck medal.
1981–1986	Studied veterinary medicine at the University of Munich.
1987–1989	Assistant at the veterinary surgical clinic of the University of Munich and received his doctorate in veterinary medicine.
1989–1991	Youth leader of the German Equestrian Federation and consultant to the FN's breeding department in Warendorf.
1994	Took over the veterinary clinic of Appelhuls and founded the veterinary clinic of Karthaus.
1998	Took over the veterinary practice of Dr. Josel Hauk in Warendorf and founded a joint practice with Dr. Dirk Remmler. Began teaching at the German Riding School in Warendorf. Designed a new veterinary curriculum for *Pferdewirt* and *Master Pferdewirt* training at the German Riding School in Warendorf: "The functional anatomy of the riding horse."
1999	Began consulting worldwide.
2006–2007	*Finger in der Wunde* published in Germany. In 2007, called *Tug of War*, the book was published in the United States and the United Kingdom. It has since been translated into 13 other languages selling over 50,000 copies up to 2011.
2008	Freelance collaborator in the Karthaus Veterinary Clinic in Dulmen, expansion of consultant and seminar activity.
2008	DVD called *Stimmen der Pferde (If Horses Could Speak)* made available in German and English. It contains the first ever 3-D animation of a moving horse in different head-neck positions.
2009	In Germany, published a children/young adult book *Mein Pferd hat die Nase vorn* [My horse has his nose out in front].
2010	Further worldwide expansion of practical seminars and presentations. Establishing training sites in Europe dedicated to the practice of the proven, Classical Training principles.
2011	This book—*Balanceakt: In dubio pro equo*—released in Germany. Companion DVD under development.

GLOSSARY

Abduction: Move or pull a body part away from the median line of the body.

Adduction: Move or pull a body part toward the median line of the body.

Aids: Cues given by the rider to the horse to communicate what the horse is being asked to do.

Diagonal aids: For example, the rider's inside leg is held at the girth to maintain impulsion and bend while the outside leg mobilizes the haunches to displace the horse's shoulders around the rider's inside leg. The inside rein maintains the bend, and the outside rein, aimed straight back toward the rider's outside hip, maintains collection.

Leg aids: The rider's legs are used singly or together with pressure on the horse's sides to cue the horse to go forward, increase impulsion, step sideways, and/or bend against the rider's leg.

Rein aids: The rider's hands communicate through the reins to the horse's bit primarily to control the horse's head and shoulders. The hands work as a restraining aid to contain the horse's forward energy, or as a guiding aid to encourage movement in a certain direction.

Seat aids: Control of forward or restraining movement of the horse through the rider's seat and weight. A supple seat is one in which the rider sits quietly, following and absorbing the horse's motion.

Back mover: Thrust and energy created by the hindquarters can freely travel through the horse's relaxed, working back toward the poll and subsequently to his mouth, causing the horse to be in a state of "relative elevation."

Balance: Relative distribution of the weight of horse and rider upon the fore and hind legs (*longitudinal balance*) and the left and right legs (*lateral balance*).

Driving seat: When done with a supple feel, the rider sits softly and balanced in the saddle with minor shifts of weight to encourage the horse to go forward with a supple back or to ask the horse to slow his pace. With a driving seat that is forced or braced, the rider shifts her hips slightly backward and down, pushing both seat bones into the saddle much like the act of "pumping" a swing.

Fall apart: The horse is said to "fall apart" when there is loss of positive tension in the back, and the back drops and loses connection between rear and front ends. The horse is completely off the aids.

Fascia: A sheet or band of fibrous connective tissue enveloping muscles.

FEI: International Federation of Equestrian Sports (Fédération Equestre Internationale), the governing body of international equestrian competition.

Forward riding: The rider encourages the horse to move forward—without restriction—with carefully measured aids.

Forward and downward: The ability of the horse to connect well and stretch to the hand as the rider dictates, with the neck stretched first forward then downward to lift and stretch the back.

Half-halt: A momentary slowing or increase in collection to rebalance the horse back toward his hindquarters. This is done by momentarily "closing" the seat, leg, and rein aids and then quickly releasing.

Haunches-in: See Travers.

"Hover" trot: A trot in which the phase of support of one diagonal pair of legs is prolonged while there is a hesitation in the forward travel of the other diagonal pair of legs, giving a passage-like, floating, hovering impression. Also called a "show" trot or a "circus trot."

Hyperflexed back mover: A head-neck position that is much too deep is indicative of a horse that has "lost" his back, with his back elevating upward: the back is too high and thereby tense.

Impulsion: Thrust developed from the horse's hind legs with the release of stored energy created by sinking of the haunches (increased flexion of the lumbo-sacral and hind leg joints) during the support phase of the stride. This imparts power and push to the horse's stride.

Kur: A freestyle riding test set to music.

Leg mover: The horse's head-neck axis is positioned higher—and with the neck made shorter—than his stage of training and muscle development allows, and the back hollows so he moves with limited or no connection of the back between the front and back legs.

Leg-yield: A lateral exercise moving the horse sideways away from the rider's leg pressure. The horse is fairly straight or looking slightly away from the direction of travel.

Lengthening: The elongation of stride while maintaining the same rhythm and tempo as in the working pace.

"Lost" back: The rider's seat aids have no connection to the horse's back and the horse also loses connection between his front and hindquarters (falls apart).

Piaffe: Rhythmic trotting movement performed nearly on the spot with no forward movement.

Positive tension: This refers to a state of muscular contraction in the horse's back that facilitates self-carriage.

Renvers: The horse's haunches are out on the outside track and shoulders are on the inside track, and he is bent to the outside; also called haunches-out.

Rollkur: Hyperflexion of the horse's neck often achieved through aggressive, forceful means and/or mechanical devices currently banned by the FEI.

Rhythm: The recurring characteristic sequence and timing of footfalls and phases of a given gait.

Self-carriage: The horse is able to carry himself in balance without support from the reins.

Shoulder-fore: Lateral movement that is a prelude to shoulder-in; the horse makes four tracks, that is, one per hoof. The horse is straight rather than bent.

Shoulder-in: The horse's hind legs track straight forward along the line of travel while the front legs move laterally, with the inside foreleg crossing in front of the outside foreleg and the inside hind hoof tracking into or beyond the hoof print made by the outside foreleg; the inside hind leg steps beneath the horse's center of gravity to passively bend and lower the haunches as the horse's trunk shifts over the diagonally placed hind leg.

"Show" trot: Same as "hover" trot.

Stepping over: These lateral movements include exercises such as leg-yield, shoulder-in and turn-on-the-forehand with the horse moving sideways without the demand of longitudinal flexion.

Straightness: The horse's body from poll to tail runs parallel to the path of travel or the line of reference.

Suppleness: Flexibility, pliability.

Swing: A springy motion that occurs when the thrust off the hind legs is transmitted through a stretched topline by trunk muscles that contract and relax in a rhythmical fashion rather than remaining either rigid or slack.

Tempi changes: Multiple flying changes in a row, every one, two, three, or four strides.

Tempo: Rate of repetition of the horse's rhythm or the strides.

"Through" and "Throughness": State in which the rider's aids/influences go freely through to all parts of the horse, from back to front and front to back.

Topline: Profile of the area extending from the poll to the tail along the top of the crest of the neck and along the spine to the haunches.

Training Scale: Also called the Pyramid of Training, this scale moves a horse's training through six sequential steps: Rhythm; Suppleness; Contact; Impulsion; Straightness; Collection.

Travers: The horse's haunches are in on the inside track and the shoulders are on the outside track, bent in the direction he is moving; also called haunches-in.

Volte: A small circle, roughly 6 meters in diameter.

I.

HORSE SPORT

A Current State of Affairs

What does it mean when someone says "I ride a well-trained horse?" What are the criteria that define this? What is Classical Training understood to be? Why do we talk so much about this subject? Why are there so many controversial discussions, writings and arguments about horse training and its underlying philosophies?

Apparently, we have great difficulty putting into action the knowledge that has been handed down and tested over centuries. It is customary to recite the key principles and to memorize the Training Scale (see p. 59). Unfortunately, what happens in actual practice is often just the opposite.

It would be a mistake to sweepingly glorify history; there were poor riding skills in the past as well. Despite a rider's limitations, following training strategies that are correct for the horse should be an absolute principle. Training methods handed down and tested over centuries are still valid even for horses that are kept only for the purposes of sport or pleasure, as they are today, and despite how distinctly the relationship between man and animal has changed.

Why is it that the concepts and images laid out in those teachings are not reflected in the current practice of riding and training? Where did the divergence between theory and practice come from?

From my point of view, there are many causes to explain this conflict. A few of them are worth looking at in detail:

- We have a different societal background from that of the old masters of the first half of the last century.
- Riding has become a popular sport.
- For a large number of riders, the desire to compete is more important than the joy of training a horse. Training is frequently designed primarily to meet test requirements with the needs of the horse relegated to second place.
- The type and body build of our horses has significantly improved in some ways. In many respects, this has brought advantages to the rider, but it has also created new problems for advancement in training.

> THE APPLICATION OF CORRECT METHODS SHOULD BE AN ABSOLUTE PRIORITY.

THE EVOLUTION OF RIDING SPORTS

Whoever can afford it can now buy a horse despite having no previous knowledge of how to care for the horse or how to ride. Riding schools are abundant and available and they offer the possibility to learn to ride on a school horse. Thankfully, the opportunity to become a rider is no longer limited to social status or belonging to a privileged class. However, riding is becoming more expensive, as is the case with many other sports. The cost of buying, keeping and training a horse varies considerably. At the highest level of competition, the league in which a rider participates is more dependent on financial wherewithal than on rider ability.

Top athletes are subject to special circumstances that don't compare with those of pleasure riders. High levels of expenditure and achievement goals elicit pressure on excellent performance and the need for financial support to pursue these goals.

With all the justified criticism of the sport, one must not forget how much knowledge, ability, patience, effort and years of personal sacrifice are required for a rider to achieve a high level of performance with a horse. That dedication deserves respect. A sweeping condemnation of all top athletes is neither useful nor appropriate.

Many competitive riders live not only for horses, but also make a living from horses, from horse sport and above all from commerce. Prize money has increased substantially at the upper echelons. However, it should be taken into account that while the number of top athletes performing at high levels, especially in international competition, has increased, prize money overall has decreased. So the majority of top athletes cannot cover their costs, especially in dressage and eventing (as compared to jumping, which is more lucrative).

Within competitive sports there are contradictory developments. Professional events with very good athletic competitions and an attractive starting field can market themselves well and grow—even in lean economic times. This is especially the case when they can guarantee media presence, display a certain glamour, and are broadcast on television. Small local competitions, however, of little interest to equestrian sponsors, must fight for survival. The number of riders, horse owners and equestrian sport fans has grown.

The demand for instruction and trainers has also increased. However, competitive sport at the lower levels is trending down. The divide between the highly subsidized top athletes and the sport at the lower levels gapes mightily.

Furthermore, in Germany (for example), traditional riding organizations have been losing members for

several years. A possible reason for the decline in membership is that riders who don't participate in competition often find it unnecessary to be a member of a riding club. Another reason could be that the training given in the riding clubs and riding schools doesn't meet the needs and wants of horse fans.

The riding and horse world has changed dramatically. Now there are many different riding styles and "schools," as well as a striking number of different breeds—not just the Warmbloods: in Europe one sees Quarter Horses, Haflingers, Knabstruppers, Arabians, Icelandics, Andalusians, Lusitanos and Friesians, to name just a few. These "special breeds" are experiencing growing popularity.

THE LACK OF EQUESTRIAN INSTRUCTION AND ITS CONSEQUENCES

The instructor situation has also changed greatly since the 1970s. There are large differences today when it comes to the quality of the instruction and the competency of the instructor. On one hand, the most competent instructors are generally not willing to give beginning lessons or to provide a solid riding basis because their earning potential is much better with upper-level competitors or ambitious amateurs.

On the other hand, many riders today are searching for relaxation and pleasure in their free time. Not everyone wishes to discuss theory or gain an extensive body of knowledge about horses or about riding. Many don't realize that even good horses can spook and react unexpectedly, or understand how much riding experience it takes to control a horse in a critical situation. Furthermore, the less experienced riders often tend to overestimate their ability to handle emergencies.

One of the biggest problems is that many riders lack broad and solid basic instruction. Why are the basics important when competition is about tests? Why should a rider learn to sit with a supple body, balanced with independent hands and sensitively ride the horse on the aids from back to front?

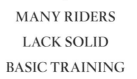

MANY RIDERS LACK SOLID BASIC TRAINING

Financial limitations often dictate that a rider find a quick and easy way to performing in competition. A prospective rider buys herself a fantastic, well-trained horse and engages a good trainer to assure that the four-legged partner "functions" on the jumping course or in the dressage arena. When this isn't met with success, there are many possible reasons ranging from the wrong horse to the wrong saddle to the wrong barn to the wrong trainer.

Most riders love horses, especially their own. They want to do everything right. However, in many questions regarding training there are different answers. The multiplicity of "schools" and riding styles masks the danger of losing one's bearings. Only when given a clear path can a rider progress in the instruction and training. There is no easy answer or only one way to learn; every horse and every rider is different. Consequently, the best possibility for each rider is to find the right path for human and horse.

Most errors occur from ignorance or inexperience.

No rider is immune to misjudgments about herself or her horse. Sport riders are not alone in being driven by excessive ambition paired with an overestimation of their own abilities, asking too much of themselves and their horses. Over the long term, this can lead to difficult problems.

Many mistakes could be avoided through correct understanding of fundamental training principles. This presupposes that the rider understands training theory. Unfortunately, such preparation is as little evident as is the faculty of self-criticism by many riding enthusiasts. Why should a rider question herself about a problem and search for the answer in the traditional teachings? When a competitor has already achieved success—dozens of wins and placings—the implication is that this rider can surely ride. It is not often suggested that any difficulty with the horse could be due to rider incompetence and/or incorrect training. So the rider searches for a problem with the horse and asks an expert to remedy the stiff poll, the dislocated vertebra or the presumed suspensory injury.

There are often physical causes of lameness and training issues that require treatment; and, horses do suffer from diseases that require care. However, training difficulties that are caused by the rider are often passed off to a ready and waiting armada of "problem solvers." The "expert" then makes a diagnosis that explains the problem; as a general rule, some therapy will improve the situation.

When there is a disruption in the horse's movement or he shows a new resistance, look to the way the horse is being ridden and trained for clues to the origin of the problems.

Far too many horses are run through numerous therapy options until some owner finally recognizes that correct training is the path to a healthy horse. Admittedly, it is not simple for a rider to assume responsibility and to accept the possibility of years of errors in the horse's training. Nevertheless, critical self-analysis and openness in the face of constructive criticism are the first and most important steps to a well-ridden horse.

ETHICS IN HORSE SPORTS AND THE ROLE OF THE JUDGE

Top equestrian athletes have the world before them. A new superstar is born, the masses are jubilant, the press falls over itself with hymns of praise, but suddenly this accomplished horse just disappears! "Hurt in the trailer," goes the official version. No one really notices since a replacement is quickly ready—and this time the legs fly still higher. People cheer; judges bestow world-record scores on him. Still, only a few realize that this horse is being regularly questioned at the vet check, not able to pass the veterinary check point easily.

Meanwhile, do we condone that our aesthetic sport of dressage wears out its main artists like a racing cyclist his machine? Has it become "normal" for a horse to no longer be able to perform without constant medical and physiotherapeutic care?

When key principles of riding theory like maintaining the physical and psychological health of the horse no longer play a role, what is the reason for having judges at competitive events? Couldn't the list of placings just be determined by the applause of the public through the loudspeaker?

The philosophy behind the teachings of the governing body of all the Olympic disciplines, the Fédération Equestre Internationale (FEI), builds substantially on an ethical code of behavior, which places the well-being of the horse in the center. Is this concept now only "on paper" or can we find it put into practice?

This is the important question: Is it okay to write and say "lovely" things and then simply do the opposite? Isn't this the reality in today's world?

Innumerable businesses that revolve around the horse strive to bring their products and methods to the public's attention. There is nothing wrong with earning one's living through breeding or competition; however, one of the biggest threats to a traditional and time-tested training system may arise from the steadily growing economic interests of an ever larger number of people.

The classic riding and training philosophy must continue to be taught and actively implemented as an effective training method. Otherwise, commerce will drive it out with the show riding that is currently in favor and good for marketing purposes.

Given this background, competition riders play an ever larger and more important role. They are the most important authority, the one that can insist on animal welfare. For this reason, judges should assure riders that training methods that disregard horse welfare will be eliminated from competition grounds. Judges must set an example by judging performances in the dressage arena according to the guidelines of the Training Scale, letting improperly trained horses, such as "leg movers" or hyperflexed "back movers" fall by the wayside. Only a true "back mover" should have a chance at placing in competition.

A "leg mover" is a horse whose head-neck axis is put in a higher position—and neck shorter—than his stage of training and muscle development allows.

A true "back mover" describes a horse where the thrust and energy created by the hindquarters can freely travel through the relaxed, working back toward the poll and subsequently to the mouth, causing the horse to be in a state of "relative elevation."

A hyperflexed "back mover" is a horse whose rider has placed his head-neck axis in an extremely round and deep position, or a forced longitudinal position (well-known today as Rollkur) in order to get the horse to lift his back too high and "swing" it. Doing so with this method puts enormous tension on the upper neck muscles and ligament system, and the back.

The concern about rewarding horses with improper training was expressed about 60 years ago by Erich Glahn in his book *Reitkunst am Scheideweg* [Equitation at the crossroads]. At that time he felt that the German judges' organization was finally recognizing this problem and considering the consequences. Is this recognition still present today? An improperly trained horse should never be placed in the ribbons, even with a technically perfect performance. The first and most important task of the judge is to separate leg movers from back movers. Perhaps this is not being done because judges fear they won't be invited back by the competition organizers.

The judges' invitational system still practiced is, in my opinion, unsuitable and long outdated. We need qualified, independent, strong and assertive judges. The associations are under scrutiny. Judges should be employed based on their technical competency and conviction for the cause rather than their agreeable personality and their ability to be "flexible."

Without strong, independent judges, ethical principles and animal protection cannot be defended against increasing economic pressures. If not the judges, who will see to it that these important principles are upheld? In my opinion, this is their most important job.

Responsibility for the qualifications and the incontestability of judges at a competitive event lies with the oversight of the national or international organization. Complete independence and absolute technical competency of the judges can stop today's trend and bring riding sport back to the only acceptable path: rewarding correct training principles. If the hunt for spectacle at the cost of horses is not slowed down, it is likely that other institutions and animal rights' activists will undertake to correct this for us.

Oskar Maria Stensbeck, an important author of the last century, described the then sought-after "show" or "hover" trot as "not pretty" on aesthetic grounds in accordance with classical riding teachings. How can it be that the subjective perception of "pretty" and "not pretty" has changed so? At one time considered unaesthetic, in today's riding world, this trot is now favored.

Oskar Maria Stensbeck wrote:

◆

"... the horse must move in increasing collection while maintaining light and free steps, without decaying into 'hovering' through too severe a collection. The only remedy for a hover trot is to immediately increase the tempo until the hovering stops and a lively trot is reestablished. One should not confuse active steps with rushing, which often happens today. One should reject hovering but also rushing strides as well."

Oscar Maria Stensbeck, "Reiten" in a collection entitled *Grundzüge der Reitkunst* [Guidelines of equitation], New edition 1983, Olms Press, Hildesheim, Zürich, New York, p. 41

◆

The hover trot is one in which the phase of support of one diagonal pair of legs is prolonged while there is a hesitation in the forward travel of the other diagonal pair of legs, giving a floating, hovering impression. This trot should be regarded as a considerable training problem, not celebrated with dream scores and not glamorized as the measure of all things.

In addition, there is a misunderstanding of the term "forward" and today, as in the past, you can still see "rushing, fast riding." This also should be considered an "error": *Forward* never has anything to do with *speed*!

Shouldn't the quality of training be scrutinized in a dressage test? What is the purpose of seeing how high the horse can throw his front legs when such activity doesn't appear in any criteria of classical riding theory and actually contradicts most of the principles? (*See Reitkunst am Scheideweg* [Equitation at the crossroads] by Erich Glahn, Erich Hoffmann Verlag, Heidenheim, 1956, pp. 89 and 93.)

THE NINE ETHICAL PRINCIPLES OF HORSEMANSHIP

❶ Anyone involved with a horse takes over responsibility for this living creature entrusted to him.

❷ The horse must be kept in a way that is in keeping with its natural living requirements.

❸ Highest priority must be accorded to the physical as well as psychological health of the horse, irrespective of the purpose for which it is used.

❹ Man must respect every horse alike, regardless of its breed, age and sex and its use for breeding, for recreation or in sporting competition.

❺ Knowledge of the history of the horse, its needs, and how to handle it are part of our historic cultural heritage. This information must be cherished and safeguarded in order to be passed on to the next generations.

❻ Contact and dealings with horses are character building experiences and of valuable significance to the development of the human being, in particular, the young person. This aspect must always be respected and promoted.

❼ The human who participates in equestrian sport with his horse must subject himself, as well his horse, to training. The goal of any training is to bring about the best possible harmony between rider and horse.

❽ The use of the horse in competition as well as in general riding, driving and vaulting must be geared toward the horse's ability, temperament and willingness to perform. Manipulating a horse's capacity to work by means of medication or other "horse unfriendly" influences should be rejected by all and people engaged in such practices should be prosecuted.

❾ The responsibility a human has for the horse entrusted to him includes the end of the horse's life. The human must always assume this responsibility and implement any decisions in the best interest of the horse.

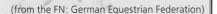

(from the FN: German Equestrian Federation)

MODERN BREEDING AND ITS CONSEQUENCES FOR TRAINING

I see an important cause of the current evolution of equestrian competitive sport arising because of the phenomenal achievements attained in breeding. Breeding associations have made a huge improvement in the rideability of horses over the past 30 years.

The quality of today's dressage horse with his ability to "round" the neck and offer the rider a feeling of softness and a big elastic movement is amazing. Fifty years ago, a round neck could only be achieved by good training—usually after several years of work. However, today, many horses "round" the neck and the poll almost from the time they are first ridden.

Paul Stecken asked a salient question at one of my presentations:

"How can you explain to young riders that they must not accept the, 'wonderful,' necks of these young horses demonstrate when they begin their training?"

This question points to the fundamental problem: The neck of today's horse rounds itself; that is, it creates this desired outline naturally, even though the horse lacks balance and hasn't yet developed the body to maintain this neck position. It's for this reason that we shouldn't accept this position, even though the "picture" looks so good. It is deceptive and leads

Neck of the modern riding horse, balanced and in self-carriage.

A wonderful neck, but in this case, the horse is curling it, going behind the bit and not giving at the poll.

the rider away from the path of good training into the "abyss" of forced and mechanical methods.

So, while the great achievements in breeding are a blessing in some ways, they are also creating a significant problem: The acceptance of a rounded neck too early in training is one of the greatest early errors of horse training. This characteristic of the modern horse is, in my view, the source of the development of hyperflexion (Rollkur). I also believe that current breeding has achieved the maximum volume of gait: The greater the volume in trot or canter, the greater the likelihood that the horse's back cannot pass such strong impulses to the front end without causing tension.

Even slight seat errors and clumsy hands cause the horse's neck to curl under and his back to stiffen, leading to a massive disruption in balance as is seen with the hover trot.

A horse that is "hovering" can never really be collected.

This situation is exacerbated by the efforts to breed a shorter back at the same time as many of today's riders are getting larger and/or heavier. How does this work? The saddle should only be placed in the area of the thorax and not extend over the loins, otherwise, it can cause lasting tension in the back muscles. Unfortunately, a clever rider can use such tension to cause over-spectacular-looking trot and canter movements, even though these "tense" steps are—for many young horses—the beginning of the end of their career!

It would behoove the breeding world to pay attention to a more appropriately shaped frame (rectangular) in order to enable a horse to correctly carry a larger rider on an 18.5 to 19-inch saddle. A good riding horse requires a powerful, well-muscled, medium-long back with a smooth transition from the thoracic region through the lumbar spine and musculature. He must be powerful, but "through" (state in which the rider's aids and influence go freely to all parts of the horse from front to back and back to front) and supple, in order to provide the rider with a good and soft feeling in the seat. The horse's back needs a significant ability to swing.

On the other hand, a back that is too long or too deep tends to be too weak—it hollows easily with the horse tending toward being a leg-mover in the absence of correct training.

Another reason for regarding the mechanics of an exaggerated gait as dangerous is the susceptibility of the horse to ligament injuries, particularly the suspensories.

A way of moving that is not overly big yet is rhythmical and elastic, an active hind leg, and a mobile back are prerequisites for a rider to be able to balance the horse and later achieve collection. It is the same for every riding discipline.

II.

RIDING

Art or Commerce?

YOUNG HORSES—THE "HOPE" MARKET

The supply of "quality" young horses is large but the animals for sale by trainers and breeders are not always promoted or presented in such a way that their potential is apparent at first glance, particularly if the young horse cannot yet be ridden. Exterior characteristics are not the only indicators of potential performance excellence. When a young horse has been started without the necessary calmness, without feel and with a hyperflexed neck, as is so often the case, then the buyer has an additional obstacle to overcome. In fact, many of the young horses sold at sales in Europe are already in need of retraining.

In Germany, for example, the picture or ideal image of a young horse is influenced strongly by the important young-horse events like stallion selections, auctions and championships. At today's stallion selection events, it is common to see two- and three-year-old stallions with stunningly developed musculature; at first glance, many appear fully developed. Also, because in recent years, there has been a tendency to breed for an extremely large size with a stick measure of over 17 hands, this early physical development gives the false impression that one is looking at a grown horse. It is the same thing with the three- and four-year-old riding horses at auctions, state and national championships.

The preparation of horses for sales and championships has long been a special discipline. Riders who work in this realm have particular experience, and know how to highlight the strengths of the youngster and play down the weaknesses. With dressage horses, an over-spectacular "show" trot particularly awakens desire in the buyers; it is not by accident that an animated trot is the gait that brings in the

THE TROT IS THE GAIT THAT BRINGS IN THE MONEY.

money. With jumpers, it is all about style and capacity. The fences are set at 4½ feet for three-year-olds and put up higher in an effort to heat up purchase interest. However, it has been shown that such free jumping predicts little about later success on the show jumping circuit.

The demands on these youngsters at auctions and sale barns are very high. They must typically attain top form in a relatively short period of time. In addition, there are the challenges of the horse moving from one barn to another, changes of feed, and different riders. Not all potential buyers are competent and sensitive when trying a horse and not every young horse can cope with such "toughness" tests. Often, the foundation that is laid at the sale barns for young talent with potential turns these horses into ones that need retraining.

The young stallion candidates and the novice horses at sales and championships are often developed physically beyond what might be expected for their age. Many demonstrate a particular willingness to perform in addition to possessing very good gaits and/or above average jumping ability. Skillfully presented by specialists, they are regarded as having significant potential even as foals. However, these "made" horses don't always develop as hoped: Many a "dream" horse turns out to be a disappointing prospect.

Over-spectacular trot movement arising from intentionally created tension in the horse's back is not only worthless, it is also very harmful.

Many young horses—especially those for sale—are presented at competitions in top form, and they win ribbons. Not all survive such an impressive performance undamaged. The driving forces behind these displays can arise through ignorance or excessive ambition, but also are frequently motivated by money. Winning or placing—especially at championships—increases the horse's value. Naturally, every championship is also a marketplace—many medal wearers change ownership following their competition performance.

Today, economic interests increasingly drive breeding, training and the horse market. Since time is money, training must be developed as quickly as possible. Horses with a willingness to perform—and with rideability—often respond to rider demands to come into the desired frame before they are physically and mentally prepared: Early physical wear and tear is programmed into them. However, with systematic development and solid correct training, there would be no need for such "sales riding." To parade novice horses around and around in a "show" trot or to demonstrate their talent for piaffe and passage (despite "hover" steps) may well impress buyers and spectators but it completely contradicts the philosophy of starting the horse with basic and Classical Training principles (see. p. 59). Anyone concerned about the health and long life of the horse should be thinking long-term.

> *"The good ones grow in gold."*
> *Walter Wadenspanner*

It is difficult to balance economic realities with accountability for a living being—in this case, the horse. Racing and Western horses are ridden at two years old and must be top performers by three. Their sports career is often finished by age five or six. There are many jumping, dressage and event horses that don't reach their zenith until 12 or 13 years of age, and today, there are even horses that remain top performers at 18 or 19. However, the career of most horses has long since ended by middle age.

There are no available numbers on how many horses fail to fulfill high expectations due to poor health and early "retirement." Likewise unknown, is how many horses are given the necessary time to become physically and mentally mature in their early years. There is an obvious connection between asking too much of a horse too early and the horse's health. When the training is solid, is correct for the horse, and the demands are gradually increased, he has a good chance of growing old as an athlete.

THE YOUNG HORSE "CAROUSEL"

When marketing a horse at all costs becomes the deciding principle, it can be "fatal" for the horse. In many countries, success at foal premium inspections, at championships, or at sales depends on how the foal presents with his mother. For two-year-olds, there are also liberty and free-jumping championships. Three-year-olds are presented at breed shows, at state shows, at stallion selections and markets. There is also preparation for these exhibitions that don't always conform to the needs of the breed, the age of the horse or to recognized training principles.

Today, most young stallions must be earning

Young horses year-round in the pasture—being turned out all day with a herd is necessary for a healthy body and strong character.

money at the age of three. After the stallion selection, these new "stars" awaken the interest of
breeders, especially the champion and premium
stallions. The sons of proven stallions are attractive
because they offer favorable genetic proclivities in
their pedigree, but for a more favorable breeding
fee than their sires. To increase the chance of obtain-
ing a good foal, it is a better option to breed to the
selected, proven stallion rather than to his younger
progeny—no one knows how prepotent the young
stallion will actually be.

When next year's offspring don't meet expectations, the breeders' interest dies away.

In Germany, a stallion's childhood is over after his
second grazing season, at the latest. The youngsters
are kept in stalls, fed and prepared in order to be fit
for inspection. Most stallion selection events occur

in the fall when the stallions are two years of age.
Most young stallions are already under saddle before their third year of life since they must be shown
at the stallion shows in the spring. While three-year-
old riding horses are not allowed to compete before
the first of May for good reason, there are no restric-
tions for stallion shows. Thankfully, these stallions
are frequently shown only in hand. However, many
people aren't satisfied with this.

Most sires complete their 30-day selection test in
the spring of their third year, or in the fall at the latest. Without a performance test or certificate, as a
rule, a stallion loses his coverage permit. Since how
well breeders think of a stallion depends on his performance, most three-year-old stallions get their first
competition experiences during their first coverage
season, and if presented at championships, they

must be ridden. The riding horse tests, which include serpentines as well as lengthenings (elongated stride yet the tempo of the working pace is retained) in trot and canter, are demanding and require conditioning and a rideability that can only be achieved through training. To present at a competition isn't enough; success is especially important for young stallions, since it increases breeder demand. With a championship title, or an excellent performance score, the value of the stallion increases along with the number of booked breedings. With a view to the future, two chances at a career are advantageous—if breeding demand falls, the stallion can still be marketed as a sport horse.

The double burden of breeding and sport is considerable. Whether a stallion is up to it depends on the individual's development, his breeding, physical constitution, mental capacity and above all, whether the demands on him are increased in a reasonable way by allowing the necessary breaks for musculoskeletal tissue recovery and repair. There are no rules proscribing use in breeding and competition; rather, participation in these activities lies in the judgment of breeders, stallion stations, horse owners and riders who will only behave responsibly if they are conscious of the problems caused by a load that is too heavy and asked too early.

Riding cross-country, rhythmically forward over small jumps, makes up an important part of the work for all young horses, regardless of the future intended discipline.

Diverse testing opportunities for all ages of horses offer many opportunities to serve the development of the novice horse. The standard to be met is very high. Whether a horse can actually reach the training goals considered the norm for his age class de-

THE DOUBLE BURDEN OF BREEDING AND BEING USED AS A SPORT HORSE IS CONSIDERABLE.

pends on many different factors. The high demands and strong competition in the tests lead to early specialization. Less experienced and sales-oriented riders and owners may go astray by training a young sport horse much too intensely: they take the horse to competitions too often, or prematurely start a horse in a difficult test. A training plan that is correct for the horse should focus solely on the individual horse's physical and mental development. Exceptional horses fulfill the established standards without a problem. In other cases, the established standards lead to horses being thoughtlessly "souped up" to reach the class goal.

In Germany, many buyers are impressed when they see a long list of good show results in the horse's performance book. A full performance book, however, is no guarantee of success. On the contrary: For long-term, healthy development, demands should only be increased very gradually, especially at a young age; this allows the horse the necessary time for recovery, particularly after intense training. Overtaxing the horse affects him negatively, both physically and mentally. It is very difficult and sometimes impossible to retrain horses that have become "sour" and don't want to work with their rider in or out of the arena

No one can predict if a three-year-old exceptional talent will later be a Grand Prix horse or an international quality athlete. How well a horse develops depends on many different factors, not the least of which includes solid training and good health.

There are riders who allow their novice horses a lot of time, not showing them at a young age at all, or only a few times in jumping and dressage tests. For them, it is not about winning and placing, but only about getting the young horse comfortable with the

Carefree time in the pasture "just being a horse" ends all too soon when it's time for stallion selection and performance tests.

Riding cross-country, rhythmically forward over small jumps, makes up an important part of the work for all young horses, regardless of the future intended discipline.

competition atmosphere. The rider who is thinking long-term will train her horse systematically over years, increasing demands slowly, so that she can ride the horse a long time and preserve his health.

The demand for healthy, honestly trained horses at the top echelons of the sport is larger than the supply. This has caused prices to reach astronomical heights for high-performance equine athletes. In isolated cases, even young horses achieve six-figure sales—at least when they are marketed by prominent sale barns. The auction sales business functions according to its own rules, similar to the stock exchange: The background of what is being sold is not publicly known. Only those involved in the business actually know whether the bid is ever really paid, if a horse actually changes hands, or what bid-

◆
FARSIGHTED RIDERS
THINK LONG-TERM
AND TRAIN
THEIR HORSES
SYSTEMATICALLY
◆

ding strategy and price were agreed to before the sale. In contrast to the private high-price market just mentioned, at auctions there are a huge number of almost unsaleable, young horses.

As long as the only goals of commercial interests are to see the front legs of potential dressage horses go as high as possible in a flailing trot and receive endless, fantasy-sized sums of money, the majority of riders won't find an appropriate equine partner at shows or sale barns. At the breed sales it is hard to find horses that have been ridden without negative tension—horses that could be fun for pleasure riders and athletes.

Unfortunately, training is a long and difficult process, and because time is money, it is also associated with financial risk. Not everyone can or will wait for a young horse to develop. Professional riders are under great pressure to succeed and have a hard time explaining to horse owners—and students—the importance of solid, patient basic training. The temptation to fiddle with quick money is large—to earn the most possible in the shortest time. Driving young horses to perform at a high level, thus destroying them early, contradicts the concept of horsemanship. Taking time to train and develop a horse opposes financial interests. As a result, horse trade doesn't depend on riders who provide their horse with a "job for life."

It depends, instead, on many horses being sold as expensively as possible. This is explained as a "truth" that it is "good for business," when, in fact, as many horses as possible are worn out as early as possible and replaced with new ones.

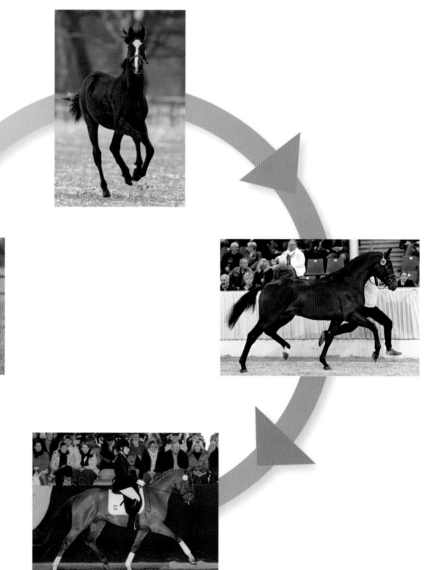

An essential part of our horse industry is the marketing of our young hopeful prospects. Here lies the interface between breeding and sport.

III.

HORSE AND SPORT
An Irreconcilable Conflict?

WHAT DOES "HORSEMANSHIP" MEAN?

It requires a permanent balancing act to be sensitive to the needs of a horse—a steppe, herd and prey animal—while at the same time asking him for high performance in sporting competitions. Whether it can be done depends on breeding and the sport's requirements but a bigger question is whether, at the same time, it is possible to remain loyal to the ethical principles of proven training methods.

In the last century, famous riding masters and trainers proposed the following hypothesis: "Competition is one thing; classical equestrian art is another." This suggests that the two areas *can't* be united, but must this be the case? Or can a competitive rider also train classically and keep the horse in the center of the effort? I would like to believe that this is possible.

The booming development of a "horsemanship movement" shows a previous deficit in this area. We live today between two extremes. On one side are a group of professional and semi-professional riders and trainers for whom horses have become devalued as "marketable wares," subject to training methods that do not fundamentally protect the animals. On the other hand, there is a large and growing group of riders and horse lovers who anthropomorphize horses to the point that the essence of good "horsemanship" and good riding is watered down to a farce. In this group of horse fans, you find mostly people who mean well but are not competent in their interaction with horses or in their training to make the necessary judgments or to assess someone's work. This is especially true in regard to the

Peter Kreinberg doing groundwork.

retraining of a ruined horse by an expert or to recognize improper training methods.

Occasionally, riders with extreme beliefs come from this latter group. Nothing more needs to be said about this than to observe that more and more people are attracted to bitless riding. With this development, the argument turns on its head. To say the use of a bit is against animal protection is, per se, an inappropriate idea. Those who say it are exposing themselves as ignorant—and inexperienced. Of course there is abuse with bits. But their correct use leads to harmony, which is the core of good riding.

An ignorant person might say that all knives must be disposed of because someone was murdered with a knife. Every instrument or tool is only as good as the person who uses it.

---◆---

There are more and more people with horses, but fewer and fewer horsemen.

---◆---

The people who could be called "horsemen" in the traditional meaning are disappearing. The number of people who grew up with good examples of horse business and learned the necessary technical knowledge is falling steadily in comparison to the number of riders. It doesn't take just years but decades to gain the necessary knowledge and ability to be a good horseman or horsewoman. What we learn from working with horses brings us further along as a rider and, perhaps, also as a person. It's not just that horses learn from us. When we are ready, we can learn much from them. This is a great opportunity!

Many young people who grow up in the professional horse world learn the "business" from an economic perspective, and perhaps a few important, core principles of the trade. The moral-ethical components of the business are often left by the wayside.

For this reason, I maintain that the preservation of the knowledge that underlies the "ethics in horse sport" to be of the highest importance (see p. 9).

WHERE DO I STAND AS A RIDER?

When experts ride, it looks as easy as child's play. Observers don't know how hard it is to achieve the path to true expertise. It is not enough to buy a horse that has as much training as possible or one that jumps "automatically" over walls, ditches and oxers. Whoever really wants to ride must be prepared for a lengthy and sometimes sweaty learning process. It takes a long time before a rider can maintain balance on a horse's back at the trot and canter. To be able to define the tempo (rate of repetition of the rhythm or strides) and direction are further training goals. It is extremely demanding, and not achievable for everyone, to learn the ideal: to sit with an independent hand; to swing supply with the movement; to sit at every moment balanced in the center of gravity; and to be able to influence the horse with very fine, specific weight, back, leg and rein aids. However, less talented or ambitious riders can have fun and a lot of success with a horse that is right for them.

Good balance, rhythm and feel for the movement are prerequisites for learning riding technique. Many riders don't realize how their physical fitness and their mental state affect the horse. Not everyone considers all that the horse must carry around: a crooked pelvis, back pain, frustration with school or job, relationship issues, and extra pounds. Whoever takes the trouble to think about this can only marvel at the extent to which most horses make up for their rider's deficiencies.

Many riders focus on riding exercises. They don't understand that exercises are not the goal of training. Exercises are merely a means of developing "throughness" and rideability. The exercise itself isn't the important factor, but rather how it is executed. Success derives from good riding technique, with the horse responding to the rider's balanced seat along with development of muscle strength that allows him to progress through increasingly advanced skills. In contrast, if a trainer prematurely introduces

Irrespective of the horse's breed or riding discipline, a supple riding seat and the natural balance of the horse must be developed before including more advanced training exercises.

difficult exercises into the work of a young horse, both horse and rider will be frustrated and bad habits may develop.

We have good horses. Now we must breed good riders.

Systematic training is an important objective. For beginners and returning riders, good results in competition serve as a learning incentive. These riders are investing time, money and effort. And, of course, everyone enjoys receiving recognition; An award confirms your competence and strengthens self-confidence. But what does this really say about a rider's capabilities? Naturally, it is an achievement to place well in a test or complete a jumping course with a solid, well-trained (school) horse. But is this rider then in the position of being able to train a young horse or retrain a poorly ridden horse?

It is difficult to realistically assess our own ability. Beginners and inexperienced riders frequently believe they can ride and know all; experts realize that they can never know everything. Experienced riders don't say "I can do it!" That may seem paradoxical, but it is easy to explain. Everyone at the beginning of a long path enjoys each forward step: the first canter, the first ride outdoors, the first ribbon. However, the farther we come along, the more difficult the process. With each step, the demand on the capabilities of the rider and the trainer amplifies. We see our own limits more and more distinctly. At some point, we are forced to admit that one human life is not long enough to really learn to ride.

The good news: Our sport will never be boring!

CORRECTION — NOT PLEASANT, BUT NECESSARY

While no one likes to be criticized, everyone needs correction from someone else in order to improve. When you ride alone, errors of the seat and giving the aids often creep in. These can be avoided through competent instruction and support. Most good and successful riders work regularly with competent trainers. Watching videos of yourself riding and of other riders is also helpful.

The beautiful thing about riding is that you always have more to learn, assuming you are ready to work on yourself and to examine yourself critically. Developing skill sets through training is a process of evolution. How successful this is depends on your ability to accept criticism and your readiness to be involved with that living being, the horse. Good instruction leads ultimately to independence. It takes many years, even decades to reach this goal. The best teacher is the horse!

When the problem is in your head
Athletes in many sports, including swimming, skiing, running or tennis benefit from consulting sports psychologists. In riding, sports psychology training has played almost no role. Without always realizing it, riders frequently have the key to a problem in their own head. When a horse "makes a mistake," it usually is the fault of the rider on his back. Fear, performance pressure, or another unknown "programmed failure" can lead to a mental block that causes a rider to do the wrong thing at a decisive moment. Almost

A rider in the "light seat." A balanced seat helps the horse find his balance.

everyone knows the situation: the starting bell to enter the ring has just rung and you hold your breath and stop riding. Or, you really want to do well and get so tense that the horse doesn't know any more what the person on his back wants him to do because of abnormal pressures and body language.

Whether you like it or not, negative experiences, especially when repeated, will stick with you. Unfortunately, fear always causes a bad reaction. Sports psychology training, therefore, is good for riders.

Fear is another important issue. There probably aren't any riders who haven't been in a situation at least once when they were afraid because they lost control of their horse. As a rule, you get back on and ride off after a fall—that wasn't so bad. But it doesn't always go so well.

Falls and accidents can have consequences that take the fun out of riding. Not because the rider doesn't like her horse anymore or suddenly doesn't want to ride, but rather because she is afraid of losing control or falling off again.

Like it or not, a negative experience, especially when it is repeated, sticks with the rider for a long time. The worst part is that fear can lead to poor reactions. Here's a typical example: A beginner or inexperienced person is riding and the horse spooks and starts to canter. The rider is afraid. She tenses, falls forward and holds tightly onto the reins. The horse, naturally, runs faster. He is not being "bad," rather just following his flight instinct.

The more times the rider loses control, the more dominant the horse will become and the rider becomes more afraid. The horse takes over the leadership role and the rider is moved to the number two position in the "herd." The rider can't usually emerge from this "negative spiral" alone. The horse needs a competent rider who can correct him and boost his confidence. The rider needs support in order to regain confidence in herself and her horse to restructure her negative reaction pattern. The trainer who accepts this job needs not only to possess equestrian competence, but also a huge degree of empathy and patience.

Frequently, certain obstacles, jump combinations or exercises will trigger blockages. The same tape plays in your head that leads to repeat mistakes. For example: Your flying changes or tempi changes are always wonderful at home, but at least one change fails to be correct during a test. It isn't the horse's fault, but rather stems from your subconscious that causes the famous "performance effect." You concentrate so hard on avoiding errors that you cause exactly the ones you are trying to prevent.

Here's another example: A mare shies with her owner at the arena door; but with a different rider, the mare scarcely moves a muscle. Why? The owner has the same program running in her head: "I know the 'beast' is going to shy again." Naturally the horse jumps again to the side—because the rider has tensed her muscles unconsciously. The new rider doesn't know about the misbehavior and stays relaxed. She simply concentrates on riding—and the mare follows the rider's lead and does likewise.

When something goes wrong, other riders, the trainer, sometimes also parents and partners are ready with pithy comments that are not necessarily helpful. Psychological problems and fears are frequently underestimated in riding sports. Perhaps that is one of the reasons why we are so uncomfortable looking at ourselves and our own deficiencies and subconsciously blame the horse instead. Happily, more riders are looking at problems from a different vantage point, working toward unique solutions.

> PSYCHOLOGICAL PROBLEMS AND FEARS ARE FREQUENTLY UNDERESTIMATED IN RIDING SPORTS.

The problem with vanity

Unfortunately, dogmatism plays a strong role with riders: Many teachers travel to barns and proclaim that they know the right way. Dogmatism often makes it difficult to talk openly with one another.

Only a few trainers are confident enough to explore doubts or examine critical questions from riding students or colleagues. Many immediately feel threatened and react negatively. Even in riding, many people believe they alone know—or have just discovered—the truth. They exhibit self-aggrandizement, vanity and emotion. It would be so much more effective to deal with each other respectfully and seek a dialogue rather than to exclude another who thinks differently. It is clear that cliquishness and exclusion of others ultimately harms our horses.

We can only learn from one another when we treat each other openly and with respect.

It can't be about erecting a memorial to oneself. It is about the horse!

RIDING AS DIALOGUE BETWEEN HUMAN AND HORSE

Riding can best be compared to ballroom dancing. Similar to a dancing lesson, every training session and every exercise should be new and unique. No moment can be duplicated exactly. Rider and horse are not always in the same mood. They encounter each other again and again at different points, but it is always about finding a common rhythm, inner and outer balance and coordination together. It doesn't always happen: The shape the rider and the horse are in that day, as well as other external considerations, play important roles. It makes a difference whether both are relaxed or stressed, or in a known or a new environment. Finally, it has to do with the understanding and partnership between human and animal.

Whether riding or just being together, human and horse should always maintain a dialogue. To assure successful communication, riders need experience and routine, wisdom and cleverness, empathy, inner peace and patience, good reactions, discipline, courage, persistence and consistency.

"Most people don't ride as well as they are capable of doing: Moods, problems on the job and anger at themselves are all vented onto the horse—often without their realizing it."

Rudolf G. Binding, *Reitvorschrift für eine Geliebte* [Riding regulation for a loved one] Rutten & Loening, Potsdam, 1943, p. 49, new edition: Olms Press, Hildesheim 1995.

I would add to Binding's list: arrogance and egotism! Riding is not a "fighting" sport. Actually, riding isn't a sport in the literal meaning of the word. Aesthetics and harmony are as important as physical competency. Riding is about cooperation: The rider doesn't just mold the horse; the horse also molds the rider. This is precisely what makes interaction with horses so meaningful for many people.

Riding builds the person—in a holistic way. Whoever abuses horses for the satisfaction of his ego and ambition hurts himself.

It is such an unbelievably beautiful feeling when human and horse find themselves in mental and physical balance and in harmony with one another. For most pleasure riders, the friendship and the shared joy in movement are the goals; the connection to the horse plays the major role for them. Even for athletically ambitious riders, the understanding between human and animal is the key to a living communication. When the chemistry between a rider and a horse isn't right, the pair doesn't become a "dream team" or achieve high performance.

The horse is neither a piece of sports equipment nor a substitute for a family or a partner, even though it sometimes seems that way. He is an independent living being with species-specific behaviors and needs. His value should no more be reduced to his current athletic achievements than a human's value should be reduced to her job or her bank account. Whether you have a friendly or a professional relationship with a horse, he deserves that you value him and respect his personality.

"The greatness of a rider is seen in his interaction with his horse."

(Adapted from a quote from Mahatma Gandhi)

RECOGNIZE STRENGTHS AND RESPECT LIMITATIONS

To treat a horse fairly, he must be evaluated correctly and with abundant sensitivity and experience. Like every rider, each horse is an individual with his own character and different strengths and weaknesses. Like every rider, each horse has his limitations. His capabilities—in respect to the training goal—depend on his inner "spirit," not just on conformation and performance ability. Many a horse makes up for physical deficiency astoundingly well with a strong character and desire to perform. Consequently, a solid "core" of a horse is more important to many riders than big gaits, huge jumping ability or extraordinary physique.

Breeding for a performance sport frequently develops horses with capabilities that far exceed those of the average rider. Too much impulsion in a horse makes it difficult for trail riders and pleasure riders to find their own balance as compared to riding a horse with "normal" movement.

Likewise, a horse can be overwhelmed by the demands of the rider. Famous names in his pedigree don't always guarantee that the horse will have comparable jumping or dressage talent. The trainer and the rider must figure out what job the horse is best suited for and in which he'll be most comfortable. Every horse needs a rider who can adjust to the horse's temperament, his natural desire to move, and his unique qualities. He also needs a rider who is able to get along with him. Human and horse will enjoy each other for a long time only when the performance ambitions of the rider are in accord with her own ability and that of her horse.

IV.
TRAINING
Part One: More than Riding

EARLY EDUCATION

Early education of the young horse comes before training. He must get used to interacting with people, become accustomed to his new world, which, generally speaking, conists of a stall, a paddock, indoor and outdoor riding area, and, if lucky, turnout with a herd in a pasture. He must learn to be led and tied up; to pick up his hooves for inspection and cleaning; and trust his new herd boss, the human. Above all, he must learn to respect the person caring for him and/or riding him.

Good training can only be built on a reciprocal relationship of respect and trust. When respect is lacking, and a horse doubts the person's leadership role, then it becomes more difficult and less safe to start and train the horse. Life-threatening situations can arise when working with horses. Many people

A horse is a flight animal. His senses are always alert. Eyes and ears play a dominant role.

WHY DO HORSES "THINK" DIFFERENTLY?

Humans are only aware of what is important to them. They have goal-oriented behavior. In contrast, horses are aware of the tiniest details and only make direct connections. Unlike humans, horses cannot think abstractly. Horses learn by trying something and either succeeding or failing; experience becomes knowledge.

Horses react out of instinct, experience and observation. To help a horse understand me, I use his horse-specific behavior in his early education and training. When he learns to accept me as the lead animal, he will connect with me and follow. As a herd animal, he naturally follows others of his own kind so with new challenges, like the first time he goes on a trail or into water, it makes sense to bring along an experienced and quiet companion horse that will lead the way, if necessary.

don't realize that they can also ruin a horse through "love" for the animal. When you interact inappropriately with a horse for a period of time, character weaknesses may develop. Eventually, retraining will be needed by using clearer, and sometimes harsher, measures from an experienced trainer. On the other hand, "rude" and rough treatment of a horse, especially a novice horse, can lead to fear and his loss of trust in people.

It is very important for the horse's early education to include sensitivity and calm while promoting the horse's self-confidence. A mature, experienced horse person is best equipped to raise a quiet, self-confident, obedient and reliable riding horse.

RESPECT AND TRUST

Respect and trust belong together. Horses sometimes test the limits. The higher the horse is in the herd's pecking order, the more frequently he will ask, "Who is boss?" This can happen while he's being led or groomed, with the farrier or the vet, being loaded into a trailer, or ridden. Horses low on the pecking order seldom raise such questions.

Dominant horses ask questions of the boss regularly and they need an experienced rider and trainer who is up to the challenge. Undesirable actions require a quick reaction, especially the first time. When a horse pushes or lashes out at a person, he needs to be given a clear response that makes the boundaries unmistakable. Horses understand a direct, quick reaction very well and as a rule, they respond appropriately. Nevertheless, this reaction must come immediately, and be measured and commensurate.

Human instruction or reactions that are insecure, hesitant or inconsistent may confirm or possibly strengthen a horse's bad behavior. Horses have a fine sense as to whether a person is impatient, fearful, or aggressive as opposed to possessing a commanding sense as the dominant member of this two-member "herd." It makes a big impression on a horse when he is allowed to intimidate with bad manners or resistance and, as a result, the next time it is harder for the person to assert herself in control.

Overreactions that the horse doesn't understand work the same way, but negatively. For example, a horse that is difficult to catch may be on the receiving end of aggravation and punishment when he's finally caught. Consequently, he then associates the punishment with being caught, not with running away, and the next time he startles and runs away, catching him will be even more difficult. But when calmness and praise are extended to the horse that finally allows himself to be caught, he connects being caught with a good experience. Positive and negative experiences mold the behavior of a horse.

Respect and trust are required for good communication.

Trust between rider and horse is fundamental if both are to enjoy the ride.

WITH ONE ANOTHER, NOT AGAINST ONE ANOTHER

It is not always easy to know whether an undesirable reaction, blockage or resistance in the horse stems from a lack of understanding, or if he's mentally or physically overtaxed, fresh, tired, feeling fear, reluctance, pain or something else. In the course of training and in general interaction, a variety of situations can arise. Experience helps, but the behavior of horses is often a puzzle for even experienced trainers. Only a few problems are solved according to a certain pattern. Usually, you must ponder over it a long time until you find the key. Under such circumstances, keep in mind: Whoever tries to accomplish something through force may have only short-term success. Over time, pressure always creates counter-pressure—or resignation.

You want to have a horse that is healthy and happy to work with, a horse that reacts to light aids and trusts you even in dangerous situations. If you want to achieve this goal, you must use training methods that are fair to the horse. I strongly advise against training methods that use questionable equipment designed to force subordination. They lead to a dead end, I guarantee you. The concept of an even relationship based on give and take also applies to the partnership between rider and horse. No one can dance with inspiration when there is a pistol held to her head. What I cannot or won't do, I can't expect the horse to do. I achieve trust and respect from a horse only when I offer him trust and respect. With forced methods, punishment or abuse, I only create a horse that doesn't want to or can't, is afraid of me or reacts in panic. That can be dangerous. Consequently, as a rider or trainer I shouldn't let it get that far.

"The horse is your mirror. He never flatters you. He reflects your temperament. He also reflects your ups and downs. Don't ever be angry with your horse: you might as well be angry with your mirror."

Rudolf G. Binding, *Reitvorschrift fur eine Geliebte* [Riding regulation for a loved one] Rutten & Loening, Potsdam 1943, p. 48, new edition: Olms Press, Hildesheim 1995

Consistency is essential when interacting with a horse and when riding so that the horse learns to understand what the person wants. At certain times, I must assert myself. But the question is, "How?" Asserting myself doesn't mean creating a fight that I must win at any price. By "asserting myself" I mean to show the horse his place in the "herd." The human must be the leader. In contrast, force and fighting usually lead to training problems related to resistance such as stiffness or a lack of suppleness, which usually make things worse. A human has no chance against 1000 to 1400 pounds of living weight. Impatience, rage and anger are completely out of place. Complex training situations require systematic analysis and a clever solution.

You can only ride well when you have your emotions under control.

Consistency is necessary. When a rider or trainer "lays" into a horse, jerks him in the mouth or otherwise mistreats him, it is no sign of ability or power, rather just ineffectual signals that stem from a rider's feeling of helplessness or lack of technique. Methods using force that the horse doesn't understand and that he experiences as punishment are counterproductive. Nothing can be forced from the horse in riding! Depending on the horse's character, forced and excessive reactions from rider or handler achieve either nothing at all or the opposite of what you wanted.

It is fundamentally better to avoid punishment altogether. When something doesn't work right away, try it again. When you run up against resistance or a blockage, analyze the situation and look for a solution based on the desired reaction. Unlike the horse, you can think logically. When something doesn't work, ask yourself, "Why?" Have you used the right aids? Has the horse understood you? Was the exercise reasonable? Does the horse have a muscle cramp from yesterday or the day before? As a rider or trainer, you have the responsibility to present the exercise in a way that the horse can understand—and execute it.

One of the prerequisites for success is to set realistic goals, and to correctly assess yourself and your horse. As rider and trainer, you must bear in mind the horse's fitness, the shape he's in that day, his ability, limitations, character, temperament, and possible health issues.

MOTIVATION

Most riders would like an agile, expressive horse that is obedient, reliable and willing. A horse's motivation is the decisive factor for charisma and cooperation: The horse must want to perform, to exert himself and attempt to perform to his limits.

Horses have to experience positive responses to be motivated. Instead of being irritated over mistakes, it is much more reasonable to provide positive experiences for the horse as well as for yourself. Even the smallest progress is worthy of being praised and celebrated. The recognition can be expressed in different ways but it should always come so that the horse connects his behavior with a positive experience. Whoever praises her horse and enjoys small forward steps motivates not only the horse, but also herself!

You won't achieve the goal that you've set for yourself at every moment. It sometimes takes longer than originally thought to achieve a new step in training. It makes no sense to work past the point of fatigue. Many training problems result from horse or rider being tense or fatigued and then suffering from blockages.

You cannot force tense muscles to relax. You can only ride intelligently so that they do relax.

When demands cause tension and blockages in the horse and/or the rider, it is best to take a step back and analyze the situation. Muscle tension and mental blocks are never resolved with force but rather with sensitivity and understanding.

Relaxation is critical to solving a problem. Often, it helps to leave a subject or exercise for a while; horses and people need time to assimilate an experience. When you try again after a break and systematically prepare for the exercise, there is a good chance that the problem or lesson will be mastered.

A brisk canter on the trail is motivating for horse and rider.

V.

TRAINING
Part Two: Physiological

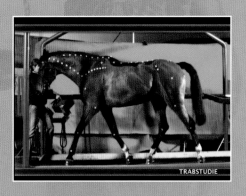

STRUCTURE AND DEVELOPMENT OF THE MUSCULATURE

This chapter does not address an athlete and her sport horse. Instead, I present some thoughts about daily physiological training appropriate for any horse. It is important to note that every rider who decides to get her horse out of a stall is a trainer! Everybody who decides when, what, how much and how long a horse works is a trainer, and she should observe a few ground rules for the good of the horse.

The goal of good training is to develop the specific musculature needed for the discipline, so that the equine athlete is able to meet performance demands. The right muscling only develops when both the mental aspect, as I've already discussed, as well

as the basic muscle physiology are considered. Only a calm horse that is alert and willing to work can be sensibly trained. Nervous tension, excitability, fear and unruliness distract him from appropriate training.

Riders must be conscious of the fact that every single ride or training session is training in the physiological sense! It is not uncommon for training to lead to micro-tears in the muscles or to production of lactic acid in the muscles when working beyond the horse's aerobic capacity (muscles working in the presence of oxygen). These physiological effects lead to "muscle aches." You may be familiar with this feeling from your own body experiences with demanding exercise.

Only a supple body can build the correct muscles.

Patient, physiological training and systematic gymnastics are prerequisites for correct collection.

Strong exertion potentially leads to pain in the muscles, ligaments and joints, particularly if the horse is unfit for the requested tasks. Measurement of muscle enzymes can determine recovery, but stiffness arising from training effects usually abates within one to three days.

The *H.Dv.12* (German army regulations of 1912), recommended that three-year-old horses should work three times a week and four-year- olds, four times a week. This simple guideline demonstrates that, even a century ago, people considered the effects of intensity and duration of training on the horse's musculoskeletal system. Ideally, a training plan should not be too strictly defined.

Every trainer and rider should be aware of the fact that a young horse, especially, is likely to experience muscle soreness the first or second day after a strong training session. It would be counterproductive to ask the horse for another intense training session during this period of soreness. Recognition of the horse's discomfort may be evidenced by specific signs: stiffness, unrideability or resistance. If you attempt to modify the horse through force and rough-ness when he exhibits such signs, you are likely to hurt him!

Physical stiffness particularly leads to chronic tension, nervousness and permanent resistance in horses with a strong personality. The psychological anticipation and resistance is revealed in the physical!

To summarize, you should carefully reflect on and analyze a horse's resistance to training. In the case of an older adult horse that needs retraining, figure out if what needs to be corrected is due to old mis-takes in training and chronic tension, or is related to pain that has arisen from a recent training—"fresh" muscle soreness. Movement, particularly voluntary exercise such as turnout, helps to relieve muscle ten-sion, so following a day of intense training, the horse can be given a day off with turnout, exercised lightly on the longe line without side reins, and ridden out on an enjoyable trail ride or in the fields.

As I've already emphasized, it is ultimately up to the feel of the rider to work out the right train-ing plan.

An older, correctly trained athlete can work ac-cording to his capabilities and the energy his feed provides. Note: A healthy, well-trained horse may not reach full capacity until he is nine to ten years old.

A horse that is being retrained must be regarded much like an older, novice horse. A horse won't al-ways have a series of good training days or bad days; the horse's reactions to training depend on a sensitive rider figuring out how to maximize the good days.

Tense muscles can only be made soft through "giv-ing" (the reins), and not through force and "taking" in with tighter reins or more collection. Shortened, tight muscles work best if encouraged to stretch; this is not done with force or by pulling on the reins. I would like to cite another philosophical perspective and understanding of dressage from the authors of the book, **Gallop to Freedom**. About the development

of "long" muscles, Frédéric Pignon and Magali Del-gado write:

"As I develop a horse, I try to ensure that he has what I call 'long' muscles. These can only be formed when muscles are relaxed while they are working. If a muscle has tension, then the horse will inevitably develop 'short' muscles. With ex-perience one can see this quality or deficiency just by looking at a horse. Horses with short muscles can have frequent physical problems and suffer from niggling complaints. People sell their horses because they get fed up with all the things that seem to go wrong and my experience is that this is often the reason. Horses working in tension do not develop harmonious musculature."

Frédéric Pignon and Magali Delgado, in *Gallop to Freedom,* Trafalgar Square Books: North Pomfret, Vermont, 2009

These two trainers aptly describe the effect of poor training on the musculature of the horse. It is one of the most important tasks of good riding to avoid tension when training and when retraining, to encourage its release!

A solid education about training horses should be required of every rider!

In my practical work, longeing with a longe caves-son (and without side reins) is the most effective training method as a supplement to work under saddle. I haven't been able to find a better longeing method for a horse needing retraining.

As valuable as longeing is as supplemental work, it is not a substitute for work under saddle and should be done with purpose and forethought. Longeing incorrectly and too frequently can be counterproductive with a tense horse, and can sometimes damage a horse's health. Longeing, as an exclusive exercise, also doesn't work well, long term. The goal of good longeing work is to relax the horse's topline, lessen tension in his back, and develop the horse's tempo with a rhythmically swinging back. Longeing should not be used with side reins as a training method to force a tense horse—one that is not "through"—into a certain frame; it is unrealistic to expect to achieve softness, "throughness" or suppleness in this way. Forcing a stiff horse into a frame to achieve throughness is not promising: It contradicts all training principles and damages the horse's health.

An additional rule to keep in mind:

The more movement, the better!

Some still believe that limiting a sport horse's voluntary exercise makes him move more expressively and able to jump more powerfully. However, this has long been scientifically disproven. The more movement your horse gets daily, the healthier he is! Joint physiology (such as nutrition to the cartilage) depends on movement. A horse that is brought in from the pasture for riding doesn't need as long a warm-up phase as a stalled horse.

For horses that are required to stand confined for 22 to 23 hours a day, an extensive walking warm-up phase is of great value to counteract the negative effects of lack of movement. During colder seasons, warm-up activity becomes even more important to prevent strain or injury.

The training plan you develop for the sport horse works best if it is flexible and well thought through. It is especially important to plan according to the horse's age and experience.

The point of training is to strengthen the horse physically and mentally. Harmony develops when rider and horse are in balance with one another.

SYSTEMATIC GYMNASTICS

For thousands of years people have trained horses. Despite the differences between individual "schools," certain principles maintain their validity. This is especially true regarding the laws of biomechanics. No riding instruction can leave out the biological basis for controlling the movement of horse and rider. Dressage doesn't mean "to train" a horse. It is not about conditioning a horse so that you can press a button and he performs as many difficult exercises as possible, or jumps high fences. The purpose of training is to strengthen a horse physically and mentally through systematic gymnastics so that he develops according to his aptitude to be able to fully unfold his potential.

◆

"The principle of harmony precedes the principle of performance."

Peter Kreinberg, *Stimmen der Pferde* [Voices of the horses], Wu Wei Verlag, Schondorf, 2008

◆

Systematic gymnastics are essential to readying a horse for competition and for the horse's musculoskeletal health. Good riding technique and training provide practical animal protection. Riding sports require solid basic training, physiologically and psychologically appropriate advanced training, with measured increases in demand. Competition—regardless of type—is best viewed as a test of systematic and continuous training. For competition to become a goal in itself contradicts sound riding theory.

VI.

THE SEAT

Supple and Balanced

TENSE RIDER—TENSE HORSE

The rider's seat is the most important form of communication, serving as the interface between rider and horse. The seat is described and analyzed in numerous books and videos. Today many people, including children, don't exercise nearly enough; many adult riders suffer from on-the-job tension. Sports medicine techniques provide exercises for riders to improve their seat. Appropriate exercises can warm up and loosen muscles in preparation for the person to sit on the horse. (See also: Michael Putz, *Richtig Reiten* [Riding correctly], FN Verlag, Warendorf 2010, p. 19 and on.)

Trainers and professional riders also benefit from gymnastics to enable them to sit on the horse with better balance and flexibility. Regular work with tense horses or on horses that need retraining often causes tension in the rider's body, which, in a never-ending cycle, spreads to the horse. Sports medicine principles offer sensible ways to counteract these negative effects.

Traditional knowledge about a rider's seat has been preserved and refined by famous institutions like the Spanish Riding School in Vienna. In their training system, the quality of the seat is developed and constantly improved, whether for an ambitious beginner or an advanced and experienced rider. Longeing the rider plays a large and decisive role: Regular correction of the seat on a well-balanced and well-trained horse is counseled by an experienced trainer doing the longeing. Charles de Kunffy, a classical trainer who lives in the United States, recommends regular correction of the seat on the longe, even for advanced riders:

In dressage training, it is a fundamental requirement to have secure balance at all gaits.

"Only a supple, well-balanced seat allows the possibility of subtle influence. This is also true for rein and leg aids."

Charles de Kunffy, *The Ethics and Passions of Dressage*, Half Halt Press, Boonsboro, Maryland, 1993

I see the static, tense driving seat as a problem of our time: It is often used and, unfortunately, regularly taught. This seat is not soft, and its force leads to a tight back in the horse.

The state of the back of the horse mirrors the rider's!

You may have seen the pictures of a rider sitting on the edge of the chair who by tensing the lower back is able to tip the chair forward. This demonstration of back tightening is very valid and true. Tightening the back makes sense but can only be done correctly once the seat is balanced and supple.

Riders often hear, "Sit down and put your legs on!" In my experience, such a command leads many of them to tighten their back as they try too hard to sit. A riding instructor doesn't tire of telling students such concepts as "Grab hold of the horse" or "Keep the hand still and sit against it." This static driving yet bracing seat is frequently taught and even the expression of this "mechanical concept" contradicts the essence of good riding. As a consequence, the rider loses suppleness; the horse becomes either lazy and is pressed forward or forced with jabbing spurs or he does the opposite by running out from under the seat of the rider.

One thing is for certain: Such a horse often hollows and/or tenses his back, making it hard for the rider to sit well. The rider then has little to no ability to generate an active seat. Moreover, the horse develops secondary problems such as issues with rein contact, tempo and rhythm disturbances, increased crookedness and more. Many training problems result from an unbalanced, tight, backward, gripping, and/or braced driving seat.

The rider's seat is the center of good training.

Only a rider who sits with a good and supple seat is able to actualize her knowledge about horse training. A rider with a poor seat can never see her knowledge put into action even when she is a good "horse person" who understands riding theory and its psychological and biomechanical foundation.

THE PSYCHOLOGICAL COMPONENTS

The rider's seat is not just the result of human biomechanics. Psychology also matters—for human and horse.

I would like to make a very important point from my perspective about something that plays a central role, if not *the* central role, in the development of a good seat: Mental relaxation is critical, at least for advanced riders who no longer have to think or

The perfect balanced seat is the most valuable asset of every rider.

be anxious about their physical balance. A rider in a hurry, or one who can't—or won't—mentally connect with her horse, will never relax sufficiently to sit well. Excessive ambition, pressure to succeed and an exaggerated sense of self-worth make a quiet and supple seat impossible!

A supple influence on the back and the movement of the horse is only possible when the rider can literally "let herself fall" into the saddle—psychologically. "Letting yourself fall" depends on a rider's healthy, but not excessive self-confidence, determination, sensitivity and character. When she rides with constant worry that the horse might become difficult, or if she is frightened of making a fool of herself in front of colleagues, it will affect her seat. She may react in any of a number of ways: Either she collapses on the horse's back, sits passively with little effect, or tries to dominate the horse by pulling on and seesawing the reins, which results in pulling the horse "backward." She may be sitting straight and braced, rather than supple and riding forward.

Psychological pressure makes it impossible to sit according to recommended guidelines. The trainer plays a decisive role here: One who yells and intimi-dates his students no more belongs in the arena than does an indifferent trainer who goes by the "book," or an inattentive one who makes phone calls or holds conversations with others when he should be focused on the horse and rider. A trainer's job is to reduce anxiety, establish a positive mood and exe-cute a systematic training plan. Working with horses should be fun for everyone involved. I would also

A calm, self-confident rider gives a horse security in any situation.

like to suggest that sports psychology works best for calm and even-tempered people. The body of knowledge about biomechanics and physiology in humans and horses is best applied when psychology is also considered!

Riding should not be like hard work with the rider sweating and stone-faced!

The rider's seat cannot be mechanically and physically forced. Good riding is a question of character, state of mind and self-control. A friendly, happy, even-tempered and self-aware person has an easier time of sitting really well—and consequently riding well.

Most riders work their horses in an environment that often produces tension and psychological pressure. Because many horses are stabled and ridden at boarding barns, a rider is seldom alone in the arena and may not want to attract attention. In addition, the rider who has positioned her horse's nose "down" is frequently considered a good rider.

The constant focus on the horse's outline (round poll, round neck) contributes to a rider's mental and physical tenseness to maintain her horse's posture in this way. Waldemar Seunig refutes this focus on the frame of the horse as the most important goal of a good rider:

"Longitudinal flexion and elevation are not essential goals of dressage training, but are the effects of proper work."

Waldemar Seunig, *Von der Koppel bis zur Kapriole* [From paddock to capriole] 1943, Olms Press, Hildesheim, Zürich, New York, p. 134.

Anybody who struggles to get the "head down and the neck up" does not yet understand the basic principals of riding theory. Longitudinal flexion and elevation are formal criteria. If Seunig's sentence was only taken seriously, thousands of riders could relax while sitting on their horse and finally be able to ride well with a good seat. The reality, however, is unfortunately quite different.

FORCED LONGITUDINAL FLEXION AND ITS CONSEQUENCES

The nose must go down! And, with physical force if necessary! Many riders climb on their horse with just this intention in mind. Longitudinal flexion is seen today as the first prerequisite to being able to gymnasticize the horse. Consequently, many riders land in a "pull-and-drive" seat. They seek to jam the horse between the seat and the hand, or actively drive him together: His hind legs are supposed to step under through the holding of a rider's clamped-on legs, rigid driving back, and counter- or backward-pull-

ing hands. The rider may hear, "Sit down and put your legs on!" Riding like this is all too common—even at top performance levels. But no horse in the world can balance himself under such a seat. Suppleness and "throughness," basically the whole Training Scale (see p. 59), are relegated to the sidelines in the process.

I believe that the basic cause of this current state of affairs relates to the formal judging guidelines and design of the riding tests. Even in the lowest introductory tests, the frame and the exercise are often

A horse being mechanically longitudinally flexed with an extremely tense and stiff poll.

placed higher than the quality of the seat. It would be better if the focus were on how wonderfully balanced and supple the young rider sits and how obedient and calm the horse is rather than how well a Training Level horse goes on the bit. The outline (round poll and elevated neck) is not the goal of good work; rather, it's the result! (See Waldemar Seunig's words, p. 47.) Too often, the rider with the good, supple seat and the rhythmical and relaxed horse isn't in the ribbons, but instead it's the horse that is the most constricted—with his nose pulled under regardless of whether the neck is shortened in the process or not.

The job of a dressage judge, according to Dr. Gustav Rau (in Erich Glahn's *Reitkunst am Scheideweg* [Equitation at the crossroads], Erich Hoffmann Verlag, Heidenheim, 1956), is to evaluate first, and most importantly, the quality of training and gaits, and then the technical quality of the execution of the test. But what about the 13-year-old girl sitting softly in a Training Level dressage test on her obedient horse that isn't on the bit? If the horse's head isn't "down," she may feel forced to increase bit contact to pull the horse's head down so she doesn't look like a bad rider in front of the spectators. In my perspective, this sort of adherence to strict guidelines, especially at the lower levels, destroys the seat of many young riders. Even in pony clubs, "the squeeze-and-drive" seat is commonly taught. At this age, riders should be taught that the pony's health and well-being are the most important things—not a ribbon!

I see a big task for the future: The sport of dressage must focus on horsemanship and education for all young and new riders, regardless of their interest in competing. A good seat and the harmony of the execution should be at the center of training efforts. These two criteria should be heavily weighed by judges and placed far ahead of the usual adherence to the formal correctness of the test. Each horse should be allowed to have his nose well in front of the vertical—a much lesser evil as compared to the horse that no longer seeks contact with the rider's hand, curls his neck in with his nose consistently behind the vertical.

Sometimes I smile when I listen to officials who verbally declare the formal guidelines to be correct but then say that a "little behind the vertical" is not so bad—and sometimes even necessary. I would like to emphasize that adherence to the formal expectations of head and neck position is not only absolutely unnecessary, but also that it is simply and overwhelmingly wrong! It takes quite a bit of time to get the nose consistently back out in front in horses that have developed a very tight back from being ridden into a compressed frame: a situation commonly seen in horses that need retraining. This style of riding is absolutely undesirable and should be resisted at all costs!

Classical training techniques are correct!
Good riding comes from a good seat!

Good physical and mental balance of both horse and rider.

Cantering in a two-point or forward seat makes it easier for the horse to relax his muscles. It is important that the rider is well-balanced and staying centered.

THE FORWARD SEAT AS AN ALTERNATIVE

For several years, I have enjoyed having an increasing number of professionals and very experienced amateur riders in my seminars. This group is generally aware that the ability of the rider to influence through the seat grows favorably and steadily with increasing age, experience, rider fitness and, not least of all, body weight. With longer legs and more body mass, the rider can be more effective and in harmony with her horse. However, some riders incorrectly use that body weight to the detriment of the horse. She can ride so that the horse "fakes it" or in such a way that actually damages the horse over term.

With certain riding techniques, a horse with a strong back can be lifted into a passage-like "hover" trot or tensed up to impress unwitting spectators. However, it works differently when training young horses or retraining older ones where problems can be "programmed" into horses with a weak or extremely tight back (novice horses, hyperflexed back movers, or leg movers). A rider who is heavy-handed or sits heavily while using the aids actually makes it very hard for such a horse to be balanced, to relax, and to be a supple back mover. Nothing is achieved by using all of your weight and power on a horse with a stiff back. On the contrary, if a rider sits completely down in the saddle on a horse with a stiff back, the horse's back muscles tense even more.

From my experience, about 90 percent of horses are not capable of bearing a full load on the back. Consequently, their sensitivity to the rider's aids causes them to react by further tightening the back. To get out of this vicious cycle, an experienced rider must learn to keep the horse's back supple or to make it supple again. You should be able to sit supplely and quietly on a novice horse or a horse that is being re-trained. Whoever causes constant tension and pres-sure on the horse's back and in the rein contact, cannot relax a horse. Good riders are able to vary their influence intermittently from being totally pas-sive and supple to using a lightly tensed lower back.

It doesn't make sense to sit the trot when the horse is tense and blocked in the back, even if the rider can sit with sensitivity and suppleness. A horse that carries himself (in self-carriage), lifting his back and able to swing through his body, is one that a rider can sit on well. (Self-carriage implies that the horse is able to carry himself in balance without any support from the reins.) With novice horses, hyper-flexed back movers and leg movers, and horses with weak or sensitive backs, it is recommended to do a posting trot or a balanced forward seat.

Professionals and experienced amateurs should be comfortable with all seat types, saddles and stir-rup lengths. A really good seat also requires the ability to ride in all stirrup lengths, except with ex-cessively long stirrups. For example, an experienced trainer should be able to balance her weight over short stirrups in a soft forward seat to avoid creating more tension in a novice horse or a poorly trained one with a sensitive or tense back. It is impossible to balance a horse by riding with excessively long stir-rups that preclude a bend in the knees, especially on a novice or ruined horse.

Professional riders should work diligently and reg-ularly on their seat, particularly since suppleness of the seat is easily lost when working with many stiff horses. The rider's back absorbs the negative tension from the horse's back. A soft, balanced seat and fit-ness are essential for the rider's health and success in training.

The fork seat robs the rider of the ability to influence the horse with balanced weight: The pelvis of the rider is tipped to the front.

The braced driving seat, the most frequent seat error in dres-sage, leads to a stiff poll and back: The back of the horse mir-rors the rider's.

VII.
INFLUENCE
Tactful and Effective

AIDS FOR THE LIGHTEST POSSIBLE COMMUNICATION

Many riders believe that they must always be "doing" something while riding. They are often continually busy pulling their horse's head down. They clench, squeeze and push, hold the reins tight, pull or seesaw to force the horse to yield through mechanical means. The "clothes–pin" seat makes it impossible to give an intentional, tactful aid: Thighs and knees are clamped on, lower legs hammer away, constantly drilling spurs into the horse's sides as a continuous irritant. The horse's response is to tighten; the rider then has more problems getting through to the horse with her aids.

The "squeeze-press-pull" type of riding is a vicious cycle, ultimately leading to a horse that becomes ever stiffer and dull, or psychologically tense and nervous. The horse ridden with a clothes-pin seat resigns himself and lets each step be driven out of his body or he attempts to get out of the situation by running out from under the rider.

In practice, many think that they can produce suppleness and "throughness" with pulling hands, a clamped driving seat and squeezing legs. Aids are, however, not meant to be a means to dominate a creature. They should serve to establish tactful communication between two partners. A supple, well-balanced seat does that!

The supple, well-balanced seat enables the rider to influence the horse with carefully measured levels of weight, leg and rein aids.

Without a supple, well-balanced seat, tactful and correct use of the aids is impossible.

A delicate tuning of the aids requires rider body awareness and coordination. The rider's muscles have to be loose and the joints mobile in order to feel the movements of the horse and to influence the horse with artfully measured weight, back, leg and rein aids. The rider should sit balanced and relaxed on the horse's back in order to blend with the horse physically and mentally, to gain his trust in the seat and therefore with the rider. A crooked or wobbly head, shoulder pulled up, elbows stuck out, hands that move too much or are rigid, a bouncing seat, gripping with the thighs or constantly beating legs are all signs of tension and they prevent the rider from finding the horse's center of gravity. When the rider is mentally and physically tense, harmony cannot exist between horse and rider.

Before the rider can mold the horse, she must first mold herself—that is, her seat.

Effective riding requires being able to feel the movement of the horse, and to react appropriately with your own body. Only when you give clear aids can the horse understand and follow them. Consequently, you must not just physically sit on the horse, but also blend with the horse psychologically. In order to develop the necessary feel, it helps to be conscious of the horse's movements. At the walk, you can distinctly feel when the right or left hind foot is set down, and how the right versus the left seat bone feels with each step.

Feeling from the seat

"Feel" by the rider comes from a soft, independent seat. She must wait on the horse and "listen." The less pressure used, and the softer and more independent the seat, the more the horse will wait for and "listen" to the rider. This is what is needed for communication: to be in balance with each other.

Only when there is balance between the rider and the horse, and the horse focuses on the rider, can the rider influence the movement and the balance of the horse.

"Getting into each other" starts with the rider. A horse will only be calm and permit being driven forward when the rider is also calm and is sitting in a supple manner. A forceful rider that pesters the horse by refusing to let him relax will never ride a through horse. Suppleness can be neither forced nor mechanically produced. In the ideal, carefree movement in unison between horse and rider is what creates the desirable harmony in riding.

To develop a horse, the horse needs the rider's support: This includes targeted strength and energy expenditure. Just as experienced in fluid dancing, the effort is barely noticeable when both horse and rider's bodies are relaxed and the energy flows.

Alarm signals: resistance and laziness

Horses are naturally sensitive. Every fly on their skin is immediately shaken off and they react to light aids when ridden appropriately. In this book, there are numerous citations from authors who stress how important it is for horses to accept the aids, especially the leg aids. If a horse doesn't react anymore to the leg, rider's seat and/or rein contact, the cause is usually not in the horse, but with the rider. The horse's sensitivity is encouraged and maintained only when your aids are precise, clear and coordinated. The goal of training is for the communication to become increasingly subtle until you give almost invisible aids coming almost exclusively from the seat. It is an alarm signal when a rider must use increasing pressure or harsher bits or devices in attempts to avert resistance. In such cases, scrutinize the equipment, the general condition and health of the horse, the training of the horse and your own riding.

REIN AIDS AND HOLDING THE REINS

I would like to present a few thoughts and experiences on the subject of rein aids. In the practical part of my seminars, I regularly encounter horse-and-rider pairs for whom communication is distorted. A major problem is that the rider pulls her inside hand back toward the thigh: Pulling on the inside rein leads to a corresponding counter-pull from the horse. The horse tenses his shortened head and neck muscles on the outside. And, pulling on one side more than the other has a corresponding effect on the rider: She tenses her shoulders and back, leans back and pulls the legs up. This becomes a vicious cycle! Being conscious of how you hold the inside rein is very helpful.

We try to create a line from the rider's elbow through the rein hand to the horse's mouth. If there are problems with poll tension and poll rounding, lift the inside rein hand higher so that it moves in a radius around the bit. This leads to a distinct release of cramping for both the horse's poll and the rider.

Horses ridden with rough hands can only move tensely. Suppleness cannot be forced!

When it is difficult to position the poll, the Littauer method of holding the reins is recommended. It keeps the rider from pressing the hand down and pulling.

With Littauer reins (driving reins), the rein goes over the hand and more quickly gives the rider the feeling of carrying the hands.

The clearly defined enemy is an inside hand that pulls backward and pushes down!

Littauer reins for retraining

Experienced riders with many years or decades in the saddle who are having problems with contact may find it helpful to hold the reins in a completely different way from their previous habits. One helpful technique is to hold the reins according to Vladimir S. Littauer: The rein goes over the index finger into the fist—this allows careful and subtle movement of the rein by the index finger to develop a completely new "hand feel." The rider becomes conscious again of the movements of the rein hand, making it easier to resist the negative, but automatic, movements. It also becomes easier to get the feeling of carrying the hand, which is especially important with the inside positioning rein. This method is especially helpful on the side where the rider is most likely to pull. To develop a riding hand that is independent from a supple seat, every now and then substitute methods, such as the Littauer method, of holding the reins that differ from the standard method.

When you focus on developing a sensitive, giving, independent hand, you will be a long way down the road to improving the seat.

VIII.

BALANCE

The Most Important Criterion

THE TRAINING SCALE AS A GUIDE

The significance of solid basic training cannot be overestimated. Every riding horse needs this foundation regardless of whether the intent is to develop a pleasure horse or a competition prospect. During the first years of training, the physical and mental qualities are developed that enable the horse to do his job and stay sound.

The Training Scale provides the essential criteria used in training and in daily work. The scale includes:

1. Rhythm
2. Suppleness
3. Contact
4. Impulsion
5. Straightness
6. Collection

The first three—*Rhythm, Suppleness and Contact*—are the basics. The following three—*Impulsion, Straightness and Collection*—build on the basics and cannot be achieved without them. Conversely, Impulsion, Straightness and Collection improve Rhythm, Suppleness and Contact. All the steps on the Training Scale are linked in a close and complex relationship that is based on biomechanics.

It is slow and difficult to make up for gaps in basic training that negatively affect further training. The ideal is a versatile, reliable riding horse that happily goes to work, willingly accepts the aids and trusts the rider in every situation. This goal presumes that the rider and horse are physically and mentally in balance: In this state, harmony and lightness are possible. This is true for every discipline (dressage, jumping and trail riding) and every breed.

A horse at liberty is balanced. During the first year of training, he'll find his balance under a rider.

JUDGING HORSES—WHAT MATTERS?

The enormous progress made in the breeding of modern riding horses affects training. The better the conformation and proportions achieved through selective breeding, the easier it is for a horse to find his balance with a rider on his back. Even a horse with near perfect conformation can and must reestablish his balance while developing the muscles necessary for carrying a rider.

Foals and young horses already show their natural talent for balance and suppleness. Elasticity and the natural gaits are genetically fixed to a large degree and can be evaluated very early. Many foals leap easily as they change directions at the canter; others are less agile, moving in a disunited, arrhythmic canter or in counter-canter. Some don't canter much, preferring instead to trot. When young horses are excited and tense, they can look very impressive, yet this can be deceptive. An over-spectacular action of the forelegs at the trot is worthless when the hind legs sprawl out behind and the horse's back is tight.

The "motor" is in the horse's back end.

What one wants is a harmoniously proportioned horse with a correct foundation, a powerfully muscled hind end with good angles and an energetically moving hind leg that steps far under the horse's center of gravity. A beautifully "carried," softly swinging tail is an indication of a supple swinging back that allows the movement of the hindquarters to transmit through to the front end. Well-defined withers with a good area for the saddle, a well-formed and well set-on neck, sufficient girth and lots of shoulder freedom are additional "plus" points, along with rhythmically correct gaits in walk, trot, and canter. Conformation weaknesses must be considered in training, and may be compensated in part with appropriate gymnastic exercises.

Conformation, the so-called physical structure of the horse, gives an impression of how well suited a young horse is for a particular equestrian sport discipline. The mental state of the horse is just as important: Characteristics such as willingness to perform, rideability, intelligence and strong nerves are great advantages.

Typically, a horse running at liberty is balanced. Four legs and a neck are all he needs to achieve balance in walk, trot, canter—and in the wildest caprioles! There is no need of support devices in his mouth to keep him from falling over. No one has to pull his head to his chest, or up or down to make the horse look good.

A well-bred horse with correct conformation and solid gaits displays natural balance when moving at liberty: Gait changes and direction are executed easily without losing balance.

Horses that show significant imbalances in free movement when not ridden have either significant conformation faults or health problems. Spinal ataxia (incoordination) can be the cause of a "hover" trot with abnormally exaggerated or slow movements, frequent bouts of cantering that are poorly connected from front to back, or poor balance in gait transitions. Frequent leaping in a disunited canter while on the longe indicates back tension, which is not always due to poor riding: Medical issues with the spinal column can also cause such symptoms. Changes to the inter-vertebral joint spaces can also cause abnormal clinical symptoms. Mild to moderate pathology may be managed to some degree with correct training but may require medical therapy. Inexpert riding can create tension in a horse's back that otherwise has no pathology.

POOR, INCORRECT RIDING CAN HASTEN THE APPEARANCE OF CLINICAL PROBLEMS.

Poor, incorrect riding in the face of pathological changes leads more quickly to training and lameness issues.

Diagnosing pathological changes of the spinal column, especially the spinous processes, is especially difficult for the veterinarian and may necessitate radiographic and ultrasound studies. The quality of the horse's training has a prime influence on the development of clinical problems such as lameness. In the hands of a tactful, good rider, mild to moderate bony changes in the spinous processes may have little effect on a horse's performance. On the other hand, minor changes may quickly lead to problems if the horse is ridden by a poor or inexperienced rider.

DEVELOPING BALANCE

What does *balance* mean for a riding horse? The term is often used without a real definition. As just mentioned, a healthy, unridden horse is balanced, and can easily and supply move his body in any situation.

The first intervention by man brings the horse's body out of balance, as for example, while longeing on the circle or when mounted. The large muscles of every young horse are strained when the horse is started under saddle as muscles tense in the effort to balance the unfamiliar weight of tack and rider: The body part that is directly loaded, the back, re-acts with protective tensing, which affects the neck, the poll, and natural motion.

After groundwork, the first goal of training is to restore the horse's natural balance.

In the first months of training, the young horse should learn how to move his body with the rider as if he were, ideally, a part of the whole. The horse should learn to maintain a consistent rhythm in all gaits while in a natural carriage with a softly sitting rider.

Such natural balance may be referred to as "basic balance" since it is fundamental for further training. Both the ability to stretch and the later ability to collect begin their development from this point.

A young horse in a longeing cavesson in natural balance.

A young horse must first learn to stretch. In the course of correct training, the poll angle opens more and the nose moves in front of the vertical.

BACK ACTIVITY AS A REQUIREMENT

Before we can further examine horizontal (basic) balance, let's look back at the underlying theme: The back is the center of movement of the horse (see: *Tug of War*, Trafalgar Square Books, North Pomfret, Vermont, 2007).

The anatomy of the horse's back is not made to carry weight without developing noticeable tension. As Udo Bürger writes:

◆

"In summary, the long back muscles are clearly movement muscles that enable forward movement and carriage, but were not necessarily designed to carry a rider's weight. The back connects the front of the horse with the back of the horse through the broad back and croup muscles. As a result, they are integrated into the rhythm of movement and can't be isolated. A free, voluminous and rhythmical gait is only possible when the long back muscles swing naturally with elasticity. It is primary, then, to achieve suppleness of the back. During all training, systematic development of the back musculature is required..."

Udo Bürger: *The Way to Perfect Horsemanship*, Trafalgar Square Books, North Pomfret, Vermont, 2012

◆

The important message in this passage is the characterization of the long back muscles as "movement muscles." It is logical to strive to maintain the elasticity of the back of a ridden horse in every phase of training. Burger also suggests that there is a connection between the back and the limbs. He explains why the natural basic gaits are immediately and negatively affected—and frequently destroyed—when the horse is not in balance (see also Otto de la Croix, p. 65. This is why the quality of the basic gaits is so significant.

The skeleton of the trunk and the attached ligament system provide great passive stability and are capable of supporting a large mass without breaking. This basic structure of skeleton and strong ligaments is the foundation of the trunk musculature, which should work actively, powerfully and supply, especially when movement needs to be elegant and energetic.

Tight/tense back muscles increase the pull on ligaments and tendons; the horse's trunk stiffens as a result. A tense trunk increases the load on the legs, which can cause damage to them.

The trunk musculature should not be abused by passive holding work! The more freely it can work, the more relaxed the whole muscle system.

Based on this structure the two large and very strong, long back muscles (*longissimus dorsi*), which run between pelvis, sacrum and neck, are responsible for large movement tasks. Furthermore, they are connected to the croup and gluteal muscles through the large sheet of fascia extending over the back. To the front, the large back muscles are connected through the wide back muscle (*latissimus dorsi*) to the upper arm of the front leg. A 100-year-old quotation from Otto de la Croix is appropriate here:

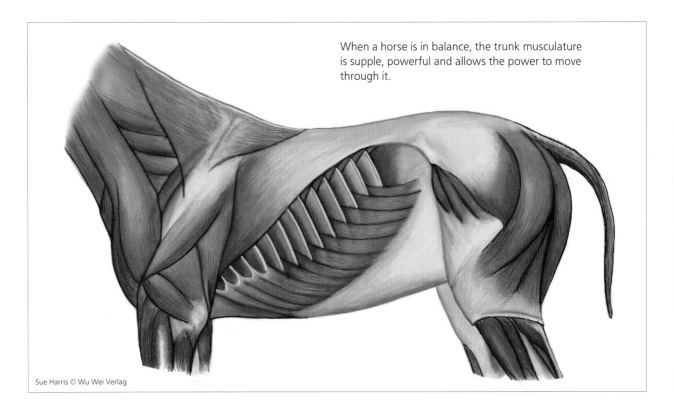

When a horse is in balance, the trunk musculature is supple, powerful and allows the power to move through it.

Sue Harris © Wu Wei Verlag

The Back and Its Importance for the Horse's Gait

"Everyone has already heard that the horse's back plays a large role in horseman-ship. Some have read it here and there. But seldom does one hear about it in the riding school, even though all instruction should focus on the back as the foundation of all work. This silence about the activity of the back shows that there is a lack of clarity in the riding world about the function of the back. In fact, most only know that a weak-backed horse doesn't like to carry a heavy rider, that a very strong back easily ruins the legs and leads to short steps, and that a moderately weak back is often correlated to a lot of action of the forehand.

"A few experts tried to go deeper into the essence of the subject earlier; but nothing can be found anywhere about the activity of the back and its all powerful influence on gaits and control of the horse—neither in the authoritative texts nor at institutions where one expects the best instruction to be available. Above all, it is not recognized that the mere anatomical characteristic of more or less strength is relatively unimportant when considering the condition of the back. Of prime importance is the activity of the back in movement, which is to be found in the work of the back muscles.

"We thank Herr v. Holleuffer for first presenting this great truth in his book about work at the pillars, basing it on the anatomy of the horse. His theory about swinging will remain for all time the starting point for reform of our current dressage method.

"It is almost miraculous that such a simple and natural cause for a swinging gait, the work of the back muscles, could have been hidden for so long from the equestrian theorists. It is still more amazing that this theory, once expressed, didn't break new ground with elemental force."

Otto de la Croix, *Natürliche Reitkunst* [Natural equitation], Olms Press, Zürich, Hildesheim, New York, 1989, p. 26

After reading this text, it could be asked, "Where is this knowledge today?" There are experts or those who see themselves as experts, who in all seriousness maintain, "Rollkur is a training method." There are those who accept spectacular-looking trot steps without connection of the back and hind legs as a component of a record-breaking dressage test! This development should make observers speechless, if not outright angry.

BACK MOVERS, HYPERFLEXED BACK MOVERS AND LEG MOVERS

The back muscles work as holding or carrying muscles only when a horse is standing or poorly balanced. They either actively carry the trunk and the rider's weight, or they actively press the back down through contraction. In rider-speak, the back is then "lost," the horse moving "without a back."

As a result, you see the so-called hyperflexed back mover or leg mover. In contrast, a horse in balanced movement, with or without a rider, carries his trunk and back in a natural position, allowing the musculature to work freely and relaxed.

The back muscles contract when the hind leg on

A back mover.

A hyperflexed back mover.

A leg mover.

the same side touches the ground; that is, when the stance phase of that limb begins. According to the gait, this contraction happens almost at the same time left and right (in canter and when jumping—asymmetrical gait) and alternating (in walk, trot or tölt—symmetrical gaits). Through correct positioning of the neck, the back is brought to a natural and anatomically necessary position, making relaxed use of the back muscles possible under the rider (see also: *Tug of War*, Trafalgar Square Books, 2007).

Having the neck of a young horse as natural and as long as possible is decidedly important. The shape of the neck, the roundness and suppleness of the poll and a suitable neck position with the poll at the highest point come only after several months (or years) of correct training.

In 1913, Otto de la Croix described the central importance of the horse's back. To fulfill the first three points on the Training Scale (Rhythm, Suppleness, and Contact), it is necessary to have tactfully "won" the back. That means: The rider needs to be able to sit on a supple back that allows the thrust from the hind end to flow through to the front; and to be able to receive this power in the form of a lively contact ("chewing" mouth) that is soft but constant.

De la Croix speaks of a spring that allows the "swing to come through." He also describes average tension (in this case, *positive tension* that is *not* to be confused with tightness), which is present in any horse (see negative and positive tension. De la Croix further stated:

◆

"The expression 'back mover' takes this demand more into account than any previous term. Lifting the back isn't possible with a high nose or without the hind legs stepping under. Lifting the head and neck causes the back behind the withers to sink due to the S-shape of the cervical vertebrae. The neck ligament loosens and the swing of the hind end can't come through to the forehand. It is clear that the lifting of the back and the stepping under of the hind legs are closely related."

Otto de la Croix, *Natürlicher Reitkunst* [Natural equitation], Olms Press, Zürich, Hildesheim, New York, 1989, p. 39

◆

Udo Bürger precisely describes the anatomy and physiology of the equine back in the section, "The Activity of the Back Muscles" in chapter 5 of his book *The Way to Perfect Horsemanship*. One of his key statements is: the long back muscles can lift the fore-hand and arch the back only from their rear attachments to the spinous processes of the sacrum and the ilium of the pelvis. If the back muscles work from their opposite front attachment or are shortened in tension, then the back is stretched to become hollow or stiff. Bürger says: "The back is then hard as a board."

Bürger delves further into the biomechanics of the back in the different gaits, distinctly emphasizing that the long back muscles most completely contract and relax at the canter. This explains the suppleness as well as muscle building benefit of correct canter work. At the walk and trot, each long back muscle contracts unilaterally with the movement of the hind leg on that side. The back arches in the process and lifts the seat bone of the rider. At the same time, the opposite side is passively stretched. Bürger sees a stiff rider's seat as the greatest challenge to undisturbed activity of the long back muscles. He summarizes:

◆

"The main cause of problems for the activity of the back musculature is the incorrect seat of the rider. The long back muscles cramp in tension at the trot when a rider with a stiff back is vertically hammering the back with her seat bones. The rider should sit with the seat bones supplely to the front in the direction of the run of the fibers of the long back muscles.

"The back will more quickly relax the less it is loaded and the more carefully the rider sits.

"Consequently, the rider should always begin the riding lesson on a young horse in a posting trot or canter and only sit in the saddle when invited by the horse to do so because the back swings in a relaxed way."

Udo Bürger, *The Way to Perfect Horsemanship*, Trafalgar Square Books, North Pomfret, Vermont, 2012

◆

All of the deeper treatises about horse training of the last century up to B. H. v. Holleuffer (1896) concluded that the back is one of, if not the most important structure in the horse's body and that it must be carefully considered in training. Suppleness, willingness to work, "throughness" or "swing" as Holleuffer describes it, are of primary importance.

◆

Every horse must give the back before he can move in balance. The back of the riding horse is precious!

◆

The abdominal and inner lumbar muscles work antagonistically to the back musculature as trunk flexors. Like the back muscles, these muscles are not primarily designed to carry the trunk but rather are muscles of movement affecting the pelvis and hind legs. The abdominal muscles work synergistically (mutually supportive) with the inner lumbar muscles to bring the pelvis and the hind legs forward under the body. Only musculature that is able to relax will lead to a beautiful and harmonious way of going.

It is easy to be convinced of the correctness of this statement. It is obvious that horses in extreme hyperflexion (Rollkur) or a long, deep round posture (LDR) have a tight back and belly. The mechanics of the trot degrade to the dreadful hover trot, with the hind legs making small, tight, earthbound steps or hops. To delve deeper into the importance of the trunk musculature, I refer to B. H. v. Holleuffer. He explained the understanding of his time regarding the biomechanics of the back in his book:

"I count as movements not only all gaits, walk, trot and canter, but also jumping over obstacles and the so-called school airs, including those performed on the spot. The horse cannot perform any of these movements well without arching (tension) and relaxing the spinal column, which we call 'swinging.'

"Swinging starts with the hind legs, travels through the spine to the head and the front legs and brings the horse into contact with the bit.

"The swings can be seen, felt and heard; the elasticity and power of the movements, the whole worth of the riding horse comes from them. One differentiates between back movers and leg movers: The latter move without using the spine. The movements are hard or tense, not ground covering, are either rushing or too sluggish and earthbound. The leg mover is either behind the aids or leaning on the reins, and is not reliably obedient.

"Back movers use swinging to reach forward and down in all movements; the stronger and more playful the swinging, the more active and ground covering, the softer and more elastic, the more vigorous and resolute the movements are. The rider and horse stay healthy and the former beats the latter in perfect obedience."

Bernhardt Hugo v. Holleuffer, *Die Bearbeitung des Reit- und Kutschpferdes zwischen den Pilaren* [Training the riding and driving horse between the pillars],Reprinted 1985, Olms Press, Hildesheim, Zürich, New York, p. 33

This text from 1896 marks the first usage of the terms "back mover" and "leg mover." It is the first time in the literature when the central theme is the back of a saddle horse. He not only makes a connection to correct riding but von Holleufer also notes the importance of keeping the horse healthy. It is important to strongly reinforce this concept!

The back has been regarded as the critical center of movement in the horse since 1896.

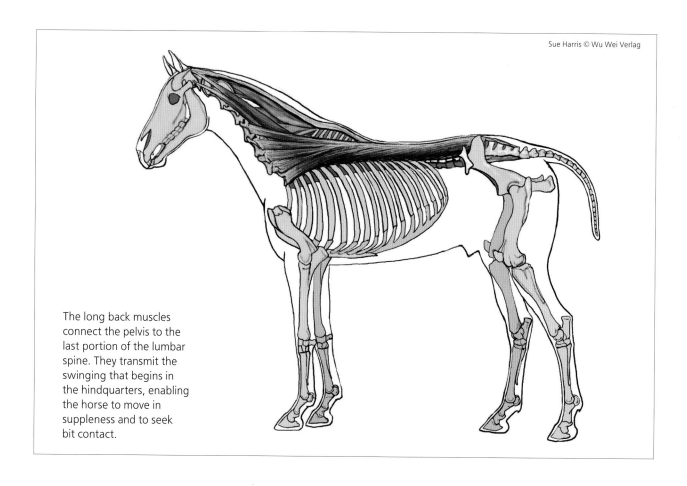

Sue Harris © Wu Wei Verlag

The long back muscles connect the pelvis to the last portion of the lumbar spine. They transmit the swinging that begins in the hindquarters, enabling the horse to move in suppleness and to seek bit contact.

CONTACT AS A RESULT OF A SWINGING BACK

Along with the importance of swinging for finding balance, von Holleuffer also highlights the fact that contact is always a result of back activity. To say it another way, if a horse doesn't give his back, correct contact can't be achieved or produced, not even artificially with constraining equipment.

———————◆———————

The whole trunk musculature in a correctly ridden horse is designed for movement—his back was not built for direct weight-bearing.

———————◆———————

The importance of the natural, uncurved neck, of the supple back and relaxed abdominal musculature is mentioned repeatedly in the literature of the last century. It can't be overstated that only a swinging back allows soft and powerfully working abdominal muscles; a tense back creates a tense abdomen with all the resultant issues. Perhaps you, too, have experienced the retraining of a severely mechanized, tense horse that resents even light leg contact on his side.

I have experienced horses that reared at the lightest touch of the leg, ran backward, kicked at the rider's leg, or simply started fighting against the rider.

The horse's alternative is to withdraw from the leg aids, becoming totally numb to all aids, especially of the rein and leg. The rider's leg is accepted only when the horse is a back mover. A tense back causes a tense abdomen with all the adverse riding consequences! It's important to discuss the whole trunk and its musculature when evaluating balance or its disruption.

Contact results from a swinging back.

THE IMPORTANCE OF RHYTHM FOR PUSHING AND CARRYING POWER

Felix Bürkner (1930s) describes the early training of a young horse:

---

*"For the first two years of training...
I developed his pushing power in a lively
rhythm at a free trot and canter. I didn't
touch his mouth or neck, left him long in
the neck, brought the back muscles lightly
to swinging and gave him only a very light,
even contact on both reins, which he
willingly accepted—forward horizontally—
without stretching down!"*

C.F. Mossdorf, *Kavallerieschule Hannover* [The cavalry school of Hannover],
FN Verlag, Warendorf, 1986, p. 75

As Bürkner describes the development of "horizontal balance" in a young horse, it is noteworthy that he spent two years stabilizing basic balance!

This passage repeats the concept akin to that expressed by von Holleuffer and de la Croix: The back is the all-determining structure of the horse's body. When it swings, the horse swings. Rhythm comes, impulsion follows, accompanied by the first appearance of throughness! The path to collection (the ability to shift the balance back) is laid and collection will improve impulsion.

Gustav von Dreyhausen wrote about the interplay of pushing and carrying power:

---

*"At the same time, impulsion is improved.
With greater flexing of the joints of the hind leg
during lively, energetic steps, the hind legs take on
more weight. The weight causes more bending of
the leg, resulting in more impulsion,
which is transmitted over the swinging back
musculature to the front legs. This results in
rhythmical stepping of all four legs, which no
longer brace against the load, but rather carry it
with great energy in a very regular rhythm. First
impulsion created collection, now the collection
improves impulsion. Rhythmical stepping begins
much earlier to a lesser degree."*

Gustav von Dreyhausen, *Grundzüge der Reitkunst* [Basic course in
horsemanship] new edition, Olms Press, Zürich, Hildesheim, New York,
1983, p. 14

Von Dreyhausen expresses the connection between impulsive power and carrying power. From that you can derive the enormous importance of the first, and perhaps most important step on the training scale: Rhythm makes the music. You must find it and improve it.

With the development and strengthening of pushing power, rhythm improves, and with that throughness and readiness to collect. Natural or basic balance is described in the Training Scale with the first three components:

RHYTHM • SUPPLENESS • CONTACT = NATURAL OR BASIC BALANCE

A rhythmical trot brings the horse into suppleness with good contact.

IX.

SUPPLENESS

From Rhythm to Contact

Natural balance is the platform for developing good lengthening.

THE QUALITY OF CONTACT

The horse has learned to step to the tactful hand with a relaxed trunk, in a secure basic rhythm, with a supple neck. He carries his head and neck in a natural position so that the poll is the highest point, even for a young horse. The correct head position, with the nose in front of the vertical, follows. This requirement of Classical Riding theory cannot be repeated too often. Only in this carriage can true contact develop. On this subject, I would like to present a passage by Waldemar Seunig that makes it clear that harmony is about the quality of the contact:

"To this end, the horse must put himself in the hand with a relaxed poll at the highest point, and an extended neck. A more secure contact results from the driving aids. This indicates, incidentally, that longitudinal flexion, which always has a 'flavor' of active hands about it, can be replaced to advantage."

Waldemar Seunig, *Von der Koppel bis zur Kapriole* [From paddock to capriole], Olms Press, Hildesheim, Zürich, New York, 2001, p. 132

The horse can maintain a secure rhythm without running away or getting lazy. Rhythm depends on the supple seat of the rider—a rider can sit in the saddle with such feeling and suppleness that the horse builds only the slightest defensive tension in his back. And, very importantly, the rider can begin using an appropriately driving seat. "Driving" requires that the horse accepts encouragement to go forward, which he must learn to do. A continually braced back is the wrong way to encourage the horse to move freely forward. (see Wilhelm Müseler *Riding Logic*, Trafalgar Square Books, North Pomfret, Vermont, 2007, p. 32).

Von Holleuffer relates contact to the swinging of the back, explaining that contact arises from the swinging. Moving with a secure rhythm causes the back to swing and encourages the horse to seek an even contact with the rider. In this way, the horse has again found his natural, basic balance.

This reestablished natural balance is the rider's work platform. From this point, the stretching ability of the horse can be developed in order to later achieve relative elevation in correct collection.

The sentence "a young horse must be ridden forward and downward" is correct to a certain point. You need stretching, but before that you need natural balance. Without balance, there is no correct stretching. The next step is to develop the stretching ability of the horse. This is accomplished effectively by "letting the reins be 'chewed' out of the hands" as the horse seeks to stretch his neck further. These exercises can dramatically improve the suppleness, strength and mobility of the long back musculature.

UNDERSTANDING FORWARD

As the ability to stretch improves while in natural balance, an important platform is created for the next components in the Training Scale: Impulsion and Straightness. The training plan is founded on three elements:

| QUIET FORWARD STRAIGHT |

A trainer friend, Andrea Jänisch, once suggested to me that the famous saying by Gustav Steinbrecht, "Ride your horse forward and make him straight" should be changed, since forward riding is often misunderstood as going fast. She suggested: "Ride your horse forward—as well as slowly—and make him straight!" A wonderful sentence! It hits the nail on the head.

Peter Kreinberg explained the adverse effects of "chasing" the horse with your seat. He has his students walk in front of him on foot at a normal speed, walks behind them and regularly shoves them forward. Ask yourself how this constant shoving would affect your balance and your physical suppleness, particularly while someone was forcing your head down at the same time!

An even temperament and physical suppleness are especially important equestrian attributes. A good seat with appropriate stirrup length is a critical part of this. A cowboy friend from Montana said:

"Wait for your horse!" – Roland Moore

"Wait for your horse." This sentence has been one of the most significant for me; in it lies the recognition that every action by the rider causes tension in the horse's back. The harmony for which we strive requires a quiet and waiting posture that is also alert and active with sensitive, driving aids.

Especially in basic training, regular forward riding out on the trails and fields is an almost essential component. Natural obstacles encourage the attention and agility of the horse.

The better command a rider has of her art, the less she works physically.

Everything good comes from a quietly waiting, effectively tense but supple seat! Alertness and the rider's wish to ride forward have nothing to do with pushing and squeezing. Correct forward riding is more about body posture and attitude than nonstop "forward nitpicking!"

The measure and importance of the effect of the seat are determined by the level of training and the anatomy of the horse. A supple seat gradually takes over more of the driving aids. This has absolutely nothing to do with commands such as "Sit down; legs on; more leg!" The driving effect of the leg and seat should not stem from tension in the rider or from force or power. Forward riding has nothing to do with strength and squeezing legs or a continually tense rider's back (see also "The Seat," p. 41).

WAIT AND FIND THE RHYTHM

Roland Moore's advice, "Wait for your horse!" wonderfully describes sensitivity in the body that leads to finding the rhythm of every individual horse. As a result of the rider feeling quiet and calm, the horse begins to wait. Then the rider begins—very carefully at the beginning—driving from her supple seat. It is sensible to creep up carefully with the driving aids for both the young horse and a horse in retraining.

In Volume 1 of *Richtlinien für Reiten und Fahren: Grundausbildung für Reiter und Pferd* [Guidelines for riding and driving: basic training for horse and rider] rhythm is defined as the "spatial and temporal exactness of movements" (FN Verlag, Warendorf 1997, 28th edition). A further, very important criterion is finding the right tempo. Either a rushing or "low-revs" horse can also move in spatial and temporal precision. However, when he isn't moving at the tempo that matches him, the horse won't find his rhythm. If a horse goes above or below his individual tempo (most horses rush and go far above the appropriate tempo), he can neither relax nor find horizontal bal-

ance. I like to compare rhythm with the pendulum of a mechanical clock. In order to find the rhythm of a horse, the rider must find the horse's own frequency and bring him to swinging movements.

Swing together in rhythm

A key for further training lies in finding the individual rhythm for each horse; finding this rhythm lays the first foundation stone for harmony. B. H. v. Holleuffer speaks of "swinging," a motion that needs to be developed. The horse can only begin to swing when moving in his own individual rhythm. Swinging is the expression of rhythmical movement with the first steps of suppleness.

A comparison with an adept dance couple comes to mind. Harmony lies in finding rhythm, which allows the dancers to relax and the dance to become enjoyable. If the lead dance partner suddenly quickens the tempo and starts a completely different rhythm from mine and the music, I would tighten up considerably and not have a feeling of harmony. Allowing yourself to "fall," in suppleness assumes that rhythm has been achieved. Similarly, only in the rhythm is it possible to find suppleness in both horse and rider. When this occurs, the feeling is good and the rider is balanced and supple. The horse begins to swing in reaction to the rider's supple seat that swings with his back.

Rhythm, Suppleness and Contact are the foundation. Everyone knows that you cannot build a house without a stable foundation!

SUPPLENESS

Suppleness or "looseness" refers to an inner calm, supplely working muscles and a lack of force. It is necessary for the horse to accept the leg (the driving aids) without running away or having to be asked for every step. When this state is achieved, the horse waits for the rider and willingly allows himself to be "driven" to contact from a supple seat. Suppleness describes a state where a horse is active without negative tension. A supple horse is ready and willing to work, not lazy hectic, spooky, nervous, rushing or running away.

The real task of the first three points of the Training Scale is preparing a horse to be able to move in balance. The criteria of Rhythm, Suppleness and Contact are non-negotiable! A horse can only develop to his best when you allow him enough time for his physical and mental development. When this correct foundational work isn't done early, it will need to be done later in the horse's retraining. A hasty training schedule that concentrates on mechanical work (exercises) always leads to problems.

The swinging of the back, which leads to suppleness, was described for the first time in 1896 by Bernhard Hugo von Holleuffer.

X.
STRETCHING
Always in Balance

UNDERSTANDING FORWARD AND DOWNWARD

"One rides a young horse forward and downward" or "I am a good rider, I ride my horse forward and downward." Such comments are heard often in connection with training, especially of young horses. They contain a certain truth as they primarily imply a correct motivation. Nevertheless, I would like to explore the logic of correct stretching. "Forward and downward" is no end in itself! The forward-and-downward stretch is an essential component of correct gymnasticizing of the horse's back. Without being forward and downward the horse cannot develop into a decent back mover. Correct and sensible stretching can only be asked for when a horse has found his natural balance. The first three components of the Training Scale should be so well established that the horse accepts the driving aids of the rider and willingly follows a giving hand.

The phrase "forward and downward" includes two words. The first word, "forward," describes the ability of the horse to connect well and stretch to the hand as the rider dictates. To develop an effective stretch, the horse must open the neck and poll angles more or less in a horizontal orientation, meaning with the neck lengthening forward without losing the convex (arched upward) topline and supple poll. The rider will immediately sense the quality of the stretch as the back behind the withers comes up.

Many trainers and riders describe this by saying "The withers lift up" or "The horse's shoulders have come up." In a correct stretching posture, a temporarily greater, passive tension builds in the back

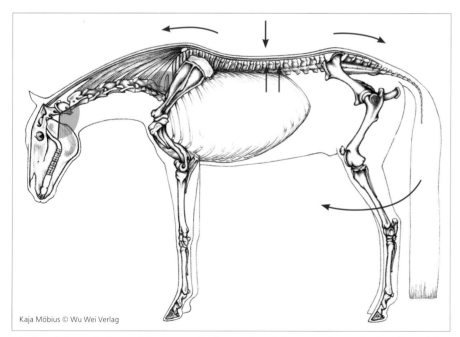

Kaja Möbius © Wu Wei Verlag

Mediated through the neck ligament, the forward-and-downward stretched topline of the neck lifts the back into the desired position. This enables the long back muscles to relax as they work and remain free to move.

Correct forward-and-downward stretching requires natural balance in every horse.

A young stallion in natural balance, the prerequisite for effective stretching.

musculature; this is not to be confused with negative tension, since there is no forced positioning of the head! With the rise in tension in the upper muscle chain of the back, the same thing happens in the antagonistic lower muscle chain along the abdomen and chest. The abdomen and chest muscles increase in tone and the *pectoralis* muscles lift the thorax between the shoulder blades—this elevates the horse, with the rider feeling that the horse "grows" in front. Along with the horse beginning to carry himself better and finally coming into the desired self-carriage,

this stretching increases the suppleness of the long back muscles. Improvement in the ability to stretch is essential for the development of the musculature, especially in the transition from pushing power to carrying power, necessary for collection.

The better a muscle is able to stretch, the more active and dynamic the contractions are.

An initial effective stretch is achieved when the horse's mouth reaches the level of the shoulder joint. The ability to stretch varies greatly from horse to horse. A horse with a short yet strong back musculature is not able to stretch spontaneously as far as a horse with a long back can. A correct stretch must be developed for each horse to fit his anatomy. A measure of correct stretching is the mobility and suppleness of the back and the preservation of the natural movement of the gaits. In contrast, an incorrectly stretched horse loses his balance and leans on the forehand.

INCORRECT STRETCHING

The correctly worked, well-balanced horse steps under his body with extra activity in his limbs in the stretch. This can be recognized especially when the rider posts the trot for a short time after sitting it and when the horse "chews" the reins from the rider's hands. In the moment when the back is given more freedom of movement and the horse correctly stretches and perhaps snorts, the rider can feel increased back swing: The back has become more mobile and dynamic. Ideally, the horse remains perfectly balanced, the steps or strides are freer and larger—that is, more round but not faster. The horse stays in his rhythm and follows the yielding hand without taking from the rider. After a correct stretch, the rider can immediately sit the trot again without a problem, with the horse moving in front of the rider by responding specifically to the rider's seat aids rather than being dependent on aids from the hands.

It is not uncommon to see this important stretching exercise executed in a completely incorrect way. The horses end up leaning on the forehand, completely losing their balance. One horse might roll his neck down and back in. Another simply elongates his neck, losing the convex arch of the upper neck (the neck drops) and carrying the head low without the upper neck having the desired effect on the back; this horse falls apart in rhythm and contact, and goes on the forehand. Still other horses push their head down or jerk the reins from the rider's hand.

Horses moving in any of these incorrect attitudes are not balanced, nor are they relaxed. The back of such a horse is mostly tight. Most don't maintain rhythm when the reins are allowed to be chewed out of the hands; they either rush or slow down. When the rider retakes the reins, it is often difficult to reestablish the desired balance. That may be why many riders don't allow their horses to stretch until the end of a practice session. They adhere to the motto: "Now that I finally have the horse's head down, I can't just let it go." This approach ultimately leads to a stiff, mechanized horse that is no fun to ride.

The curled neck
Modern, rideable Warmblood horses respond to any negative tension in their back by curling their neck. It is common to see horses being ridden with a deep round neck, with the riders believing that they are riding forward and downward.

However, it is not so! They are riding their horse with a tight back and on the forehand (hyperflexed back mover), which motivates him to run away from the rider's seat.

Riding with a deep round neck is riding a horse with a tight back, on the forehand.

A horse that has fallen apart is completely off the aids and moving with a stiff and dropped back.

The horse that has fallen apart

It is somewhat different with the horse that has "fallen apart." Usually this is a pleasure or trail horse that doesn't arch the topline of the neck: His back drops and he becomes a leg mover. Horses that simply fall apart without positive tension in their topline and without "carrying" their back are often lazy and difficult to motivate to go forward. Also, these horses are not balanced and tend to go on the forehand. They are completely off the aids.

"THROUGHNESS" AS A GOAL OF TRAINING

Correct stretching according to Classical Riding theory is a key exercise for the correct training of a horse. Consequently, stretching exercises shouldn't only be practiced at the end of a training session. The younger the horse or the weaker or tenser the horse's back, the more frequently he must be stretched. Development of the stretched position has a large influence on the back, especially the area behind the withers. Stretching in motion is most effective: Begin at the walk and then concentrate on developing a quiet, rhythmic trot, finally arriving at the horse "chewing the reins out of the your hands" at the canter, which achieves the most effective stretch of all. At the canter, both back muscle cords are used equally and almost simultaneously. Stretching at the canter allows the back to relax and achieve a more natural position. The positive effect on subsequent trot work is enormous! A horse that can stretch and is balanced accepts the aids and can be ridden from a supple seat to a sensitive contact.

Oskar Maria Stensbeck explains the relationship between acceptance of the driving aids, and suppleness of the poll, back and the hips:

"The horse must learn to accept the aids so that he goes relaxed forward, first mainly at the trot. As long as he fears—and runs away from the lower leg—his back will be tense. He will only relax and swing when he trusts the leg, accepts it as an aid, swings forward and lets the rider sit in the saddle.

"We can even see this! When the horse tolerates the leg while standing and allows himself to be moved back and forth and steps forward and backward without moving his feet nervously, you can begin to collect him in place and slowly apply the seat aids. After a while, the horse will learn to flex in the hips, relax his back and use his legs normally without making 'chicken' steps. His back will remain active and not stiff. The back activity causes 'throughness.' The poll, back and hips of the horse are all involved. When the poll does not allow a tug on the bit to come through while the horse is standing, but rather stiffens against it, the stiffness will spread from the back to the hind legs, preventing them from being able to step under the horse's body. That would not be 'through'...."

Oskar Maria Stensbeck, *Grundzüge der Reitkunst* [Basic course in horsemanship] and *Reiten* [Ride], Olms Press, Hildesheim, Zürich, New York, 1983, p. 70

In this work that originally appeared in 1935, Stensbeck clarifies the importance of the back along with the poll and haunches in achieving the concept of throughness. Throughness can only develop when the back allows the impulsion of the hind legs to pass from the hindquarters to the front, and the half-halts of the rider to pass from front to back. Without a supple swinging back, there is no throughness!

Only a horse that is through can willingly follow the rider's aids. Over the whole course of training and during every daily training session, the objective is all about improving throughness.

The reestablishment of natural balance through Rhythm, Suppleness and Contact provides the prerequisite for further steps in training. Impulsion, Straightness and Collection (remaining elements of the Training Scale) are the next projects.

XI.

IMPULSION

Loved and Misunderstood

MEASURED DEVELOPMENT OF LENGTHENINGS

True impulsion arises from the initial development of balance. Through systematic gymnastics, the horse develops more pushing power. The hind legs become more active and dynamic, moving with increasing energy like a spring. This is where we look for the origin of von Holleuffer's "swinging" (p. 69). The better the back biomechanics, the more the activity of the hind leg causes it to swing—and impulsion is the result.

Impulsion begins with the hind legs and requires a "carried" and supplely swinging back with good contact and a "chewing" mouth in order to allow for the suspension in trot and canter. The walk is a stepping pace without impulsion.

As a result of correctly developed impulsion, the contact becomes more secure. If the rider holds the horse through solid seat aids, she can easily slow the tempo as, for example, after a lengthening of stride; "throughness" is also improved. An eager young horse with especially large gaits likes to stride out with large steps and a tight back. This may feel great and look terrific but a rider shouldn't be deceived. Such a positive forward feeling and expressive "show trot" result primarily from lost balance

Foto Werner Ernst

Dr. Reiner Klimke on Ahlerich in a correct trot extension in self-carriage and with good lengthening of the frame.

and a tight back. Such horses must first be calm and find their own rhythm, before you start using the leg and seat aids. Not until a horse willingly accepts the leg and seat aids should you allow him to lengthen a few steps.

As long as a horse is not responding to the rider's seat aids and instead is running against the hand, no lengthening should be required.

As a general rule, lengthen only as much as can be taken back readily. Only when back activity, Rhythm, Suppleness and Contact are present and can be maintained can impulsion develop and throughness

improve. A further, essential criterion for trot and canter lengthenings is the lengthening of the frame. A desirable side effect of developing correct impulsion with appropriate lengthening of the frame is that the horse improves in his ability to stretch the neck and back (see also chapter XIV, p. 112).

The fourth stage of the Training Scale can only be reached when there is a clear and solid foundation of horizontal balance. A young horse that does not yet have a secure foundation can't show correct lengthening with impulsion. On this subject, Egon von Neindorff writes:

"With a young riding horse, the less experienced eye usually can notice when the gait is impure, the lumbar area is tight or other muscles are unnaturally tense. However, if a horse moves with a stiff back as is often seen at competitions—even in the Grand Prix test—many experienced riders and judges are deceived. For example, anyone who has seen many horses piaffe, but only rarely seen a piaffe where the horse is relaxed and the movement cadenced with impulsion, easily believes that a horse that shows a trot-like leg movement on the spot must be 'loose'...

"Today, exaggerated 'showy' gaits—even in young horses—impress audiences and are especially popular at horse sales. At dressage competitions, you can see—with increasing frequency—horses throwing the front legs out almost horizontally. An insufficiently schooled eye doesn't notice how little push and swing of the hindquarters there is, despite the exhausting action of the forehand in these 'fantastic' gaits. How often are young horses produced with shortened, compressed necks, high croups and deep shoulders compounded by stiff back and neck musculature in negative tension! This is clearly an unnatural (supposedly modern) misunderstanding of the concepts of impulsion and tension...."

Egon von Neindorff, *The Art of Classical Horsemanship*, Cadmos Verlag, Brunsbek, 2009

In his book, Egon von Neindorff exposes the ubiquitous show or competition trot, and evaluates it as exhausting and damaging to the horse. Nevertheless, this erroneous evolution continues unabated. Warnings and requests to remember horse-friendly principles are largely unheeded.

"SPECTACULAR" STEPS AS THE MEASURE OF ALL THINGS

Since the 1980s, the large ground-covering trot has increasingly become the measure of all things. Top prices at auctions, record-breaking scores at competitions, and honor titles such as champion stallion and champion mare are significantly tied to "spectacular" trot mechanics. Not long ago, I witnessed a judge's evaluation in which he awarded a seven-year-old gelding that was tense as he could possibly be—his front legs thrown out—with a score over a 9.0. The people cheered, this FEI judge of the highest rank proudly announced his score, and the horse stood in the salute at the end with his mouth pulled a hands-breadth wide, eyes wide with fear under a rider dripping with pride while holding the curb bit tight.

To me, this was a picture of horror! This sensational score was given to a horse with "hovering" spectacular-looking steps that at no time fulfilled the Training Scale or the content of Article 401 of the Dressage Rules of the FEI, which states, "...the head should remain in a steady position, as a rule slightly in front of the vertical, with a supple poll as the highest point of the neck...." (see p. 91 for Article 401).

The very highest guardians of our riding and training culture appear, at least partly, to be turning away from the proven principles. The question must be asked with increasing frequency and intensity: "How can we save our cultural wealth from this merciless steamroller of commerce, fame and spectacle?"

Such movement is the result of hand-dominated, backward riding, which also existed in times past. Max Freiherr von Redwitz in 1914 commented on the training methods of Paul Plinzner, the long time Equerry of the German Kaiser Wilhelm II:

"Plinzner's absolute elevation (usually nose behind the vertical) brings neck and head in a position that causes an incorrect leverage effect on the horse. The reins go diagonally across the neck to the rider's chest and don't travel through the vertebral bridge to all the joints of the hindquarters. Since the horse in any gait and at any tempo can't step farther with the front feet than the spot where a vertical line from the leading part of the nose touches the ground, Plinzner's absolute longitudinal flexion causes 'short steppers.' He thereby prevents the natural development of the gait."

Max Freiherr von Redwitz, *Die Grundsätze der Dressur* [The principles of dressage], first publication 1914, reprint Georgi GmbH, Aachen, 1987, p. 122

Von Redwitz's words explain the origination of leg movers and "running" in trot and canter. He doesn't mention the destructive effect this type of riding has on the back of the horse. He also doesn't discuss the hover steps, which develop from this form of riding. Plinzner had actually recommended them over a century ago in his book, originally published in 1879, *Ein Beitrag zur praktischen Pferde-Dressur* [Practical horse training] (Olms Verlag, Hildesheim, Zürich, New York, 2007). He had also recommended developing the passage in a cross-country horse that begins to run away at the trot! Von Redwitz does indicate, however, that such a "mechanized" horse would probably have loved to go cross-country "...to be free of his bindings."

Totilas, the horse that is the epitome of modern competitive sport, with over-spectacular trot mechanics.

ARTICLE 401: OBJECT AND GENERAL PRINCIPLES OF DRESSAGE

❶ The object of dressage is the development of the horse into a happy athlete through harmonious education. As a result, it makes the horse calm, supple, loose and flexible, but also confident, attentive and keen, thus achieving perfect understanding with his rider. These qualities are demonstrated by:
- The freedom and regularity of the paces.
- The harmony, lightness and ease of the movements.
- The lightness of the forehand and the engagement of the hindquarters, originating from a lively impulsion.
- The acceptance of the bridle, with submissiveness throughout and without any tension or resistance.

❷ The horse thus gives the impression of doing, of his own accord, what is required of him. Confident and attentive, submitting generously to the control of the rider, remaining absolutely straight in any movement on a straight line and bending accordingly when moving on curved lines.

❸ The walk is regular, free and unconstrained. The trot is free, supple, regular, and active. The canter is united, light and balanced. The hindquarters are never inactive or sluggish. They respond to the slightest indication of the rider and thereby give life and spirit to all the rest of his body.

❹ By virtue of a lively impulsion and suppleness of the joints, free from the paralyzing effects of resistance, the horse obeys willingly and without hesitation and responds to the various aids calmly and with precision, displaying a natural and harmonious balance both physically and mentally.

❺ In all the work even at the halt, the horse must be "on the bit." A horse is said to be "on the bit" when the neck is more or less raised and arched according to the stage of training and the extension or collection of the pace, accepting the bridle with a light and soft contact and submissiveness throughout. The head should remain in a steady position, as a rule slightly in front of the vertical, with a supple poll as the highest point of the neck, and no resistance should be offered to the rider.

❻ Cadence is shown in trot and canter, and is the result of the proper harmony that a horse shows when it moves with well marked regularity, impulsion and balance. Cadence must be maintained in all the different trot or canter exercises and in all the variations of these paces.

❼ The regularity of the paces is fundamental to dressage.

Von Redwitz also describes the consequences of such "forced" training on the horse's nerves and, consequently, his suitability for cross-country riding. This also applies to misbehavior during awards ceremonies that include music, applause and cheering. Isn't the purpose of dressage to ride a horse that is overall and at any time 100 percent controllable? So, shouldn't a horse be disqualified if he can't be controlled or won't stand still during the awards? In our rules we talk about terms such as "natural" and "harmonious," yet what is happening in the current competition arena?

As I mentioned, over 100 years ago, the influential Plinzner recommended the practice of the hover trot. Unfortunately, there are occasions when it is no different today, at least not when a score of over 9.0 is given to such a movement. However, the FEI rules have it exactly right and are sensible for the horse (see Article 401, p. 91).

FROM PUSHING POWER TO CARRYING POWER AND BACK

A horse begins to move with impulsion when he is able to increase the suspension of an impulsive pace. The rhythm of the pace and the balance (suppleness) of the horse must be maintained. The development of a dynamic and expressive trot or canter should come exclusively from strong activity of the hindquarters (power and suppleness). The "spring" of the haunches grows and the back starts swinging (see p. 69). Prolonged suspension emanating from a tight back and a slow hind leg has nothing to do with impulsion!

Impulsion develops when a horse moves relaxed in natural balance, in a regular rhythm, with good contact and a chewing mouth. The large joints of the haunches softly sink (passive haunches flexing) at the moment the hind leg lifts up in order to set the foot down again with dynamic energy. The greater the ground cover, the more impulsion. In a trot or canter lengthening, carrying power is converted to pushing power. Early impulsion in a young horse comes from rhythm when there is only minimal "springing" strength available. A horse can only develop impulsion equivalent to the extent to which he can be brought back and collected.

◆

For maximum development of impulsion, there must be a like ability to collect.

The development of impulsion, therefore, goes along with the development of pushing power, throughness and readiness for collection.

◆

PURITY OF THE PACES

In the chapter on "Shifting the Balance" (p. 144), it will be shown why impulsion and the development of pushing power is only possible with a corresponding lengthening of the frame. Unfortunately, riders often sit rigidly and straight, or even behind the motion, during lengthenings. Seldom seen is the rider who is thinking forward with her upper body and a "give" of the hands. Instead, the desire to make a

"Pushing" and "carrying" are both accomplished by the limbs. A horse that can push powerfully with a steady rhythm can later be collected.

spectacle causes the rider to grip the reins tightly, with the horse's neck raised in absolute elevation and a tense back with the front legs "thrashing" out as a result. With these horses, the back is usually dropped and the activity of the hind end is completely lost. Dropping of the back behind the withers, or tightness in the lower neck region, builds up so much negative tension that the front legs fly out almost horizontally.

It is almost inexplicable how such a development could occur with the FEI rules as the foundation, and it happens right in front of our very eyes! Where are the officials that should be standing against such developments that are so bad for the horse? The goal is to develop a correctly trained, happily moving horse that presents himself in his natural beauty and in harmony with his rider. Purity of the gaits is the foundation of dressage. For this reason, horses with a lateral walk or a four-beat canter receive low scores. It contradicts every principal of classical teachings that horses should receive the highest scores despite being obviously tense with a swishing tail, grinding teeth, open mouth, resistant facial expression, and exhibiting hover trot steps.

On this same subject, Eric Glahn stated about the rides at the 1956 Stockholm Olympics:

"The German reporter, Dr. Gustav Rau, frequently criticized the judges for letting tense trots and insufficient back activity go unnoticed. This critic saw the problem clearly and recognized the source. However, today no one has taken up the banner against it, apart from the German judges' organization, which admittedly hasn't been successful in stopping it... A horse moving from his back was denied [good results]. The way to the leg mover and resulting 'mechanized' horse is being followed. At the same time the aids that lead to a back mover—seat, lower back, driving aids—have been devalued and the methods leading to 'mechanizing' the horse have been elevated..."

Erich Glahn, *Reitkunst am Scheideweg* [Equitation at the crossroads] Erich Hoffmann Verlag, Heidenheim, 1956, p. 89

I am talking about a historical problem that was recognized and criticized more than 50 years ago at the beginning of modern competitive riding sport. Does this tell us that it is hopeless to try to turn back in the direction of classical and horse-appropriate training? A look in various amateur and professional barns underscores this hopelessness anew. Those focused on developing a relaxed and swinging horse are frequently ridiculed! Only our organizations can put an end to this appalling spectacle so bad for the horse's welfare.

Over-spectacular, "hover" trots deserve neither applause nor good scores!

The narrow line between positive tension and negative tension poses a challenge. Dressage judges and the dressage audiences place a lot of value on "expression" and "impulsion." Consequently, the rider who wants to win must accordingly pull the maximum out of her horse and literally turn him into mostly producing leg action. At international championships, the pressure on riders, trainers, and ultimately on the horses, is immense. The special atmosphere in the stadium or in the hall with spectators sitting right up against the dressage arena, loud music and storms of applause require maximum nerves from both horse and rider. Horses that are especially sensitive or tense can scarcely relax under these conditions, particularly when not used to the commotion. Previous problems of insufficient suppleness worsen in a competition atmosphere and expectations from judges and public alike for expression, huge movement and spectacular mechanics frequently cause riders to over-exaggerate their efforts. Rhythm and suppleness are lost. Potentially injurious hover trots develop that are most assuredly without harmony and lightness.

There is a fundamental difference between "made" expressiveness, which arises from tension, and natural expressiveness that arises from contentment, Rhythm, Suppleness and true Impulsion from the hind legs. Less is more! Frequently, this is not given enough consideration in scoring.

A tense back (a leg mover or hyperflexed back mover) leads to disturbances of the natural footfall.

XII.

THE SPORT
OF DRESSAGE

Nothing but Show?

A "SPECTACLE" OR CORRECT TRAINING?

A spectacle at any price—is this the downfall of classical dressage?

Sometimes people want a show, even a bad show. "We needed to decide between 'show' and correct training and we have decided for the show," exclaimed a judge publicly in 2010. This is a revealing statement of more significance than the originator might have realized.

The cause for this remark was the judging of a class that included the three top placing horses of a young horse championship. In contrast to the official championship finale in the morning, the evening Kür (freestyle) is traditionally regarded as a type of show without essential sport value. Riders, judges and trainers regard it as a "fun demonstration."

Rides are regularly given scores of 9.0 and higher. It is primarily about "presumed" entertainment value for the public.

The riders and the officials do their best to make their dressage sport attractive to the public. The grandstands are typically fuller in the evening than during the official finale in the morning, which is primarily attended by the technically knowledgeable riding public. The evening audience is much more diverse and includes many non-equestrian spectators. Even when the riders give their horse a good "kicking," which results in tense trotting, rhythm errors, insufficient "throughness" and rough rider aids, it doesn't seem to bother anyone. In fact, the main objective is to stir up public excitement: The spectators clap, and hopefully will return in even larger numbers next year.

Educated spectators, judges and the riders themselves know that this evening event is a performance for the public and that judges aren't using the normal standards. Scores of 9.0 and higher are the absolute exception in regular dressage. Anyone informed but not understanding this background would be irritated by this since the highest scores are given for rides that frequently don't reflect criteria fundamental to dressage.

In contrast, at a show in 2010 during the freestyle in the evening, the rider who had won the official championship earlier, declined to pull the maximum of "impulsion" and "expression" out of her barely seven-year-old horse. At the end, she placed "only" third because she had decided in favor of correct training instead of putting on a "show." She didn't want to over-challenge the young stallion and risk everything. Another seven-year-old and a nine-year-old were, on the other hand, ridden full tilt with Rhythm, Suppleness and Contact totally lacking—and there was no harmony. And in the winner's lineup, the first- and second-place horses were in no way calm, but rather displayed signs of overloaded nerves.

An occasional appearance at such a show shouldn't pose damaging health consequences for the horse if it is followed by an appropriately long time for recovery, then later by correct training according to the Training Scale. But I wonder if asking for this kind of effort doesn't set the horse back in his training and damage the trust relationship with his rider?

DEMONSTRATION OF CLASSICAL TRAINING

There are some competitions where spectators interested in dressage are taught by experts about the importance of fulfilling the criteria of the classical Training Scale. These events are highly regarded in knowledgeable circles and are well attended. It must seem contradictory that these criteria suddenly play a secondary role at other events that are only about glamorous spectacles—at the cost of the horses suffering. The judges give a signal to both competitors and the public when they award scores of 9.0 and higher for performances that are purely about entertainment and judged by the loudness of the applause.

From my point of view, these show events contradict Classical Riding theory and the dressage rules of the FEI. At seminars, members of the leading committee of FEI judges regularly voice support for Classical Riding theory. It seems ironic that the same high-ranking individuals are also involved with the show events, which must be seen as technically questionable. I don't understand how the functionaries deal with this contradiction.

It would be easy to make such events into a wonderful presentation of good, Classical Riding technique. The best young horses with excellent riders in the saddle could demonstrate to the spectators how Classical Training should look! Why not seize the opportunity? The public could be educated in a comparison of the new versus old picture of "good" versus "bad" technique as the judges explain to the spectators which trot extension they *should* clap for and when it is better *not* to! Then, riders

THE SPORT OF DRESSAGE—*Nothing but Show?*

could enjoy showing their horses at the Kür in the evening as correct riding would be rewarded rather than "showy" exhibition movements. Many riders are now considering whether they would rather not participate in the Kür in order to protect their horse from excessive demands.

THE POLITICAL BACKGROUND OF THE SPORT

 he evolution of dressage from sport to show is grounded in politics. For a long time, dressage was regarded as a "boring" side sport, which found little interest with the public at large. Unlike jumping, a sport that is judged by errors (knock-downs) and time, the evaluation criteria of dressage are not understandable at first glance. It takes many years, if not decades, to gain the necessary technical

The German Equestrian Federation (FN) in Warendorf.

99

knowledge for full appreciation of the nuances that are the essence of dressage.

Germany had an unchallenged leadership position in dressage for decades. Not everyone liked that; other nations saw themselves as disadvantaged. Furthermore, a sport where only a few nations participate and the same ones always win is not especially exciting. It was therefore debated as to whether or not dressage should be discontinued as an Olympic discipline. That would have resulted not only in a harsh loss of image but also of subsidies and sponsorships. Large competitions and championships could have lost financing.

To secure the survival of dressage in the lucrative sport arena, solutions were sought and far-reaching concessions were made. That dressage in its essence is not only a sport but also an art form is difficult to convey. The Kür, about which we currently argue, makes dressage popular. International-level sport broadens as more countries participate in championships. Music and dancing horses, show effects and spectacles are easy to market. Riders who animate the public to clap along and turn the music up provide the atmosphere. The former dream team, Totilas and Edward Gal, have raised the bar a whole notch higher. In the meantime, the grandstands of the dressage stadiums are filled to bursting and dressage is more popular than ever before. The popular story about the "world's best dressage horse" Totilas changing ownership was marketed by a professional agent and even picked up by political magazines, daily newspapers and television.

Those who approve of the evolution of dressage riding to that of a public show see themselves confirmed by its growing popularity. The balancing act

ARE PROVEN AND BIOMECHANICALLY BASED TRAINING PRINCIPLES BEING IGNORED?

is failing between preservation of recognized training principles and judging criteria on the one hand and the concessions of competition organizers and sponsors on the other. In the wake of growing commercialization and superficiality, true dressage actually loses out, especially at the highest levels of performance.

Those who followed the rides at the 2010 World Equestrian Games in Kentucky saw many performances in which the riders demanded the maximum from themselves and their horses. But only a few pairs inspired through true impulsion, harmony and correctness. Perhaps so much pressure is on riders, trainers and horses that lightness and beauty in the test are inevitably lost. Perhaps this loss of beauty and lightness will lead back to recognizing that the proven and biomechanically grounded training principles are being ignored. At the same World Equestrian Games a rider competed on a horse obviously trained through pure force. This truly appalling ride still received more than a 70 percent score and much applause. Where will this lead? How long can competent horse people stand it? How long can officials, organizers and sponsors continue to close their eyes?

Stallion presentations, auctions and young horse championships are events that have been viewed as a "meat market" for many years.

Even at large national and international championships, success has become less about the quality of the training and the understanding between horse and rider. Those who care about riding sports in general and about the horse would do well to demand a rigorous return to FEI rules. Performances rewarded with top scores should only be those resulting from correct training and education.

High expectations: Competition judges should be trained, technically competent, independent thinkers dedicated to the well-being of the horse.

THE JUDGMENT OF JUDGES

A dressage class should be won by the horse that is the best trained and executes the best test. When a horse trots tensely and loses the back and hind legs in all the trot movements, he does not deserve high scores—even when he can lift his front legs up to his jaw! Training that is correct for the horse should be the first criterion; competition success should come second: The desire for receiving sponsorship money must never rank higher than the well-being of the horse.

As can be seen in the passage by Erich Glahn (p. 94), this shift in the judges' perspective has a long history. Naturally, it is simpler to judge according to comprehensible, technical criteria. But dressage riding is not primarily technical. Dressage riding at the highest level should be art!

Have you ever heard that the paintings of a world-famous artist are only to be evaluated according to technical criteria? Experts in the evaluation of artwork also have different opinions, and in my view, it is the same for dressage judges. The desire for standardization and conformity contradicts the essence of art. Dressage technique is complex and open to creative execution. For this reason, judges should not evaluate the individual movement only according to purely technical, formal criteria; they should use the whole range of marks more often, especially the collective remarks for purity of the gaits, impulsion, obedience and throughness, seat and effectiveness of the rider—all these features deserve to be considered seriously. In ridden tests, I propose that there be two additional scores for "harmony" and the "fulfillment of the criteria of basic training." This would be easy to implement on a judging card and logical for the horse. But of what use is a ranking when the collective remarks are unfortunately just "political scores?"

In dressage, the opinion of experts is needed—judges serve best when educated, brave, and independent-minded. Above all, we need people in the judge's booth who understand the content of Classical Riding theory. We need judges who can technically substantiate their evaluations and stick to their opinions regardless of what the judge in the next booth thinks, says or writes about it!

"A rider without a horse is only a person. A judge, however, must be an incorruptible person with extensive technical knowledge, quick perception, tolerance and a clear view of what is essential! When in doubt, a judge should follow the motto: IN DUBIO PRO EQUO (when in doubt, for the horse)."

Hans Freiherr von Stackelberg, member of the Order of the Federal Republic of Germany, student of Major a.D. Paul Stecken

---

THE ROLE OF THE PUBLIC

Organizers, judges, riders, trainers and association officials assume the public wants fun and spectacles. The question is: Is this really true? Or do they only want this because for years they have been sold the concept that a tense, leg-thrashing and "hovering" horse is "extraordinary" and "sensational?" Naturally, experience determines taste. Nevertheless, one shouldn't assume spectators are

Enthusiasm for the sport: Enlightened spectators can serve as a critical authority.

ignorant. The public at the Horse International in Munich is as varied as at a folk festival. Only a portion of the spectators is technically versed in dressage but interest in dressage grows yearly. One of the most beloved tests, the dressage derby, puts the best Grand Prix riders on horses they don't know. The ride commentary is filled with humor and technical content. The moderators talk with the riders. While often funny, it is still informative. Spectators are enthusiastic for both the spectacles of the dressage and its entertainment value.

Some years ago at the Horse International, Hubertus Schmidt rode the then still young and inexperienced Wansuela Suerte, the horse he rode when he was an Olympic team winner in Athens in 2004. In Munich, the mare performed one of her first Grand Prix Special tests. Still today, this performance remains a "goose-flesh" ride in the memory of many spectators. The performance was definitely not "spectacular" nor was it without mistakes, but it was quite moving and beautiful. The concentration, harmony and lightness of this pair put everyone under a spell—it was as quiet as a mouse in the packed dressage stadium. Afterward, there were standing ovations for the clearly deserving winner. When a horse presents in his natural beauty without force and follows his rider relaxed and willingly, even laymen can see and appreciate it.

XIII.

STRAIGHTNESS

A Special Challenge

NATURAL CROOKEDNESS

Only a horse in horizontal balance can be vertically balanced—that is, straightened.

Straightness is the fifth component on the Training Scale. Straightness is immensely important because nearly every horse has a tendency to be crooked. This means that his body has a hollow (difficult) side plus a stiff (restricted) side, and he assumes the shape a little like a banana. This natural asymmetry of the horse's body is called "natural crookedness." To the rider this feels like a horse is, for example, hollow to the right and stiff to the left. Such a horse is easier to ride on a right bend. Going to the left the rider feels stiffness. A horse by his nature doesn't have the same suppleness on both sides. He isn't capable of bending the same nor is he accepting of gymnastics work equally well in both directions.

Scientifically, natural crookedness can be compared to the handedness (laterality) of the human. Science no longer doubts that handedness is rooted in the central nervous system. Scientists F.R. Wilson in 2002 and J. F Stein and C. J. Stoodly in 2006 have explored this subject focusing on a genetic locale; scientists from Oxford in England discovered a gene for handedness in August 2007 although the evolutionary advantages of handedness still are not clearly understood. (For further background information on crookedness in the horse see: Michael Putz, *Richtig Reiten* [Correct riding], p. 133, FN Verlag, 2010.)

Waldemar Seunig in his 1943 book *Von der Koppel bis zur Kapriole* [From paddock to capriole] speaks of incorrect bending on the hollow side. Most authors describe the hollow side as the difficult side that is more challenging to gymnasticize.

———————————◆———————————

A horse that isn't straight is not regular in the natural paces (rhythm), can't be collected and may not stay sound as performance demands increase.

———————————◆———————————

THE CAUSES

There have been numerous attempts to explain this phenomenon of natural crookedness. Theories range, from the position of the fetus in the womb to a cause related to the central nervous system, similar to the handedness of people. Even in the last century, crookedness in the horse was traced to tight (less elastic) muscles of the trunk. Shortening (reduced elasticity) of the trunk musculature on the so-called "hollow" side of the body is now considered the biomechanical cause of natural crookedness.

———————————◆———————————

The stiffness on the "tight side" is thought to be caused by reduced elasticity of the trunk musculature on the hollow side.

———————————◆———————————

In many horses, their right is the hollow side. The

Incorrect, mechanical means of fixing natural crookedness lead to strengthening it instead. And increasing crookedness causes the horse to stiffen even more. This results in resistance in the poll, in the back and in the haunches, as well as loss of horizontal balance. The horse may become a leg mover or a hyperflexed back mover. Such stiffness can injure the horse, in addition to causing related training and orthopedic problems. A lot of therapy work could be avoided through correct training.

Classical Riding theory maintains that a horse can only be straightened when he can move in horizontal balance.

rider perceives the horse as being bent to the right. Riding a circle in this direction seems easier at first. The horse tends to support himself on the outside rein and falls on the outside front leg. If, for example, the right side is the hollow side, the horse leans on the left front leg when going to the right. This is also referred to by many as "the horse falling on the outside shoulder." It is much more difficult to control the inside hind leg on the hollow side; the hind leg on the hollow side is weaker than that on the stiff side—it tries to avoid the load by not stepping under the center of gravity. The horse evades by moving almost in a travers (haunches-in) on the hollow side.

The other, so-called "stiff" side is usually the left side. The horse gives the rider the feeling that he doesn't like flexing and bending to the left. In extreme cases, an attempt to turn to the left leads to resistance as the horse tends to support himself on the left rein. It is difficult, sometimes almost impos-

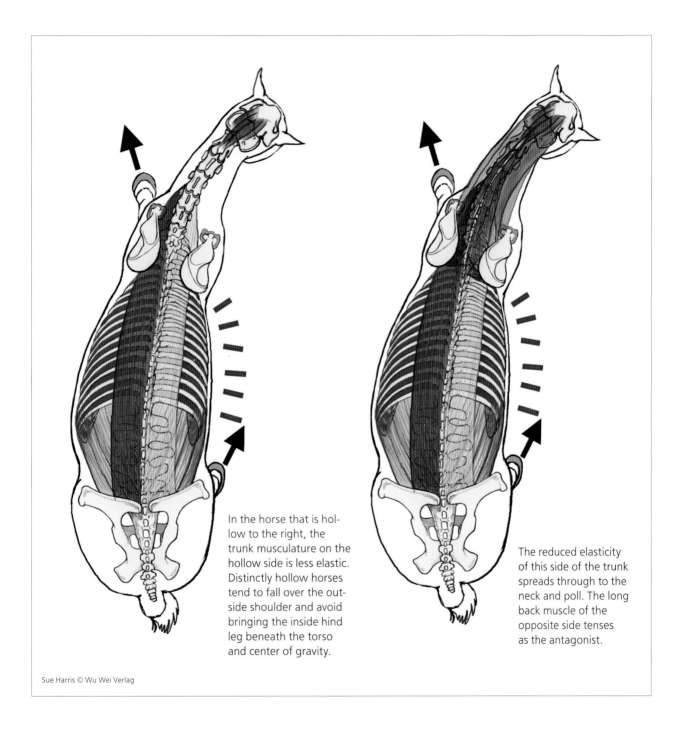

In the horse that is hollow to the right, the trunk musculature on the hollow side is less elastic. Distinctly hollow horses tend to fall over the outside shoulder and avoid bringing the inside hind leg beneath the torso and center of gravity.

The reduced elasticity of this side of the trunk spreads through to the neck and poll. The long back muscle of the opposite side tenses as the antagonist.

Sue Harris © Wu Wei Verlag

sible (especially with horses needing retraining), to achieve a constant contact on the right rein. Most young horses canter better to the left. The hind leg on the stiff side is stronger, albeit stiffer, and can carry more.

HORIZONTAL AND VERTICAL BALANCE

Alleviating natural crookedness is critical in order to achieve Straightness. The better a horse flexes and bends in both directions, the bet- ter the vertical balance. Riding the horse 100 per- cent straight is not likely to happen so expectations should be adjusted accordingly.

HORIZONTAL BALANCE

The position and length of the neck and the suppleness of the poll allow the large, long back muscles to work free of tension. As the horse moves with impulsion, the swing through his body leads to a soft contact with a "chewing" mouth. The horse has re-found his natural balance that may have been lost when first ridden. This lays the foundation for further training. The horse learns to stretch and later to move in *relative elevation*, as he gradually gains the ability to collect—that is, shifting "the horizontal balance." Relative elevation means the horse is beyond *horizontal* balance and already in *uphill* balance. Collection is the process of shifting the weight to the rear, which takes the horse out of horizontal balance. But the horse must achieve horizontal balance before this next step can occur.

VERTICAL BALANCE

Before a horse can have vertical balance, he must develop horizontal balance. He moves rhythmically (Rhythm), swinging (Suppleness) and with consistent Contact with the rider's aids. Then the horse develops vertical symmetry; that is, he lets himself be straightened and flexes and bends equally in both directions. He accepts the diagonal aids. The horse loses resistance (stiffness) in the trunk, poll and in the haunches. He increasingly stays attuned to the rider's supple seat aids. The quality of the balance steadily improves.

A large number of rider problems come from natural crookedness (see also p. 105), including "The rider can't sit," "The horse goes behind the bit," "The horse is against the hand," "The horse is grinding his teeth," "There are tongue problems," "The horse is resistant in the poll," or "The horse runs away from the rider's weight or through the rider's hand." These are also signs that are helpful to a veterinary diagnosis of an active problem. Rhythm disturbances attributable to lameness issues are fre- quently caused by muscular tension in the poll, neck and trunk. These conditions are also caused by in- correctly addressing natural crookedness and poor vertical balance. (See further expansion on this on p. 156.)

A horse can be straightened when the horse goes to the rider's hand relaxed and with a clear rhythm, and the rider can drive tactfully from a relaxed, quiet seat. As has been studied and confirmed, horizontal balance is the most critical prerequisite for straight- ening, which forms the foundation for the develop- ment of vertical balance.

A certain level of straightness must exist in order for a rider to have fairly even contact on both reins. In other words, a horse must be able to go forward in horizontal balance before more work on straightening can be asked.

A horse can only be balanced vertically when he is a back mover, which means he is horizontally balanced.

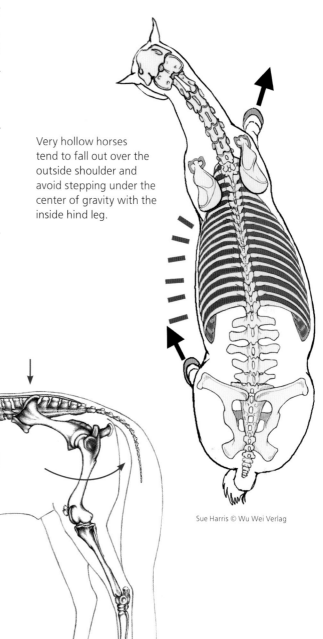

Very hollow horses tend to fall out over the outside shoulder and avoid stepping under the center of gravity with the inside hind leg.

Sue Harris © Wu Wei Verlag

Kaja Möbius © Wu Wei Verlag

A horse with a tense back (hyperflexed back mover) cannot be straightened. On the contrary, crookedness will increase and affect the natural gaits. Rhythm irregularities and rein lameness may develop.

FIRST DEGREE BEND

Waldemar Seunig describes the terms "first degree bend" (indirect bend) and "second degree bend" (direct bend). in his work *Von der Koppel bis zur Kapriole* [From paddock to capriole] (Olms Press, Hildesheim, Zürich, New York, 2001).

First degree bend is used to bring the outside of the body to suppleness and elasticity in both directions. Central to this effort is a "giving" (following) outside rider's hand on a bent line. It has to do with riding forward in a regular rhythm with equal contact on both reins. On a circle or corner, the rider tries to use this contact to the outside rein to increase the elasticity of the outside trunk musculature through sensitive giving of the outside hand.

It is about giving on the outside, not pulling on the inside.

I remember many riding lessons during which instructors tried to teach us to bring the outside shoulder along in turns. By that they meant *giving* with the outside hand—that is, a first degree bend. A comparison with riding a bicycle is helpful here: When riding around a curve, I automatically turn by leading with the outside of my body.

Common rider errors

Misunderstanding these principles leads to an increase in crookedness. When a horse is going to the stiff side (usually the left side) and isn't ridden forward enough, he tends to lean on the inside rein. If the rider accepts this invitation and simply holds against it or even begins to pull on the inside rein, the horse reflexively pulls back or creeps behind the bit. In any case, he won't accept the bit. The crookedness increases. The poll and the back tense and lock up, as does the half of the body that is turned to the hollow side.

If the rider keeps going in this way and continues to pull more, the horse's neck tilts away sideways with a stiff poll and a locked back. The horse becomes a leg mover.

I believe the rider's incorrect response to natural crookedness is one of the main sources of errors in horse training.

Next to a stiff and tense seat, one of the worst mistakes in giving aids is when a rider pulls the inside hand back and deep. Pulling with the hand generally affects the rider's seat in an opposite direction. When the rider pulls backward consistently, she starts pulling her stomach in, her legs go up, she squeezes with the thighs and then tenses her back. Such a chain reaction leads to a vicious cycle. The tense shoulders of the rider (pulling hands) causes the rider's entire back to tighten, especially the lower back. The rider can no longer sit supply, which creates the same issue for the horse. When the rider's back is tense, the horse's back is tense. This chain reaction increasingly stiffens the horse's poll, which causes the rider to pull even more. These errors are so common that the industry has responded by designing saddles with deep seats and large knee blocks. The rider then sits as if cemented in the saddle, clamping with tense thighs (adductors) behind the saddle blocks so as to better brace in front.

SECOND DEGREE BEND

After a horse becomes more elastic on the outside of his body on both sides, the rider can ask for the second degree bend, the direct bend. The horse responds to the outside aids to bend around the inside leg. If there is equal suppleness on both sides of the body, it is then possible to increase the demands on the inside hind leg of the horse. Collection work becomes increasingly important. Straightening and bending exercises improve throughness and suppleness of the back and are critical prerequisites for collection work.

The natural horizontal balance is the prerequisite for vertical balance (straightness,) and this is the prerequisite for correct collection.

A horse can only be collected when he moves in a relaxed and regular rhythm, in good contact, with impulsive, energetic steps and strides while being straight.

An expressive left half-pass: The poll angle could be somewhat more open.

XIV.

COLLECTION

Shifting Horizontal Balance

THE BIOMECHANICS OF COLLECTION

© Variation of figure by Michael Strick's *Denksport Reiten*, FN Verlag, Warendorf 2001

Flexing the haunches: All the large joints of the hind leg flex in the supporting phase—this places the "spring" under tension.

In further training, shifting the horse's "horizontal balance" plays a critical role along with "vertical balance." By shifting the balance, it is possible to shorten or lengthen the trunk of the horse—and to control the horse without resistance. The term "throughness" in Classical Riding theory describes the ability of a rider to gradually increase her influence on various horizontal balance positions. In the ideal case, a good rider on a well-trained horse can use her seat to change the balance from maximum extension of the horse's trunk to maximum shortening of the trunk. That means the rider can achieve the greatest possible lengthening of the frame to the shortest possible shortening of the frame—and back again. From the greatest possible extensions at the walk, trot and canter, a through horse can develop the highest degree of collection and vice versa: A strong canter can lead to a canter pirouette, and a piaffe can develop into a strong trot.

In the literature, we find terms like "shifting the center of gravity," "lengthening the frame," "collection as a shortening of the frame," "increased stepping under," "bending the haunches," and "relative elevation." Descriptions of various balance positions address the question of what biomechanics means to balance and collection. The term "bending of the haunches" is regularly used as a synonym for the term "collection."

Friedrich Freiherr von Krane writes from an empirical perspective about "center of gravity, carriage, balance and inclination in the gait" in his work, which appeared in 1879, *Anleitung zur Ausbildung der Kavallerie-Remonte* [Guidelines for training cavalry remounts] (Olms Press, Hildesheim, Zürich, New York, 1983). He describes a shift in the balance around the "middle posture," in which the "animal feels comfortable in a typical stance." He is referring to the natural balance. He explains collection through an analytical observation of the external form:

"The conformation of the horse (his carriage) in combination with his inclination in the gait give collection."

Waldemar Seunig likewise examines collection and describes the biomechanical process as follows:

"For correct collection, the back must undergo intense stretching. This increase in elastic tension comes from the back being stretched in opposite

directions. *The croup and gluteal muscles of the flexed hind end pull sharply backward and downward on the back muscles. At the other end, the neck and head stretch forward and upward through the neck ligament.*

"This elastic tension, which is maintained through impulsive, energetic gaits, and which has nothing to do with cramped stiffness type of tension causes a leverage effect of the raised neck and head on the hindquarters. The impulsive power is changed from forward pushing into load bearing according to the amount and direction of the rider's influence on the impulsion."

Waldemar Seunig, *Von der Koppel bis zur Kapriole* [From paddock to capriole], Olms Press, Hildesheim, Zürich, New York, 2001, p. 135

Seunig brings two thoughts into focus with his observation. First, he references the elasticity of the back. In other words, he says that only a back mover can be collected. Moreover, it is clear that without well-developed pushing power—that is, true Impulsion—there is no Collection.

It is biomechanically impossible to collect a horse correctly that has a tight back doing "hover" steps with the hind legs sprawled out behind.

LENGTHENING AND SHORTENING THE FRAME

Historically, the term "haunches" refers to the two large joints of the horse's hind leg, namely the hip and the stifle. Waldemar Seunig suggests in his work, "*Von der Koppel bis zur Kapriole*" [From paddock to capriole], that it is logical, on anatomical grounds, to also include the hock. Hip, stifle and hock joints of a well-ridden horse all flex passively in the support leg phase. The degree of flexion increases in accordance with the degree of collection at different tempos. These joints cannot flex as necessary when there is tension in the trunk and back. Consequently, these three joints are dependent on the elasticity (suppleness) of the musculature involved, including the large muscle groups of the back and hind legs.

FOR THE HIP, STIFLE AND HOCK TO FLEX, THE MUSCULATURE OF THE BACK AND HINDQUARTERS MUST BE ELASTIC.

The coffin joint functions as a spring regardless of the horse's state of balance. It flexes passively regardless of the condition of the back and hindquarters' musculature and also regardless of the throughness of the horse. The spring apparatus of the coffin joint functions no matter if the horse is a leg mover or hyperflexed back mover. I believe that this phenomenon explains the great sensitivity of the suspensory apparatus (predominantly injuries to the suspensory ligament) in tense dressage horses doing "hover" steps.

But to explain how the horse's frame "shortens in collection" or "lengthens during extension, the topline of the horse must be analyzed by looking at the upper neck-back-croup silhouette of a horse performing different paces.

The topline of a horse changes with increasing collection. First the neck lifts and appears to shorten due to the increasing arch of the neck, but without actually shortening. Second, the region of the back in front of the lumbo-sacral joint lifts slightly and arches. Third, the outline of the croup tilts down and back from its highest point at the lumbo-sacral joint.

THE ROLE OF THE LUMBO-SACRAL JOINT

The *lumbo-sacral (LS) joint* plays a key role in shortening the trunk through a tilt of the croup that increases as collection increases. The greater the collection, the greater the flexion of this joint: the pelvis rotates and changes its position (angle) relative to the spine due to the lumbo-sacral joint.

Even though the *sacroiliac (SI) joint* (the joint connecting the sacrum and the ilium bone of the pelvis) moves very little, if at all, due to the massive ligaments between the sacrum and the pelvis, it can still be regarded as a "spring apparatus" in this region. The main movement related to the tilting of the pelvis occurs in the LS joint. The sacrum follows the pelvis as it moves upward in extended gaits and downward in collection. Since the sacrum and the attached tail vertebrae are the bony structures that

115

give shape to the croup, the position of the croup changes when the horse performs correct extensions and true collection.

As the rear portion of the back is lifted and arched in collection, the croup slants. This phenomenon is explained in the strong anatomical attachment of the ilium of the pelvis to the long back muscles, the attachment of the pelvis to the sacrum and the attachment of back ligament from the sacrum to the spinous processes of the back vertebrae and the neck.

Contraction of the trunk flexor muscles causes this movement of the pelvis in collection. The main trunk flexors are the *inner lumbar muscles* and the abdomi-

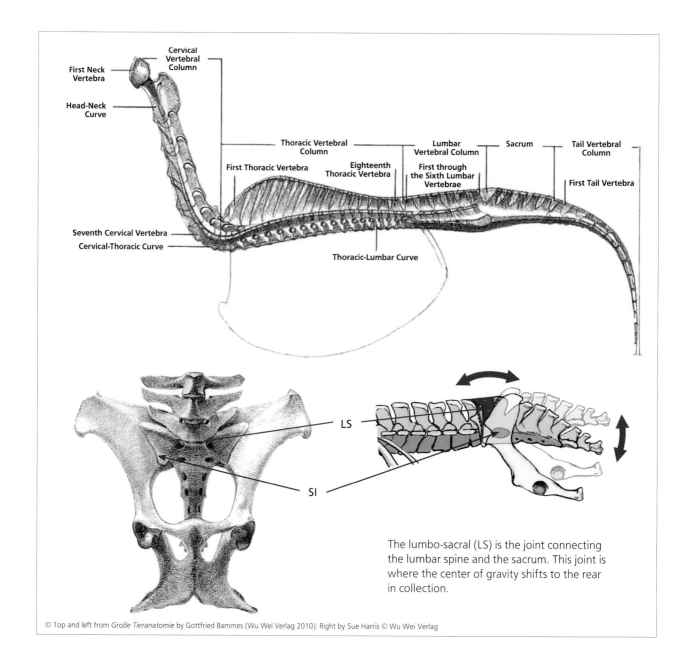

The lumbo-sacral (LS) is the joint connecting the lumbar spine and the sacrum. This joint is where the center of gravity shifts to the rear in collection.

© Top and left from *Große Tieranatomie* by Gottfried Bammes (Wu Wei Verlag 2010): Right by Sue Harris © Wu Wei Verlag

Piaffe in good balance with an open poll angle. The tail shows minor tension.

nal musculature. *The psoas muscles*, which are found beneath the lumbar spine, along with the *horizontal* and *external oblique abdominal muscles* are responsible for flexing the LS and hip joints. When these muscles contract they pull the pelvis and the upper leg forward beneath the trunk of the horse.

When considering its function, the LS joint must logically be considered part of the haunches, since it plays a critical role in how a horse looks when collected.

Except for a small role played by the arching of the lumbar spine, the LS joint is almost exclusively responsible for the shifting of the center of gravity backward in collection. As the pelvis sinks in collec-

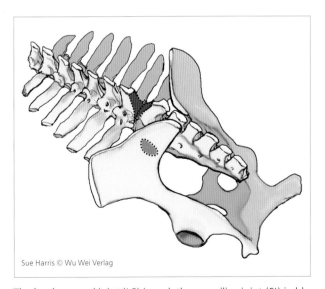

Sue Harris © Wu Wei Verlag

The lumbo-sacral joint (LS) in red, the sacroiliac joint (SI) in blue.

117

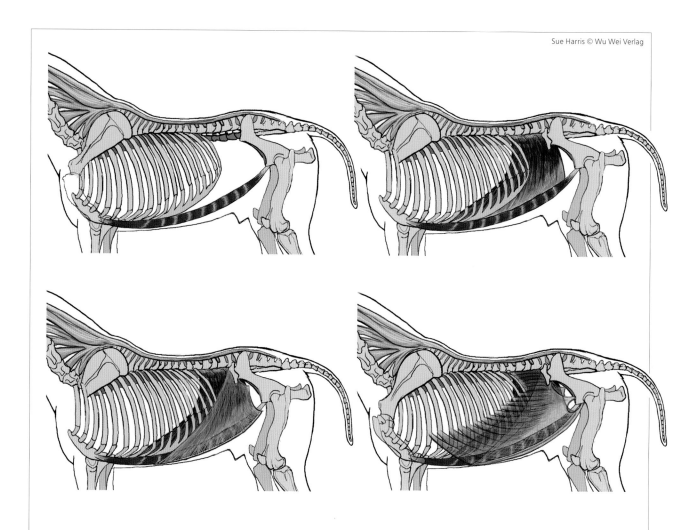

The four abdominal muscles: Upper left: *Musculus (M.) rectus abdominis*. Upper right: *M. transversus abdominis*. Lower left: *M. obliquus abdominis internus*. Lower right: *M. obliquus abdominis externus*. Like the inner lumbar muscles, the abdominal muscles are active in the movement of the pelvis and the hind legs. The passive tension of the trunk from below is due to the ligament attached to the *M. rectus abdominis*, the white line.

tion, the LS joint enables a small arching where the lumbar and the thoracic vertebrae meet.

There is one striking biomechanical difference of the LS joint when compared to the first three joints named: the hip, stifle and hock. In the correctly collected horse, these three joint areas are passively flexed in the support phase by the extensor muscles of the hind limb. The extensors of the hind leg and the muscles of the back must not only be especially powerful, but also very pliable and elastic since the carrying work increases as the joint angles get smaller (more flexed). The ability of a horse to flex in the haunches is mirrored in the rider's perception of the horse "becoming softer" in the haunches despite great carrying and pushing power. Egon von Neindorff referred to this when he said that a well-ridden horse should "hit" the rider in the seat with his hind legs.

In contrast to the hip, stifle and hock joints, the LS joint can only be actively flexed. The angle between the vertebral column and the pelvis decreases only through the action of the trunk flexors.

THE ROLE OF THE TRUNK MUSCULATURE

The trunk musculature causes energetic forward movement through the extension (pushing-off) phase of the hind leg, which is then brought forward under the trunk of the horse. These muscles are only effective when they are powerful enough, and when the strong antagonists in the back, meaning the two strands of the long back muscles, are also elastic and supple. The power of the trunk flexors can only be developed through systematic, rhythmical forward riding.

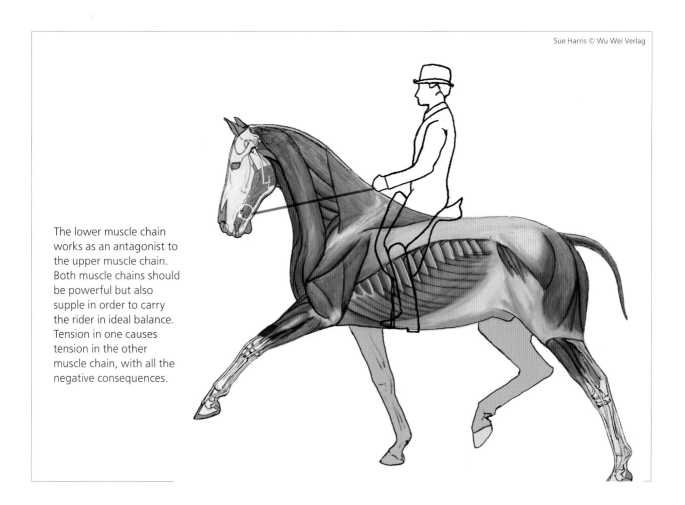

Sue Harris © Wu Wei Verlag

The lower muscle chain works as an antagonist to the upper muscle chain. Both muscle chains should be powerful but also supple in order to carry the rider in ideal balance. Tension in one causes tension in the other muscle chain, with all the negative consequences.

Before collection, it is necessary to develop pushing power!

Collection results not just from the development of strength, but equally importantly it results from growing elasticity and throughness.

Suppleness and elasticity of the back muscles and the muscles of the haunches play a critical role.

A horse with a tense back cannot go forward actively and dynamically, nor can he be correctly collected.

In his book, Dr. Robert Stodulka describes this muscular relationship in his chapter on Rollkur:

"The pull of this forced head position down and back stretches the lumbo-sacral region (where the lumbar and sacrum meet). This region should arch up due to the flexing of the haunches during collection of a classically ridden horse. The extreme head position in hyperflexion of the neck makes collection and stepping under difficult. The horse pushes his rear legs behind him rather than being able to collect. Horses trained in this way for a long time get used to it. They work without any flexion of the haunches and remain

horizontal in the back and in the hindquarters."

Dr. Robert Stodulka, *Vom Reiten zur Reitkunst* [From riding to horsemanship] Parey Verlag, Stuttgart, 2008, p 77

Inevitable consequence

Dr. Stodulka shares the above described viewpoint that a horse with a tight or hyperflexed back cannot be collected. He speaks of the difficulty the horse has in stepping under, and that the horse "becomes accustomed" to "working out behind." I would like to raise the role of the rider on this issue. It is not so much that the horse gets used to it, but more that it is impossible for the horse to step under and to collect. I believe the cause lies in totally incorrect riding. Consciously causing such a condition in a horse through forceful training methods is an inexcusable disregard of correct, Classical Training principles! All those accountable must act strenuously and as quickly as possible against such an assault on ethics, morality and, not least of all, animal protection. We should no longer merely react and treat the damage. We should finally demand consistent adherence to our principles!

Power and speed

A well-ridden horse develops powerful, yet supple and pliable trunk muscles. If these muscles must work in extended contraction with passive carrying work, it is much harder for the horse to go forward and he will resist collection. In the previous writings (B. H. von Holleuffer, von Krane, Seunig, Bürger, for example), it has been shown repeatedly that a well-ridden horse becomes not only more powerful, mobile and supple, but also "faster." The authors aren't referring to frame lengthenings in the sense of Classical Riding principles, but rather to the ability of a well-gymnasticized horse to canter fast. Have you ever tried to gallop a trained dressage horse? The horses with rigid and hollow backs can't do it; many are positively stuck to the ground, much less able to go faster. With increasing tension in the back, often for years, many horses can no longer gallop forward, losing their athletic ability. Dressage has become a goal in and of itself, in an arena.

EXPLANATION OF THE DIFFERENT STATES OF BALANCE

The terms "frame lengthening," "shifting the center of gravity," "relative elevation," and "collection" can be explained biomechanically and anatomically as follows:

1. The pelvis and the sacrum are connected to the thoracic vertebral column and the neck by the *nuchal back ligament* and the *long back muscles* and via the nuchal ligament to the head (see figure on p. 124).
2. In the process of collection or frame lengthening, the pelvis moves in an arc around the LS joint (see figures on p. 122).

As the pelvis tilts, the hip joint moves in a relative circle around the LS joint. In correct collection, the hip joint of the horse moves down and forward and causes passive flexion of the haunches (hip, stifle and hock). This leads to a shortening of both the support surface and the trunk of the horse to correspond to a shift in the center of gravity to the rear. The relative position of the distal (lower) legs is not affected in all paces in forward movement. The cannon bones of the supporting pair of legs (cannon bone of the supporting front leg and the diagonally supporting hind leg) remain parallel and are not affected at the trot. Only in the piaffe is the hind leg brought more under and the cannon bones of the diagonally supporting legs are no longer parallel.

The shortening of the support surface refers to the distance between the supporting legs (front and diagonal hind legs). The shortening or lengthening (frame lengthening) of the trunk is understood as the distance between the point of the hip and the point of the shoulder of the supporting front leg (see figures on p. 122).

THE BIOMECHANICS OF RELATIVE ELEVATION

So far we have only dealt with the lever arm of the pelvis, which sits beneath the LS joint. In the following section, we will deal with the bony parts of the pelvis that lie above the LS joint.

When the *distal* (lower) part of the pelvis (section between the LS joint and the point of the hip) moves around the LS joint down and forward in collection, then all *proximal* (upper) sections (between the LS joint and the *tuber sacrale*) move exactly opposite, up and back (see figure on p. 122). The sacrum is important because it is the insertion point for the uppermost end of the back (*supraspinal*) ligament. The sacrum follows the movement of the pelvis almost exactly, since it tightly connects to the pelvis with strong ligaments.

The long back muscles attach dorsally to the ilium

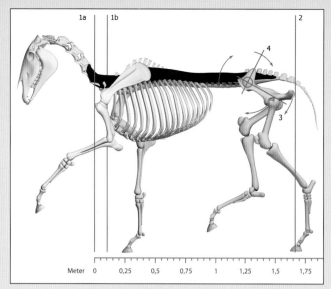

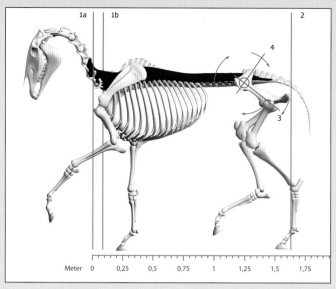

At the medium trot, the lumbo-sacral (LS) joint is slightly extended, the neck position is deeper and longer, the hind leg is pushed a little out behind. The extensor muscles act primarily.

In the working trot, the LS joint is in a neutral position; the neck is in a natural position. This body carriage can also be considered natural balance and is the foundation for developing rhythm.

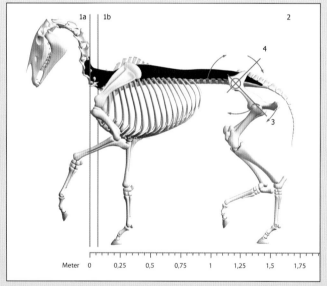

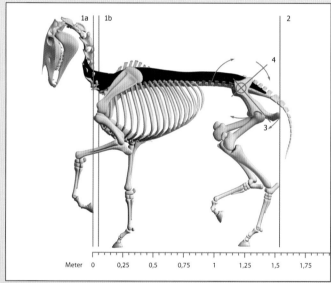

In collected trot, the LS joint is flexed, the hip joint moves farther forward and down, which causes flexion of the stifle and hock. The angle of the hip joint stays about the same, relative to the tilt of the pelvis. The neck lifts (relative elevation) through a shift backward by the long back muscles and the nuchal back ligament. The support surface of the horse shortens. The lumbar vertebrae begin to lift.

In the piaffe, the LS joint tilts more. The hind legs come so far under the body's center of gravity that the hind cannon bones slant a little to the front. The greater tilt of the pelvis leads to a greater relative elevation and arching of the lumbar vertebral column. The support surface is shortened still more.

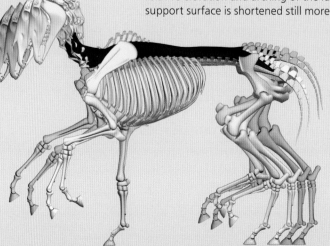

The biomechanics of shifting the center of gravity in lengthening and shortening the frame.

and the sacrum, and the hind insertion point of the back ligament is on the sacrum. This means that as the pelvis tilts in collection (or for example in the suspension phase of a fast gallop) the hind insertion point of these structures (long back muscles and back ligament) are pulled back (tuber sacrale backward and up, sacrum backward and down). The attachment of both structures (nuchal back ligament and the long back muscles) along the trunk vertebral column causes it to bow upward.

The attachment of both structures to the head and neck (long back muscles from C4 to C7; the nuchal ligament along the entire cervical vertebral column and occiput with exception of the first neck vertebra) work to raise the neck.

The term "relative elevation" is biomechanically logical and explained in this way. It results from rotation of the pelvis around the LS joint and correct flexion of the haunches, with a corresponding effect on the back, neck and the head.

Collection, then, is only a form of shifting the balance in the horse's body, so that the downward rotation of the pelvis in the LS joint causes the haunches to bend, the back to arch slightly and the neck to lift.

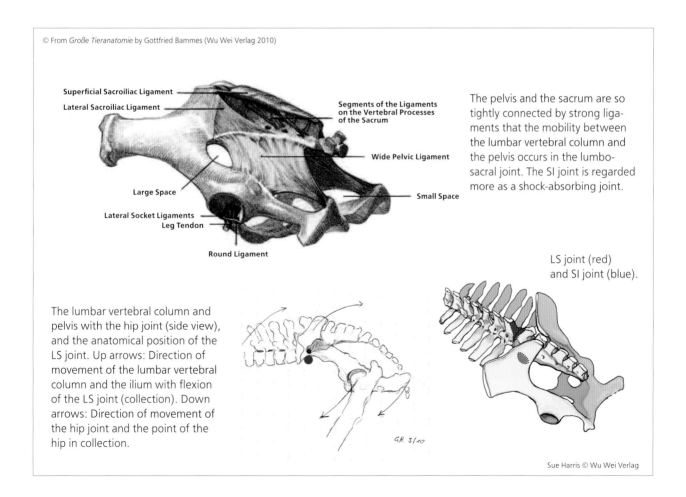

© From *Große Tieranatomie* by Gottfried Bammes (Wu Wei Verlag 2010)

Superficial Sacroiliac Ligament

Lateral Sacroiliac Ligament

Segments of the Ligaments on the Vertebral Processes of the Sacrum

Wide Pelvic Ligament

Large Space

Small Space

Lateral Socket Ligaments
Leg Tendon

Round Ligament

The pelvis and the sacrum are so tightly connected by strong ligaments that the mobility between the lumbar vertebral column and the pelvis occurs in the lumbosacral joint. The SI joint is regarded more as a shock-absorbing joint.

LS joint (red) and SI joint (blue).

The lumbar vertebral column and pelvis with the hip joint (side view), and the anatomical position of the LS joint. Up arrows: Direction of movement of the lumbar vertebral column and the ilium with flexion of the LS joint (collection). Down arrows: Direction of movement of the hip joint and the point of the hip in collection.

Sue Harris © Wu Wei Verlag

123

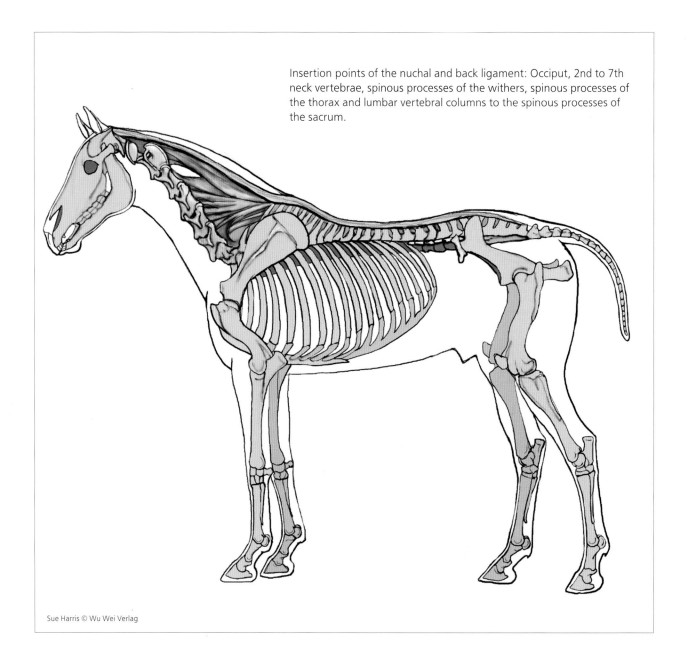

Insertion points of the nuchal and back ligament: Occiput, 2nd to 7th neck vertebrae, spinous processes of the withers, spinous processes of the thorax and lumbar vertebral columns to the spinous processes of the sacrum.

Sue Harris © Wu Wei Verlag

The support surface is shortened. The tilting of the pelvis at the LS joint and the flexing of the haunches are dependent upon elasticity of the back and power and throughness of the hind leg extensors.

Carrying power develops only when there is sufficient pushing power.

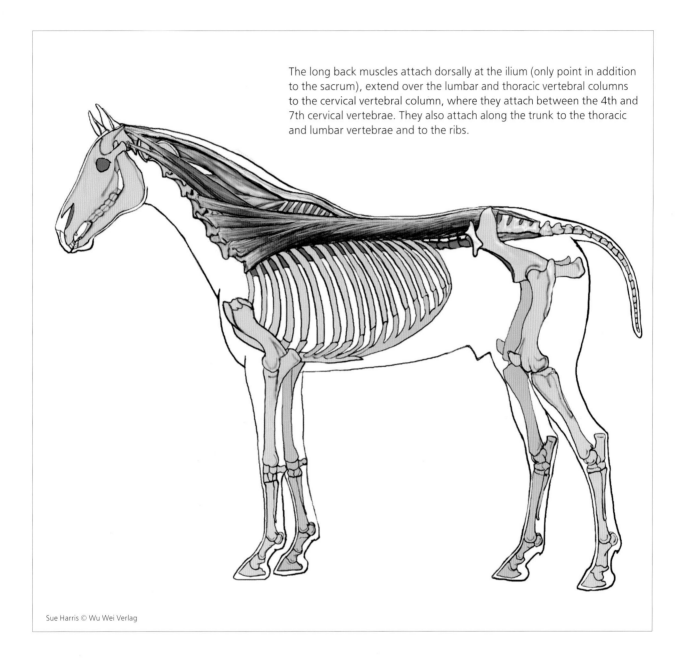

The long back muscles attach dorsally at the ilium (only point in addition to the sacrum), extend over the lumbar and thoracic vertebral columns to the cervical vertebral column, where they attach between the 4th and 7th cervical vertebrae. They also attach along the trunk to the thoracic and lumbar vertebrae and to the ribs.

Sue Harris © Wu Wei Verlag

CONSEQUENCES FOR TRAINING

Biomechanics explains the training effect of correctly ridden changes of tempo at the trot and canter. The repeated change between collected and working pace, working and medium pace or collected and extended pace requires and develops throughness. Therefore, it isn't just about riding forward for 40 to 60 meters. Like an accordion, only a few strides at trot or canter are lengthened and then

A good, seated piaffe with the back leg swinging under and slight tension in the lumbar area of the back (see tail).

brought back, to be lengthened again and brought back again. An extension should last only so long as the horse is able to carry himself in independent balance. Extensions that are too strong or last too long cause the horse's balance to fall apart, the horse comes off the aids and goes on the forehand, which can be damaging to the horse.

Likewise, a period of collected work should be followed by fresh forward riding. When a horse is ridden so long in collection that the musculature gets tired and tense, the training effect is lost and turns into the opposite! Stiffness and resistance are the result.

Continuous change between tension and relaxation is essential for training success. Horses need a lot of time to develop the necessary musculature from which pushing and carrying power can develop.

A horse with a tense back, regardless of which inappropriate balance he is in, can never really be collected. This makes it clear as to why we generally don't see collection or only very rudimentary attempts at collection, in horses with hovering movements created by tense or hover trots from tight backs. Only a back mover can develop a true piaffe!

The critical movement muscles of the back, the long back muscles, run between these two bony structures, the cervical vertebral column and the pelvis. That is why the power and suppleness of this muscle is so very important.

◆

"Only the back mover, the horse that moves with a powerful but elastic and swinging back, is a horse in balance."
—*B.H. von Holleuffer*

◆

As the haunches bend, all the angles of the hind leg get smaller. As a result, the stress on all the carrying muscles (leg extensors) is considerably increased, as is the need for elasticity of the back. These extensor muscles can only support the greater passive carrying work in collection when they have been sufficiently strengthened in rhythmical forward movement. This is the physiological reason behind the recommendation for regular outside work, especially for young horses. On the path of correct training, the prerequisites for carrying in collection are developed through the power of the extensors in forward riding.

A balanced horse is one that has the best chance of staying healthy for a long time and is the one that allows his rider to sit supply. In comparison, almost all rider problems arise from a tense or "lost" center of movement in the back. Elasticity paired with the power of the trunk musculature is a critical goal of good training.

An unexpectedly high proportion of horses are lame due to common training mistakes. Veterinarians interested in orthopedics should, in my opinion, focus more on this area. You can't have a comprehensive picture of the patient in a lameness exam without considering the quality of the training and the problems in this area (see p. 156).

XV.
THE POLL
A Joint with a Key Function

SENSITIVE CONTACT AS A GIFT

An even and sensitive contact results from a swinging, relaxed back.

A final prerequisite for vertical flexion is a supple, or as riders say, a "yielding" poll. The importance of the rounding of the poll is highlighted in a passage from *Von der Koppel bis zur Kapriole* [From paddock to capriole] (Olms Press, Hildesheim, Zürich, New York, 2001). Waldemar Seunig writes on p. 134:

"Longitudinal flexion and elevation are not essential goals of dressage training but rather results and symptoms of expert work."

All that is in front of the rider (longitudinal flexion, relative elevation) is a gift from the horse based on correct, good work from a tactful and supple seat. You need to carefully manage and organize the gift with sensitive hands. You can ask the hindquarters for this gift, and it shouldn't be more than a request, with fine leg and seat aids. Seunig says very correctly, "At the end, it is only about the rider's seat and the horse's hind legs." The sooner the rider grasps this concept, the faster she finds the harmony she longs for.

The development of diagonal aids is important in this context. In order to be able to develop first degree bend (indirect—see p. 110), it is necessary to

129

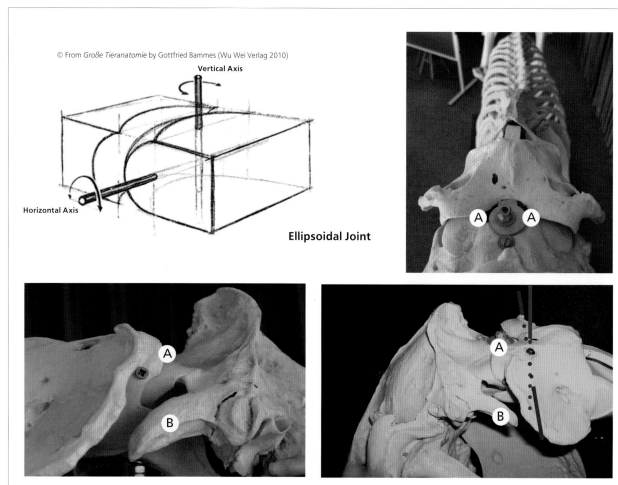

© From *Große Tieranatomie* by Gottfried Bammes (Wu Wei Verlag 2010)

Vertical Axis

Horizontal Axis

Ellipsoidal Joint

The poll (atlanto-occipital joint) (A) is the joint between the head and the first cervical vertebra. It is a crosswise-oriented, ellipsoidal joint that allows two movements: first, an up-and-down movement of the head; and second, a sidewise flexion (positioning) of the poll. A rotation (head tilt) of this joint is not possible. The *processus paracondylares (jugulares)* (B), which are two bony projections that protrude an index finger's length from the base of the skull, stiffen the poll if the head is positioned too deeply with the nose behind the vertical. Therefore, correct positioning of the poll is only possible with an open poll angle.

already have a good and consistent contact. In re-training a horse that doesn't have a well-established contact, the horse will typically support himself on the outside rein and/or stay "behind the inside rein" when going to the hollow direction. To the stiff direction, contact problems cause the horse to support himself on the inside (positioning) rein. The horse can't or won't step up to the outside (leading) rein.

Positioning plays a large role in the correction of contact along with vigorous "forward" and "straight" movement. If such a horse allows himself to be correctly positioned, he'll step to the outside rein, which is the start of first degree flexion.

Positioning the poll

Positioning occurs only in the poll. A sidewise flexion of the head (lateral flexion) is only possible in the upper cervical area (atlanto-occipital joint). The joint between the first and second cervical vertebrae prevents lateral positioning movement (lateral flexion). Based on its anatomy, two movements are possible in the poll:

a) Vertical flexion and extension (this corresponds to the lowering or raising of the head).

b) Lateral flexion, sidewise bending, depending on the length of the *procc. paracondylares*, (see the bottom left photo on p. 130), the positioning to the left or right, which is positioning in the equestrian sense.

Rotation of the head, as when the horse tilts his head, is only possible one joint farther back, between the first and the second cervical vertebrae.

Correct contact, where the horse goes to the bit with a "chewing" mouth, is only possible with a yielding poll.

To pull the whole neck all the way sideways is fully counterproductive in many ways. The poll becomes stiff and the neck is "torn loose" from the withers. The poll should be supple and the neck stabilized by muscle at the withers. A good sign of correct positioning is when the crest of the neck flips to the side to which the horse is positioned.

THE CORRECT POSITION OF THE POLL

In order to achieve contact that is correct according to the Training Scale, it is extremely important to maintain the poll as the highest point of the neck. That should not be confused with elevation. A young horse going in natural balance generally positions his neck according to the anatomy of his neck and back length so that he carries a relaxed back. For example, a short, powerful horse positions his neck somewhat higher, a long horse with a deeper backline, somewhat lower.

In order to have good contact, the rider must be careful that the horse's nose is in front of the vertical as well as the poll up. A young horse ridden with a deep, long neck constantly behind the vertical (even slightly so) always falls on the forehand and cannot find his balance. The argument that "A little bit behind the vertical is not a problem," or "Sometimes you have to get the horse 'through,'" is technically false. Every active backward effect with the intention of making the poll angle smaller is damaging and makes it impossible to achieve desirable suppleness of the poll. The horse's back reacts proportionately according to the type of horse and anatomy—it hollows (leg mover) or tightens (hyperflexed back mover). In no way will the horse arch up according to classical teachings to allow the movement to come swinging through.

It is true that it is not a big problem when a horse, usually one in retraining, now and then goes behind the vertical. But this position should not last long. As soon as the back relaxes, the correct head and neck position is automatic!

And it is especially so when the horse seeks and goes to the hand/the bit. A giving hand of the rider is fundamental to suppleness of the horse's back. The old saying is true: "The ears should be as far from

A young horse in natural balance. The back is not yet completely relaxed.

the rider as possible, the poll the highest point and the poll muscles should always be supple (soft poll)."

At this point, I would like to remind you of the passage by B. H. von Holleuffer (p. 69) describing contact as being the result of a softly swinging back. The poll position and contact are the result of good training, not the prerequisite!

DEALING WITH THE STIFF POLL

Classical Riding teachings logically stem from anatomy and biomechanics. Why is it so difficult to put them into practice? Perhaps because there is always the same problem: Many riders have little patience or time to wait until the horse finds his way to suppleness and becomes connected through training. Instead, they frequently force the manufacture of a "beautiful" frame and demand what they want to have in front of them (round poll, elevation) with physical force. Much too late many riders realize that they cannot mechanically force suppleness and throughness. Experienced riders often feel and know intuitively that something isn't right. But many riders and trainers don't go as far as really admitting to themselves that they have made mistakes—possibly for years!

Trainers who already have much respectable success in competition find it especially difficult to take this step. "How can I be doing something wrong? I have won many Grand Prix!" Such thoughts are like a bullwark against recognizing that Classical Riding theory offers a sensitive path free of force. Because the horse must function, competitive sport ultimately doesn't allow for taking the time to "smell the roses" or to dwell on Classical Riding teachings. Success is money, and money is more success. Why should there be any question? The suspicion of deficiency is repressed and covered up, and the trickery begins. Frequently, it is self-induced pressure for success that keeps a rider from taking a clear, matter-of-fact look at correct riding. Naturally, the pressure is not just of our own making since success in the current system relies on satisfying customers and officials. There is no way around feeling the pressure of training within time limits.

PHYSICAL FORCE IS NO SOLUTION TO CONTACT PROBLEMS!

I knew a trainer successful at the highest levels who regularly overpowered his horses in the worst way. When I challenged him one morning about a horse that he had strapped together with draw reins, the horse covered with foam and gasping for air, he replied, "They need this every couple of weeks!"

I also know that this is not an isolated case. The worst outbursts of force are daily business in many barns. However, I believe that these "attacks" are only very seldom really due to human character flaws. No doubt there is some despair involved, with the trainer not knowing what else he can do or how to extricate himself from a dead-end road.

Often these outbursts are the frustrated reactions to a horse that has long been ridden stiff and tight. Many riders break from this behavior pattern as they gain the knowledge that more force only takes them farther away from achieving a through horse.

A soft poll makes such emotional outbursts unnecessary.

WHAT IS A SUPPLE POLL?

Between the occiput and the first and second cervical vertebrae, there is a muscle system referred to as the *short head and neck muscles*. These muscles allow movement of the head and the neck in the first two joints of the cervical vertebral column. A "soft" poll means complete suppleness of this

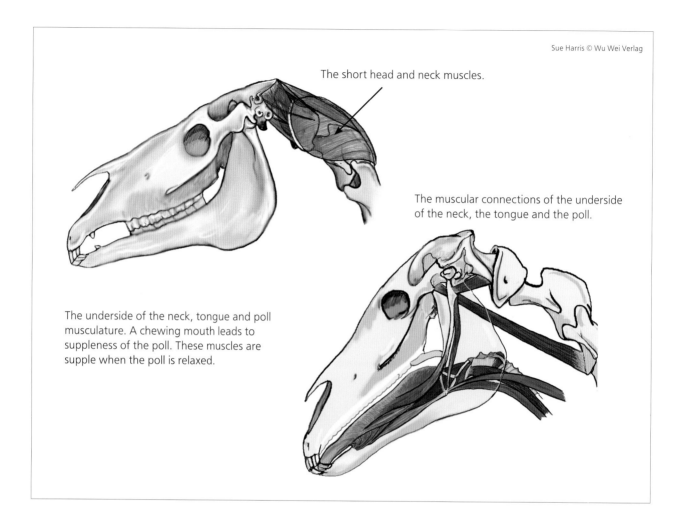

Sue Harris © Wu Wei Verlag

The short head and neck muscles.

The muscular connections of the underside of the neck, the tongue and the poll.

The underside of the neck, tongue and poll musculature. A chewing mouth leads to suppleness of the poll. These muscles are supple when the poll is relaxed.

muscle system, which then overcomes resistances that make contact difficult. The horse willingly allows himself to be positioned in both directions, and to step up to the tactful rider's hand, relaxed and with a round poll.

At this point it should be clear that a relaxed poll never results from lowering the head against resistance from tight muscles at the top of the neck and the short head and neck muscles. A forceful pull against one or several muscle groups leads to complete cramping, which naturally leads to the back tensing up. On the other hand, tension in the poll results from a tight back, since the one inevitably causes the other. The consequences of this understanding are clear: Both systems must be relaxed at the same time.

When our modern, young riding horses are put under saddle, they almost always react with defensive tension in the back, which in turn causes poll tension and over-rounding of the neck. If, at this stage, this over-rounding and "going behind the bit" is mistakenly interpreted as "going on the bit" or "giving at the poll," then the foundation has been laid for disturbance of a critical balance. Another horse needing "retraining" has just been created!

Forceful longitudinal flexion always, without exception, leads to cramping of the entire topline. This, in turn, leads unavoidably to the maximum possible disruption of balance, which causes negative consequences for training and for the health of the horse.

A horse can round his poll only as a result of his supple poll and back muscles.

SUPPLENESS OF THE POLL AND AN OPEN POLL ANGLE

The *positioning of the poll* is an indispensable prerequisite for correct bending. The diagonal aids, the leading outside rein and the driving inside leg, can only be established in a "positioned" horse. Positioning is only possible when the poll is relaxed and the poll angle is open. That requires the nose to be in front of the vertical. A horse with the nose behind the vertical rotates in the poll downward behind the vertical line. The nose points toward the chest, or at least backward. On the left and right side of the base of the skull, index-finger-long, bony processes (*Procc. paracondylares* or *procc. jugulares*) jut out caudally (to the back). When the poll flexes so that the nose goes behind the vertical, these bony processes lift under the wings of the first neck vertebra and block the poll from moving sideways. Positioning of the poll has then become anatomically impossible!

A horse going behind the vertical is less able to be positioned the smaller the poll angle gets.

With a narrow poll angle, the horse can only bend the whole neck to the side. In so doing, he breaks right in front of the withers. At the same time, the short head and neck musculature over-stretches, cramps and loses all suppleness as a result.

In daily riding, it is understandably unavoidable that a horse will go deeper for a short time now and then. The tight-backed horse in retraining, a leg mover or an hyperflexed back mover is occasionally ridden with deeper neck flexion; this position can be tolerated for a short time. However, the rider should not purposely ask for this and should not consider it correct.

Statements such as "Make him through," or "Put him deep," are misunderstood concepts. In the worst case, the central message of the teachings of Classical Riding is turned on its head. It is not about pulling the head down, right or left. It is more about the horse going from his back end to his front end to the hand, seeking the contact in trust, and relaxing the back (see p. 69, Von Holleuffer on "swinging"). Only then will he give his poll and allow himself to be positioned equally to both sides. Consequently, the basic command reads:

The nose must be in front of the vertical!

This statement was, is and always will be correct, important and absolute!

If a rider wants to ride and train a balanced and through horse, there is not a single factual excuse for ignoring this command. A narrow poll angle doesn't allow the poll to be the highest point. A narrow poll angle prevents the horse from relaxing his back and arching it. Tension throughout the trunk musculature is inevitable. Naturally, the all important elasticity can't develop from such muscular tension. Consequently, the horse can't develop forward thrust and carrying power.

It is simply anatomically impossible to correctly train a horse with a narrow poll angle. The goal—throughness—is not achievable in this way. Certainly, such a horse is capable of mechanically performing the exercises that he has been taught since what is required is more or less the mechanical control of the flight reflex. In this regard, ethnologists speak of "learned helplessness." The horse must be psychologically broken, which everyone can surely imagine also leaves behind physical traces. It is not unusual for trainers to talk about a horse in this way: "This horse is a good horse. He tolerates everything." Seriously, I have heard this said often! Obviously, horses that don't resist rough training methods are more loved than those that self-confidently fight back!

She who believes a horse must be dominated with the hand will never experience how wonderfully light a through, balanced horse feels, and how much fun he is to ride!

The poll is a key juncture of the horse's whole body. Without a soft poll there cannot be a through horse. I would like to emphasize again: you cannot force the poll of a horse to be supple.

You "receive" a supple poll; you cannot "take" it!

Many authors have observed from experience that a tense poll always accompanies a back that doesn't swing. A horse without correct contact and without a supple poll will never be a back mover. When the poll appears to be supple as a result of exclusively manipulating the mouth, it still doesn't mean that the back has relaxed and that the horse is in balance. A leg mover or hyperflexed back mover (a Rollkur horse with an hyperflexed back) with a seemingly relaxed poll remains an unbalanced horse.

CONSEQUENCES FOR TRAINING

Suppleness of the poll must result from rhythmical movement in all three gaits. A yielding, relaxed poll requires that a horse swings in a relaxed fashion under the rider, and goes to the hand from back to front.

The order of the Training Scale components cannot be reversed! Without Rhythm, Suppleness, and Contact, you can't develop Impulsion, Straightness and Collection. The first three on the Scale are the foundation upon which everything else is built.

Everything that a rider wants "in front of her" when on her horse comes as a result of what she is able to achieve with her seat and sensitive hands as a means of communication. A stiff, tense seat with hard fists and tight shoulders always leads to a stiff poll, a tight back and tight haunches in the horse. The order of the first steps in the training of a young horse should read:

Supple, sensitive, balanced, appropriate seat (e.g. adjusted stirrup lengths) → sensitive, waiting, soft contact to the horse's mouth with open neck and poll angles (nose in front of the vertical) → calm → feeling of rhythm → begin driving → rhythm → regular rhythm forward → suppleness → back begins to swing → rhythm improves with more dynamism and regularity → contact with a chewing mouth and a relaxed poll.

Basically it can be said:

Riding works only from the back to the front!

Never ride from the front to the back! In training for contact, the horse must play the active part and the rider's hand the waiting, passive part. It is called, after all, "leaning to," (the German word used for "contact" is *Anlehnung*, which literally means "leaning to") not "pulling to." A rider's hand that is too active and overused leads to "disrupted" balance from the braking, backward action of the rider. A good, supple balanced seat and independent, quiet, sensitive hands are the foundation of good riding.

XVI.

THE ACTIVE MOUTH

A Prerequisite for Basic Balance

THE PSYCHOLOGICAL COMPONENTS OF "CHEWING"

A proper "chewing" mouth is always the result of a relaxed trunk and poll musculature.

It has been known for many decades that a chewing mouth relaxes the horse's poll (the short head and neck muscles). This mechanism has a biomechanical as well as a psychological component. The process of chewing has a psychologically calming effect that acts on the muscular attachments of the tongue and the underside of the neck, and a relaxing effect on the poll muscles. In the last century, it was regarded as absolutely necessary for a ridden horse to have an active mouth. This perspective seems to be largely forgotten today and in fact, has gone so far that some riders intentionally forbid the horse to chew by "tying" his mouth shut. Even a well-intentioned, bitless bridle ties the mouth shut when the reins are taken up, in short leading to a massive poll cramp. Not everything that looks and is considered gentle is always so!

Waldemar Seunig explains that proper chewing is the result of a movement of the tongue that comes with swallowing. He says:

"While chewing, the lower and upper jaws move only a few millimeters apart, just wide enough to give the tongue room for a slight swallowing movement. Any exaggerated, cramped lifting of the tongue would be a sign of insufficient suppleness; likewise, clamping the mouth shut is an evasion. The head of the horse should find a position that is steady, natural and near the vertical; tipping backward is an attempt to get away from the bit."

Waldemar Seunig, *Marginalien zu Pferd und Reiter* [Marginalia to horse and rider] Wu Wei Verlag, Schondorf, 2011

The authors and trainers of the last century were in error in their explanation of the biomechanical causes of chewing. They thought it related to the bit (mouthpiece of the curb) in the mouth of the horse.

An incorrect bit can hinder the correct, relaxed and relaxing chewing of the horse. A bit that fits is, however, no guarantee of desired mouth activity.

THE BIOMECHANICAL COMPONENTS OF CHEWING

Good mouth activity, almost a sucking movement of the tongue, is the result of a relaxed lower muscle chain working on the body of the horse. This muscle chain begins with the external abdominal oblique muscle, includes the muscles of the chest and ends in the musculature of the underside of the neck. Therefore, the abdominal musculature is central and fundamental to the activity of the mouth. It is also a part of the trunk flexors in the horse.

A supple and powerfully working topline is considered the decisive muscle chain for the balance of a horse. Since every biological system is built on the basis of *agonists* and corresponding *antagonists*, it is clear that the system of *trunk extenders* complements the *trunk flexors*. This muscle system is located under the thoracic vertebral column.

The abdominal muscle system (along with the inner lumbar muscles) contracts while the horse is standing and during the suspension phase of a bend (arching up of the chest and lumbar vertebral columns) in a moving horse. The ability of the upper or lower muscle chains to work relaxed depends on the other one. A tight back always leads to a tight abdomen (e.g. the horse doesn't accept the leg or kicks against the rider's leg) and vice versa.

Balance refers to not just "front and back," "left and right," but also to "above and below."

If the back of a horse is supple, the side flexors also work rhythmically and powerfully. The horse goes forward with regular rhythm. As soon as basic balance is achieved, the rider can drive sensitively with the calves and seat. "Driving from the legs"

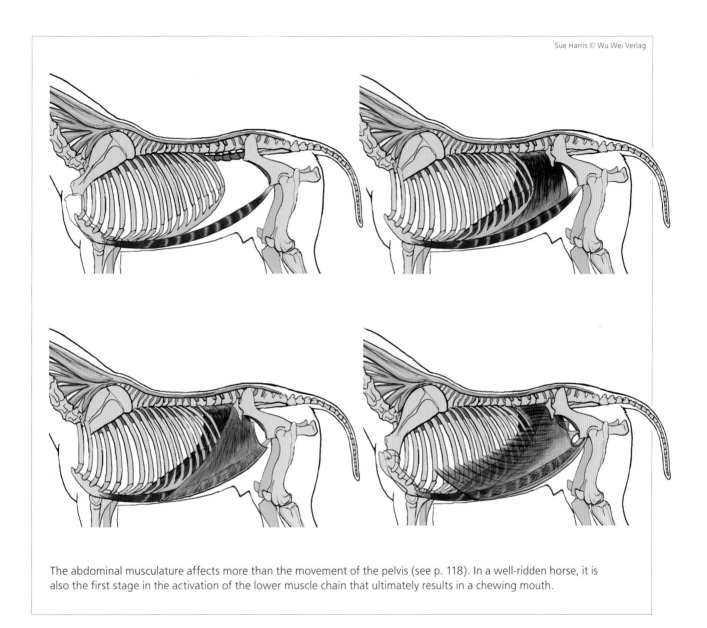

Sue Harris © Wu Wei Verlag

The abdominal musculature affects more than the movement of the pelvis (see p. 118). In a well-ridden horse, it is also the first stage in the activation of the lower muscle chain that ultimately results in a chewing mouth.

primarily activates the external oblique abdominal muscle, and influences the movement of the hind leg on the same side. The external oblique abdominal muscle lies largely against the side wall of the chest. In the forward, ventral (lower) region of the chest, this muscle attaches directly to the abdominal segment of the deep chest muscle, which attaches directly to the superficial chest muscle.

In the area of the front chest, this muscle is in intimate biomechanal contact with the musculature of the underside of the neck, which runs to the lower jaw, the tongue and the poll. (See also: "Jaw-Mobilizing Effect of the Lower Muscle Chain," p. 153.)

A back that is working well allows the antagonists (inner lumbar and abdominal muscles) to work

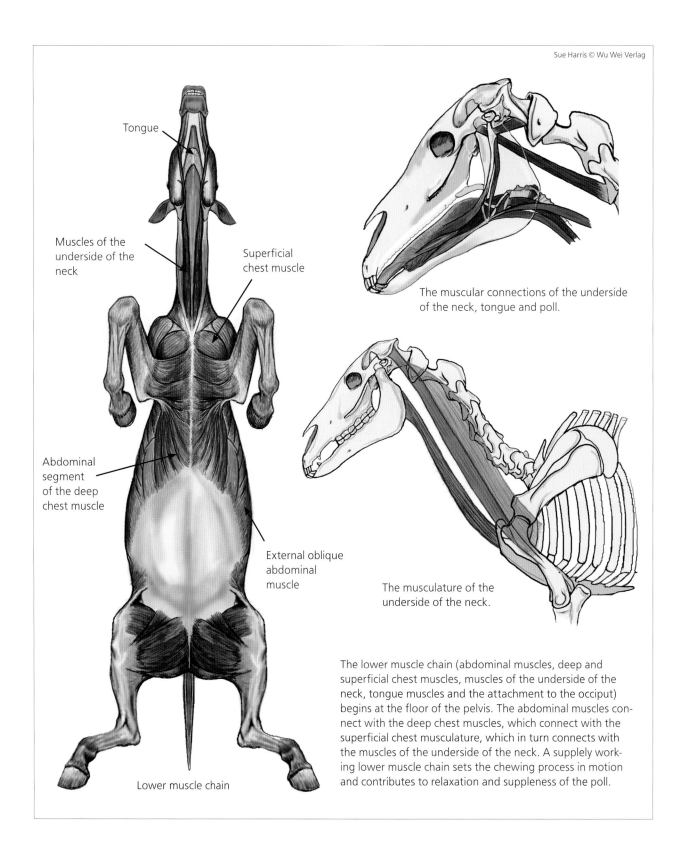

Sue Harris © Wu Wei Verlag

Tongue

Muscles of the underside of the neck

Superficial chest muscle

Abdominal segment of the deep chest muscle

External oblique abdominal muscle

Lower muscle chain

The muscular connections of the underside of the neck, tongue and poll.

The musculature of the underside of the neck.

The lower muscle chain (abdominal muscles, deep and superficial chest muscles, muscles of the underside of the neck, tongue muscles and the attachment to the occiput) begins at the floor of the pelvis. The abdominal muscles connect with the deep chest muscles, which connect with the superficial chest musculature, which in turn connects with the muscles of the underside of the neck. A supplely working lower muscle chain sets the chewing process in motion and contributes to relaxation and suppleness of the poll.

rhythmically. This lower muscle chain activates the temporomandibular joint and the horse begins to chew. This effect is the same regardless of whether the horse wears a bitless or a conventionally-bitted bridle, which allows the lower jaw to move when the reins are taken up. When the mouth is active, there is always suppleness of the poll, which is critical to the quality of the contact.

Balance can only be achieved when you regard the horse as a harmonious whole. It is impossible to seize on sections and mechanically work on them in an effort to relax and balance the whole.

Fundamental basic balance comes out of Rhythm, Suppleness and Contact.

XVII.

SHIFTING THE BALANCE

Biomechanics

FLUID TRANSITIONS

Collection is only possible when a horse is balanced and "through." Collection cannot be forced! Only a back mover can be collected.

As we saw in chapter XIV, "Collection—Shifting Horizontal Balance," collection is a special form of balance. In collection, the center of gravity of the rider and the horse is increasingly shifted to the rear. Through the sinking of the hindquarters and the arching of the back, the trunk of the horse measurably shortens. At the same time, the back musculature maintains its length and basic tension when the horse is in relative elevation since muscle insertion points at both ends coordinate the shift of the center of gravity toward the rear. The positive tension of the back can easily increase as necessary in a correctly trained horse, along with the tension of the whole body. There should never be negative tension, which results from faulty biomechanics and causes cramping of the muscles and restriction of movement.

To do the hard work of the movements, especially collected work, the horse's muscles are not relaxed—meaning they are limp. There is muscle tension as appropriate for the work, but it isn't constant: It is on/off according to the demand. This is "positive" tension.

Shifting the balance means changing impulsive energy of the hind legs into carrying power. This is a dynamic process. In the ideal case, there is a supple and fluid transition; a horse should never suddenly tip from one balance state into another. In many different disciplines and training philosophies, we see horses that trot without effective use of the back (leg mover) because the back is stiff. They suddenly tip their pelvis down into a "pseudo" piaffe and rhythmically pull the legs up high.

With comprehensive analysis from the perspective of Classical Training concepts, you can understand that this "collected" work is not really collected at all.

These horses, pressed down by the seat of the rider, have learned to rhythmically pull the legs high while in a crouching position, without relaxing the back and swinging through. There is no actual bending of the haunches! The weight of the horse doesn't lead to passive bending of the haunches because the horse didn't sit his haunches down through a process of true collection; rather, he has been forced to bend to a certain extent in the stifles by a rider sitting heavily in the saddle.

Calm stepping over in-hand or under saddle encourages mobility and supples the back in the lumbar region.

THE IMPORTANCE OF LATERAL MOVEMENTS

Collection is real only when the diagonal aids are well established, as is required for longitudinal flexion in a back mover. Otto de la Croix comments on this subject:

"All exercises are totally worthless unless they use the back, or improve the horse's ability to use the back, when going straight. No exercise can have value if it doesn't enable or perfect the use of the back.

"With that we have established the purpose of the lateral exercises, which is our next topic. First, it is important to point out the negative side, namely that the lateral movements are never a goal in themselves but rather are an aid to create impulsive gaits."

Otto de la Croix, *Natürliche Reitkunst* [Natural horsemanship], Olms Press, Hildesheim, Zürich, New York, 1983, p. 113

After basic balance is established, the lateral movements are used to improve longitudinal flexion on one hand, and on the other hand to take the first steps in the direction of collection, which also leads to a qualitative improvement in impulsion.

Moving sideways without the demand of longitudinal flexion leads to stepping over, seen in such exercises as leg-yield, reducing and enlarging the square and turn-on-the-forehand (see Waldemar Seunig quotation on p. 140). With these exercises, the horse yields to the inside, sideways-driving leg and steps with his hind leg under his center of grav-

ity. While stepping forward and sideways in leg-yields and turns-on-the-forehand, the horse crosses his hind legs. In the reducing and enlarging the square, the horse generally steps more forward than sideways. The horse should not run away from the sideways-driving leg but should step calmly. The outside leg of the rider plays an important regulating role here.

Loosening effect of stepping-over exercises
The outstanding biomechanical effect of these exercises is the loosening, relaxing effect on the croup and lumbar regions. The fascial attachments of the back musculature to the large croup muscle (*musculus gluteus medius*) enable this effect. Since this large croup muscle attaches to the large rotator (*trochanter major*) of the femur, every sideways step passively stretches this muscle chain. The large rotator moves out and back; in so doing, it passively stretches the large croup muscle.

Since the croup muscle is attached to the long back muscle by the back fascia, it also passively stretches and this improves the balance of a leg mover. In tense horses, this effect also passively stretches and relaxes the back muscles. This very powerful effect depends significantly on the quality of the rider's seat and the speed of the required movement. Young horses and horses in retraining best follow this abduction movement of the hind limbs through the back musculature when the exercise is done slowly. A horse that is recklessly pushed sideways and/or a sideways-running horse will not relax, or may even become tenser. This loosening effect occurs only when the rider sits supplely; a tense rider squeezing with her thighs cannot create a loosening effect in her horse—regardless of the exercise!

Collecting effect of the shoulder-in

Now and again, it is said that leg-yielding is not a useful exercise. "We ride shoulder-in. That is what we want." Shoulder-in is a collecting exercise resulting from the inside hind leg stepping exactly under the *center of gravity* of the horse (the imaginary vertical line through the rider and the horse's trunk to the ground). This diagonal positioning of the leg while stepping under the center of gravity passively bends the haunches. As the movement continues, the trunk of the horse shifts over the diagonally placed hind leg. This hind leg, passively weighted by the horse's whole body over the center of gravity, now flexes. The collecting effect of the shoulder-in stems from this biomechanical effect.

The haunches can only flex when the back of the horse is supple and through. A horse that is too young and not horizontally balanced, or a tense horse in retraining to resolve a tight back, is not able to bend his haunches in this way. The muscle chain (long back muscle, croup musculature, long gluteal musculature) is not supple. An incorrect shoulder-in, or shoulder-in exercise asked for too early, doesn't lead to passive flexing of the haunches. Negative tension in the muscle chain restricts the stifle (the hind leg is extended) and doesn't allow the horse's body weight to passively flex the hindquarters. The stiff back stiffens the hind legs and blocks passive flexion in the haunches. Consequently, the back muscles on the inside of the body are shoved up and the rider feels the inside back muscle rising as her seat tips to the outside.

In a correct shoulder-in, the rider sits well centered, softly, and slightly to the inside (see Waldemar Seunig's *Von der Koppel bis zur Kapriole* [From paddock to capriole]). This is necessary for gymnasticizing the horse's inside hind leg. If the rider tips away from the working hind leg and sits to the outside, the purpose of the shoulder-in is lost.

When the rider sits in front of the center of gravity of the horse, the horse runs after her, so to speak. There is no collecting effect.

Shifting the rider's center of gravity in the direction of the movement can certainly be helpful when teaching a young horse to move sideways. When the horse understands this movement, however, the gymnasticizing, collecting work of the shoulder-in is effective.

Some riding and training methods don't put the balance of the horse (the supple back) at the center point of their training philosophy. As a result, the rider is required from the start to sit to the outside in the direction of movement in the shoulder-in. Sitting in this way is the logical consequence of starting the shoulder-in too early or asking for it from a poorly balanced horse. Riders also may sit to the outside when riding horses that aren't worked as back movers. These horses run sideways and tip the pelvis back and forth, and the lumbo-sacral joint rotates at every stride. The collecting effect of the shoulder-in is also lost in this case.

CONSEQUENCES FOR WORK

If a horse is still not ready for a collecting lateral movement, then the stepping over of the leg-yield is the exercise of choice as it provides both training and loosening effects. In the eighteenth century, François Robichon de la Guérinière recognized this. In his work *School of Horsemanship* he describes the

A supple, right half-pass with correct bend. The poll should be the highest point with the nose in front of the vertical. Correct positioning is not possible if the poll is too deep.

shoulder-in with distinctly more detail than how it is taught today. He even describes leg-yield in trot and canter:

"This exercise builds the entire horse. It is true that every ruined horse, no matter how, becomes just as supple as previously when one works him a few days in shoulder-in."

François Robichon de la Guérinière, *School of Horsemanship*, JA Allen, London, 1993

From my point of view, a correct shoulder-in comes seamlessly from correct leg-yield through shoulder-fore as training progresses. I would like to state once more that shoulder-in with a collecting effect is only possible in a correctly balanced back mover. Correction of a falsely balanced horse (leg mover or hyperflexed back mover) is accomplished only through stepping-over exercises like leg-yielding.

Lateral movements are the "elixir of life" for horse trainers!

Without correct shoulder-in, counter shoulder-in, travers (haunches-in) and renvers (haunches-out) the rider can't achieve an expressive impulsion in trot and canter or advanced straightness, nor can she gain collection. The maximum suppleness and elasticity of the back musculature is only achieved through what is referred to as "straightening bending work."

Correctly ridden lateral movements from a supple seat improve the mobility of the horse through a loosening effect. They position the back in balance and improve the horse's ability to flex the haunches for a collecting effect. Correctly ridden lateral movements improve the quality of the flexion of the haunches and throughness since the musculature becomes suppler, especially through the back and in the hind legs. As a result of the growing suppleness of the poll through the rider's diagonal aids, the contact continues to improve.

Without lateral movements with open neck and poll angles, a horse cannot be correctly trained!

WHY DOES A HORSE "CHEW"?

A balanced horse in good contact "chews"! Numerous authors have long recognized that proper chewing is the first and most important true sign of a relaxed poll. For years, I studied the question, "Why does a through horse chew and a tense one doesn't?" The importance of chewing for the poll was described extensively by Francois Baucher around the turn of the last century; his body of thought is now experiencing a revival. In numerous publications, many exercises are described that trigger chewing as a reflex to gain suppleness in the short head-neck muscles. From his teachings, it is assumed that poll suppleness inevitably supples the trunk and other muscle systems of the horse; therefore if a rider "makes" a horse light in front, the horse is automatically balanced.

Such thoughts ignore, in my view, the key point: Without a supple working back, natural balance is impossible! You cannot actively "make" throughness, balance and suppleness by triggering a couple of re-flexes until the horse chews. It isn't done that way.

The reverse is also true: Without a supple poll there is no balance, and no swinging through the back! The rider, especially in the dressage world, can't get past these two facts.

The rider must have a good contact, and the horse: a chewing mouth, a swinging back and lightness. You can't simply create these attributes through mechanical means or force! Understanding the biomechanical mechanisms of balance and collec-tion can help many riders to develop a truly balanced and through horse. One thing is certain: By follow-ing commands such as, "Sit down; close your legs!" "More leg!" "Hold him and use your legs!" or "Make him through!" a rider can never achieve this goal.

Hand techniques and force must become less and less important on the path to a through horse. Actually, they must completely disappear!

The properly chewing mouth is closed and shows a little edge of foam at the front of the mouth. The chewing movement in the sense of equestrian theory incorporates more of a rhythmical suck-swallow movement, rather than a true chewing.

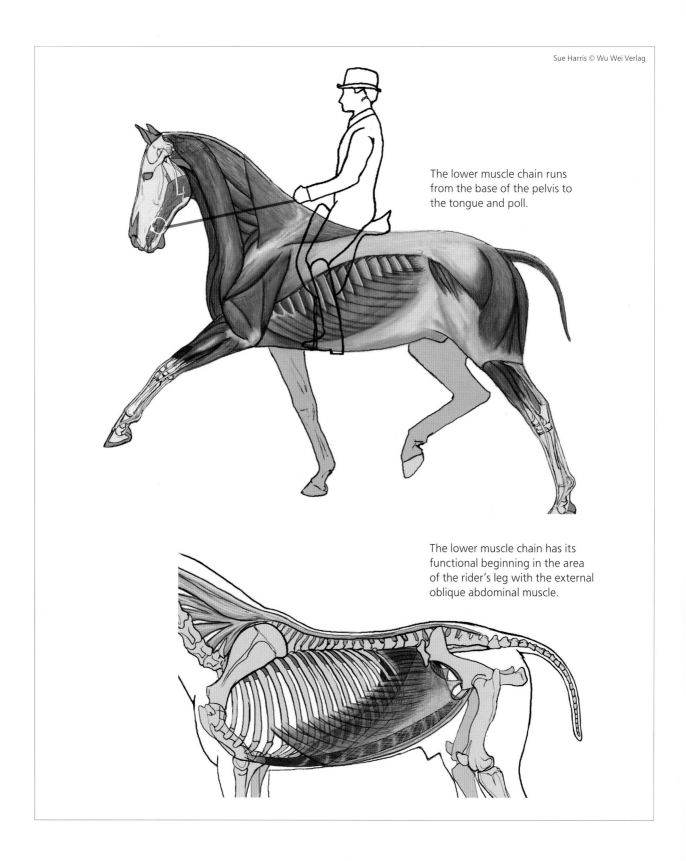

The lower muscle chain runs from the base of the pelvis to the tongue and poll.

The lower muscle chain has its functional beginning in the area of the rider's leg with the external oblique abdominal muscle.

JAW-MOBILIZING EFFECT OF THE LOWER MUSCLE CHAIN

I have spoken extensively about the *upper muscle chain*, which runs from the poll of the horse to the stifle of the hind leg. It is now clear that only a relaxed, carried back allows the dynamic of the hind legs to lead to an effective and good contact. We also know that the corresponding antagonists, the *trunk flexors* (muscles of the underside of the trunk), also work unrestrictedly in a balanced horse. Just as we can influence the back and the hind legs with our seat in a sensitive and measured way, we can likewise influence the abdominal muscles with tactful leg aids in the area of the thorax and abdominal wall.

The abdominal muscle that is the most superficial and for riders the most interesting is the *external oblique abdominal muscle*. It arises from the 4th/5th rib on the lateral thoracic wall and runs from the thorax to the lumbar fascia. There it connects with the terminal tendons of other trunk muscles and encloses the straight abdominal muscle (*rectus sheath*) before transitioning into an abdominal tendon and a pelvic tendon. It is connected through the fascia structures with the pelvis and the femur.

The influence of the rider

Riders can influence the external oblique abdominal muscle with the leg. However, you can only positively influence contraction of this muscle when using co-ordinated aids. A correctly placed and measured leg aid given at the right time strengthens contraction of this muscle—the horse steps farther under or over. The ability to influence the muscle, however, is dependent on whether the rider can feel the natural working rhythm of this muscle. With a clamped leg or a tight thigh, the rider works against the muscle; squeezing and clamping lead to tension in the whole trunk of both horse and rider. Once again it is clear that the quality of the seat is the decisive criterion for good riding!

Through alternating contractions, the pelvis and the femur are pulled forward by the external oblique abdominal muscle. Contraction on one side increases muscle tension on the abdominal wall of the same side, leading to relaxation of the abdomen on the other side. This motion is bilateral, symmetrical and rhythmical and is referred to as the "trunk pendulum" (see Herr Eberhard Hübener, regular contributor to the magazine *Piaffe*, edition 2008–2009, Wu Wei Verlag). Under a rider with a supple seat, the trunk pendulum improves contact between the trunk wall and the rider's lower leg that alternates from side to side. It can be said, "The horse gets his driving aids on alternating sides by himself." When this harmonious rhythm between rider and horse exists, the abdominal musculature begins to work powerfully and regularly.

The external oblique abdominal muscle attaches to the rear of the pelvis and the femur. It also runs toward the front of the horse along the abdominal portion of the deep thoracic muscles. Powerful and rhythmical impulses of the external oblique abdominal muscle, which regularly contract with movement of the hind leg, influence the abdominal portion of the deep thoracic muscles. The most important muscles of the underside of the neck attach in the area of the breastbone, the shoulder and the humerus. These are connected partially through fascia with the chest musculature, and are also activated by the abdominal musculature when it is working effectively. The muscles of the underside of the neck terminate at the lower jaw, the tongue and the occiput. This muscle chain is responsible for chewing in a horse with a balanced, supple trunk—chewing relaxes the poll muscles.

Only a horse that is working supplely in all the muscle chains is in balance and can correctly chew.

When a clamping or shoving rider's seat blocks the horse's back and tightens his trunk muscles, the function of the lower muscle chain is likewise hindered. A "squeezed" horse can chew no better than one with his mouth strapped shut!

Assure freedom of the mouth

Inconsiderately strapping the horse's mouth shut, as is often done today, is completely illogical and even injurious. When a horse's head is bound like a package, this restriction automatically results in a tense, unyielding poll with all the negative consequences for balance. Bridles and fastening straps should always be loose on the horse's head. The old rule is as relevant today as ever: "Two fingers, one on top of the other, must fit between the nose bone and the noseband and flash straps!"

The lower jaw must not be limited in its mobility!

Through quietly ridden stepping-over exercises and leg-yields that activate the abdominal musculature, the muscle chain described on the pages prior makes it possible to encourage a horse in retraining to chew, leading to the initial stages of poll suppleness. The relaxing effect of sideways (lateral) movement relates not just to the croup and the back but also to the jaw and the poll! The key to achieving this benefit is to do the exercises slowly and to have a supple seat. The chewing mouth and relaxed poll are the result of good work and rediscovered balance in the horse!

XVIII.

REIN LAMENESS
An Unpleasant Diagnosis?

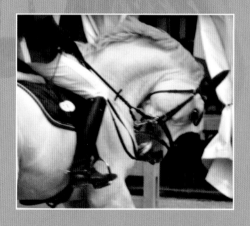

INCORRECTLY DEALING WITH NATURAL CROOKEDNESS

As was discussed in chapter XIII, "Straightness—A Special Challenge," many of a rider's problems are connected to a horse's natural crookedness. Those who ride and train their horses with heavy hands have significant problems with this natural phenomenon.

As the words imply, "natural crookedness" is a natural phenomenon. Dealing with it incorrectly causes complex problems!

Issues range from non-specific riding problems to quite specific disturbances of movement, as for example, lameness. These training questions are discussed later in detail (see p. 176).

Pulling causes counter-pulling

The cause of these problems is relatively simple to identify and to describe. A rider feels the crookedness of the horse and often attempts to correct for it by pulling on the inside rein. Every horse answers this forceful backward-oriented rein aid with tension and resistance. Many riders pull or hold the rein tightly because they do not have independent hands.

Constrained and backward riding is the cause of many horse and rider problems. It leads to disturbances in the gait, which are regularly presented to a brotherhood of therapists. A high percentage of horses brought to veterinary practices and clinics with lameness symptoms are not satisfactorily diagnosed, if at all, by veterinary means. Every veterinarian has experienced horses that present to his clinic with an obvious medium-level lameness, yet don't respond to diagnostic blocking agents. Such tests use anesthetic agents injected into the joints of the leg to identify the point of injury. Such horses, however, may respond positively to flexion tests, especially of the rear legs. Generally speaking, most "rein-lame" horses show no pathology.

"Gait errors"—a long recognized problem

In *The Way to Perfect Horsemanship* Udo Bürger describes rein lameness as a "gait error," which results when horses are "artificially elevated into false collection." He also discusses the veterinarian's dilemma when nothing abnormal can be identified in the legs of a horse that is clearly "lame." He describes the extreme crookedness that sometimes arises in such horses. He also talks about the way out that many therapists give themselves when they talk about a "back lameness." Bürger carefully describes his observations about the rider's attempts to straighten the horse in relation to the way a rein-lame horse moves. Here he is describing horses that are hollow to the right and stiff to the left:

"They get used to consistently taking a long and then a short step behind. The uneven steps impact the front legs diagonally. Horses being ridden forward will be rein lame on the left hind. The left hind leg pushes off sharply and makes the shorter step, the right hind leg steps correspondingly farther forward. The rider feels in the hand that the horse is on the left rein but behind the right rein. He has a lot in the left hand and little in the right hand."

DIAGNOSIS

I have concluded from long experience that the number of rein-lame horses has steadily risen in the last several decades. The unbelievable focus of veterinary science and research on fine diagnostic and medical equipment hinders us from seeing the whole horse as an integrated unit. Naturally, this development accords with the personal perceptions of many riders: "My horse is lame. He must have something wrong. It can't be because of me!" Many owners and riders are not open to suggestions that encourage self-critical evaluation of their own riding habits and tendencies. Physiotheraphy, osteopathic, chiropractic therapy or acupuncture may actually improve the horse's symptoms. If a therapy works, then the rider continues to assume that the original problem couldn't possibly have stemmed from herself but is rather an ongoing problem with the horse!

It appears to be a given in the rider world, that the solution is to call a "problem fixer" (veterinarian, physiotherapist, osteopath, chiropractor, acupunturist, massage therapist) who treats the stiff poll or the back that can't be sat on any more. It rarely occurs to the rider to scrutinize her own actions while on the back of the horse, perhaps to find there the cause for the horse's ineffective performance or resistance issue, such as constantly being behind the bit.

This type of motion disturbance, classified as "natural crookedness," is seen in varying levels of severity in many horses with "rhythm errors." Equine veterinarians are commonly asked to evaluate such individuals, yet these horses typically fail the diagnostic roster of a thorough orthopedic lameness exam that includes biomechanical evaluation such as trotting forward, longeing, testing for pain on turning, bending tests, flexion tests along with diagnostic anesthesia, radiographs and ultrasound.

When nothing is identified with classic lameness exam techniques, a veterinarian may find it easier to send a horse to scintigraphy (nuclear imaging scan), a CAT (computed axial tomography) scan or an MRI (magnetic resonance imaging) rather than to get involved intensely with analysis and correction of the horse's training. How can a veterinarian criticize his own clients and tell them that their manner of riding is making the horse sick or lame? The horse owner would then approach another vet who is waiting to respond, "That's ridiculous. Let's do scintigraphy and inject the back."

It is certainly a blessing to have more advanced means of medical diagnosis, to be able to find disorders in the body of a horse that up until now were not diagnosable. Intensive diagnostic methods should be preceded, however, by a comprehensive clinical exam. The availability of such diagnostic tools shouldn't justify abbreviating or throwing overboard the normal and methodical diagnostic examination process of hands-on and gait evaluation, or just offering a treatment that may have no relevance to the horse's problem simply for the sake of doing something to appease the rider.

Are veterinarians and riders closing their eyes to the training problems because the subject is too complex? Are they shying away from discussing the possibility of training problems with the rider and owner and instead choosing a more comfortable and familiar path that is based on a medical approach?

I believe the current state of the entire horse industry impacts the whole picture of how horses with problems are managed today. The focus turns further away from the actual protagonist, the horse, with solutions often decided more based on business practices and less with the horse in mind.

A pleasure horse with distinct natural crookedness.

SHORTENED, SECOND SUPPORT PHASE

Rein lameness, assuming we want to continue to use an old, historical term, is a problem of our time, and an unbelievably big one! As has already been explored, it leads back to the incorrect way the rider tries to deal with natural crookedness.

Natural crookedness is structural, in that there is less elasticity of the trunk musculature on the hollow side of the horse's body. The muscles of the lateral thoracic wall and the abdominal wall are shorter and less elastic on the hollow side.

On the other side, the rider feels stiffness, which makes it impossible to flex and bend the horse to the "stiff" side. Riders or trainers describe it as the horse generally "hangs" on the inside rein. As will be discussed shortly, the abdominal and thoracic muscles between the ribs are important in moving the hind legs forward. The stronger basic muscle tone on the hollow side—combined with the distinctly lower elasticity of these muscles—elicits the following effects:

a) Natural crookedness—the horse is hollow to this side.

b) The trunk swings more to the opposite side, the side that feels stiff. The rider feels a stronger contact of his leg on the trunk of the horse on the stiff side.

c) The hind leg on the hollow side steps under without trouble during movement due to tone of the trunk muscles. However, it doesn't stay as long at the end of the support phase due to less elasticity of the trunk muscles; the limb leaves the ground—that is, is picked up—earlier. In a horse that is hollow to the right (the most frequent case of natural crookedness), the veterinarian examining the horse sees a *shortened second support phase* of the right hind.

The first support phase begins the moment the foot is put down and lasts until that leg is vertically under the body. The second support phase begins from the moment the leg is vertical under the body until the moment it leaves the ground.

REACTION OF THE LONG BACK MUSCLES

This phenomenon is clear and obvious to the trainer or anyone examining the horse. For years I have been studying the question of how the long back muscles react in response to the ventral (lower) trunk musculature. In a horse that is hollow to the right, the left long back muscle is generally higher with more negative tension. On palpation, there is generally a distinct difference in height between the two strands of the long back muscles. The back muscle on the hollow side is generally lower and softer than that on the stiff side (stiff from the point of view of the rider). The latter is generally higher and shows great tone—it is frequently tight.

The answer to this phenomenon lies in a study of the anatomy of the skeleton of the trunk, the pelvis and attached trunk muscles.

The lumbar vertebral column, which is very stable, connects with the pelvic ring at the lumbo-sacral joint (LS). The pelvic ring is connected to the sacrum, which has only minimal mobility. At the sac-

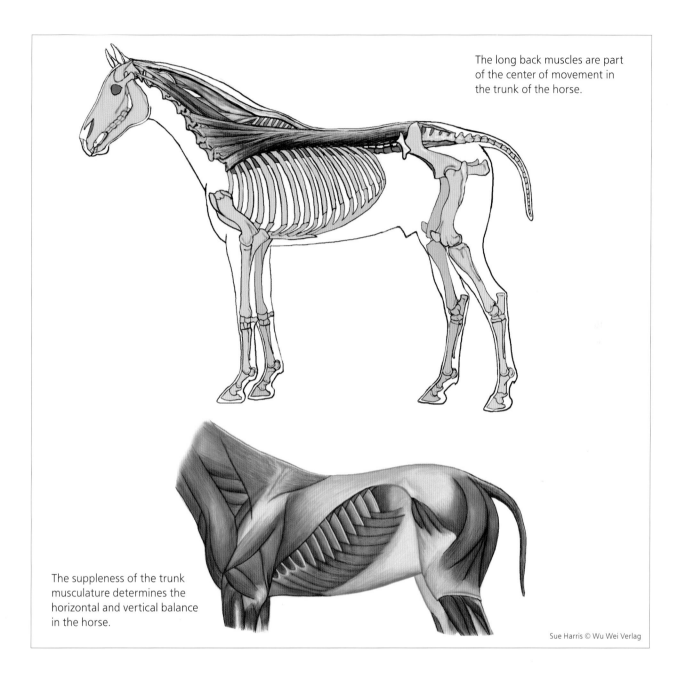

The long back muscles are part of the center of movement in the trunk of the horse.

The suppleness of the trunk musculature determines the horizontal and vertical balance in the horse.

Sue Harris © Wu Wei Verlag

roiliac joint (SI), the ilium and the sacrum are tightly bound together by very strong ligaments. The joint between the lumbar vertebrae and the sacrum, the LS, is more mobile in the vertical axis (up and down) than all the other joints in this area. As this joint flexes, the pelvis tilts; rotation of the pelvis (lowering of the tuber coxae) is possible only to a slight degree. The sacrum, which is connected to the lumbar vertebral column at the LS joint, defines the bony hind area of the horse's croup.

The muscular attachments of the abdominal and inner lumbar muscles (muscular attachment of the

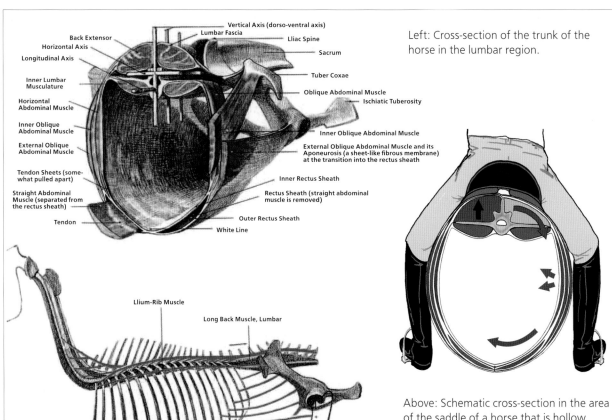

Back Extensor
Horizontal Axis
Longitudinal Axis
Inner Lumbar Musculature
Horizontal Abdominal Muscle
Inner Oblique Abdominal Muscle
External Oblique Abdominal Muscle
Tendon Sheets (some-what pulled apart)
Straight Abdominal Muscle (separated from the rectus sheath)
Tendon

Vertical Axis (dorso-ventral axis)
Lumbar Fascia
Iliac Spine
Sacrum
Tuber Coxae
Oblique Abdominal Muscle
Ischiatic Tuberosity
Inner Oblique Abdominal Muscle
External Oblique Abdominal Muscle and its Aponeurosis (a sheet-like fibrous membrane) at the transition into the rectus sheath
Inner Rectus Sheath
Rectus Sheath (straight abdominal muscle is removed)
Outer Rectus Sheath
White Line

Left: Cross-section of the trunk of the horse in the lumbar region.

Llium-Rib Muscle

Long Back Muscle, Lumbar

External Oblique Abdominal Muscle
Straight Abdominal Muscle

Above: Due to its greater tension, the external oblique abdominal muscle on the hollow side pulls the hind leg on the same side forward. The higher tension causes the trunk to arc to the opposite side.

Above: Schematic cross-section in the area of the saddle of a horse that is hollow to the right: The abdominal muscles are stronger on the right while the long back muscle on the left side is very tight. As a result, the horse's trunk shifts to the left, the rider tips to the right. Due to the trunk rotation, the rider has more contact with his leg on the left, which feels to the rider like the stiff side, and less contact on the hollow right side.

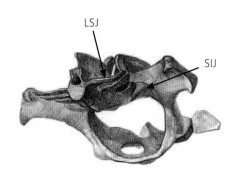

LSJ
SIJ

Left and right: The articulation of the sacrum with the pelvis (sacro-iliac joint) and the articulation of the last lumbar vertebra with the sacrum (lumbo-sacral joint).

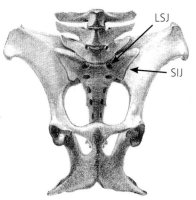

LSJ
SIJ

Top right by Sue Harris © Wu Wei Verlag; all other figures from *Große Tieranatomie* by Gottfried Bammes (Wu Wei Verlag 2010)

trunk to the pelvis and the hind legs) spread out from the ilial column below the SI joint down to the pubic bone and the femur.

A contraction or long-lasting shortening of these muscles on one side of the trunk leads to corresponding diagonal crookedness of the pelvis, insofar as the joints of the vertebral column and the pelvis allow. This phenomenon can be diagnosed clinically in many horses. In a large number of horses, asymmetrical *tuber coxae* and sometimes even different heights of the *tuber sacrale* can be felt, even in horses without any report of traumatic injury. To my knowledge, these findings are not yet scientifically connected to natural crookedness and the quality of the training of a horse.

The asymmetrical pull of the ventral abdominal muscles causes diagonal crookedness of the pelvic ring. For the bony parts of the pelvis that lie over the LS/SI joints, there is a corresponding and opposite movement. In horses that are hollow to the right, the left ilium moves backward and shifts the largest attachment point of the long back muscle to the rear. Since the ventral arm (distance between LS/SI joints and the attachment points of the abdominal muscles to the pelvis, the ilium and pubic bones) is essentially longer than the dorsal arm (distance between LS/SI joints and the muscular attachment of the long back muscles to the ilium), the back muscle cannot easily straighten the pelvis. The back muscle ends up in a long-term, one-sided spasm in poorly trained horses as a result of this growing, one-sided pull by the ab-

dominal muscles on the diagonally opposite side. In this example (horse hollow on the right), the left long back muscle counters the pull of the right abdominal muscles on the ventral (underside) of the pelvis.

In a standing horse, the legs on the hollow side are closer together. With a right-sided hollow horse, the right front leg is farther back, and the right hind leg is placed farther under. The greater tension of the abdominal muscle chain pulls these legs closer together. On the left side of a right-sided hollow horse, the horse stands with the legs farther apart: this is due to greater tension in the upper muscle chain derived from the left long back muscle (see Michael Putz, *Richtig Reiten* [Correct riding], FN Verlag, 2010, p. 133).

The rider's perception
To the rider, it feels like the right side (hollow side) of the trunk is shorter and that the horse steps farther forward, but the hind leg steps farther to the inside. This phenomenon is even more dramatic in almost all young horses and in poorly trained horses. With increasing crookedness, the long back muscle on the stiff side bulges from tension and the difficulty of straightening the horse is massively increased. The muscle chain—long back muscle, croup muscles, long gluteal muscles—carries this tension to the stifle of the horse and shortens the forward stride of the limb. This explains the second phenomenon of the movement disorders in rein-lame horses: short-long steps in passage.

SHORTENED, SECOND SWING PHASE

The right-sided hollow horse tracking to the right usually steps shorter with the left hind. "He doesn't take his left hind leg with him," a rider

would say. The rein lameness can vary: It may take the form of a rhythm irregularity, which a competition judge might identify, particularly in turns and on bending lines to the horse's hollow side. Or, it may appear as an obvious lameness, yet be very frustrating for a veterinarian to achieve a diagnosis.

On the stiff side there is generally a shortened, second swing phase. Analogous to the description of the support phases, a limb in the forward-swing phase is categorized as a "first swing phase" and a "second swing phase." The "first" refers to the phase of movement of a limb from the moment when the foot is lifted up until the moment in which the limb is vertical under the body. The "second swing phase" refers to the moment when the limb is vertical to the moment when the hoof touches the ground to the front.

Naturally, this slowed and shortened second swing phase of the left hind leg in this example (right-sided hollow horse) leads to the hoof of the diagonal front leg also setting down early in the trot. The trot has a centrally fixed (meaning controlled by the brain) movement sequence: Normally, a horse moves in two-beat rhythm at the trot, so that a diagonal pair of legs (left hind and right front, or right hind and left front) step at the same time. If one hind leg now steps down earlier, the timing of the diagonal front leg is affected. The horse doesn't break the diagonal movement since that would affect his balance. To the examiner, this appears as if the trot stride is shorter on the left hind or, as the horse trots directly toward him, it appears as if the horse is "falling" harder on the right front leg, giving the impression of a support-phase lameness on the left front. When viewed from the rear, this very distinct picture of lameness either completely or partially disappears.

In summary, a right-sided hollow and rein-lame horse moves as follows: The shortening of the second support phase of the inside (right) hind leg causes the outside (left) hind leg to set down early along with shortening of the swing phase of the outside (left) hind leg. Since the footfalls are diagonal, in this example, the horse also steps down earlier with the inside (right) front leg. As observed from the *front*, the horse "falls," with more weight on the right front leg, appearing lame on the *left front.* Observed from *behind*, the horse falls onto the left hind leg, thereby appearing lame on the *right hind* leg.

THE GAIT PATTERN AFTER A CHANGE OF DIRECTION

With purely rider-induced lameness or rein lameness, there is frequently an extreme change in the gait pattern with a change of direction. In contrast, a horse that is experiencing a pathological problem of the spinous processes, such as "kissing spines" (impingement of the tops of the bony processes of vertebrae in the back), exhibits lameness that is independent of the direction of movement.

Rein lameness is a disorder of movement that is primarily due to incorrect riding. Rein lameness is observed in horses that have been subjected to forceful training, with their whole musculature forming an inexplicable tightness. Rein lame horses rarely show gait patterns that are explained through the typical systematic diagnostic veterinary exam.

The horse might have a concurrent problem that may be identified with radiographic (X-ray) studies of the spinous processes of the thoracic and lumbar vertebral columns. Kissing spines frequently increase the gait abnormality of a rein-lame horse; however the basic problem of rein lameness is almost always due to defective training. On the other hand, a horse with mild to significant radiographic changes of the spinous processes may continue to be fully capable of performance and free of symptoms, provided he receives correct training.

An S-shaped horse is hard to correct

Frequently, horses reverse their crookedness in the poll, meaning a horse that is actually right-sided hollow becomes left-sided hollow in the poll after long exposure to heavy pulling reins. It is now easier for him to position his poll to the left rather than to the right as previously done. Such an S-shaped horse is more difficult to correct; the resulting gait pattern is difficult to explain with biomechanical analysis.

Occasionally, extreme rider effects cause stiffening in the poll on both sides or only on the hollow side—normally the ease of positioning the poll corresponds to the natural crookedness.

With single-sided poll stiffening, the long back muscle on the same side is almost always stiff and leads to a corresponding gait pattern. That means, the hind leg on the same side as the stiffened long back muscle is shortened in the forward step, since the leg on the other side is shortened in the support phase.

This shows that a rider can have such a negative impact on the balance of the horse that the natural gait pattern changes. It takes an experienced rider to successfully address this "disrupted" gait pattern in retraining.

Understanding "motion pathology" in a horse requires a foundation in veterinary science, combined with expertise in biomechanics and training physiology.

XIX.

THE VETERINARIAN
In the Arena of Political Conflict

DUTY TO TAKE ACTION FOR ANIMAL WELFARE

Forced longitudinal flexion, among other methods, is counter to animal welfare. Where is the line between what is acceptable and intolerable? When should veterinarians no longer keep silent?

In the previous chapters, I have discussed horse training and daily gymnastic work in detail. Training is supposed to strengthen the horse mentally and physically so that he is capable of performing to his abilities. It's about establishing horizontal balance and developing straightness (vertical balance) on the path to collection. A horse trained well according to classical principles becomes mentally calmer and even more powerful and supple, and thereby more "through." These developments also keep a horse healthy and sound for a longer time.

The components on the Training Scale—Rhythm, Suppleness, Contact, Impulsion, Straightness, Collection—are based on the nature of the horse. The Scale prepares the horse for work, develops his ability to perform while also preserving soundness. Based on this century-old knowledge, it can be deduced that a veterinarian's perspective is politically relevant to the development of horse sport, along with the opinion of judges and officials. I believe that the veterinary profession has the duty on behalf of animal welfare to identify reprehensible training methods and practices that inflict cruelty to the horse and to notify authorities, particularly in extreme cases.

During the last few decades, the horse world has become accustomed to inappropriate and sometimes cruel methods. The more-or-less tense horse, with some exceptions, has become the horse the public is the most interested in and aware of, due to media and social acceptance.

I see the origin of all forceful methods, into which riders have fallen in the last century, as a result of riders responding to negative tension by using methods that don't conform to desirable classical teaching. If a rider reacts consistently to negative tension in the horse with power and force, then she is likely to end up as part of an unsuccessful horse-rider pair.

The rider daily tries to fight against ever-stronger tension by using manual methods. The best known and the longest used means of putting horses in a forced position is the draw rein, which has been used since the Duke of Newcastle (1592–1676) suggested it as a means of showing a horse the way down to develop elasticity. Today, draw reins are misused as a mechanical method to force a deep, and usually *too* deep, head position.

In the 1980s, the use of draw reins was considered dishonorable. Even *thinking* about using such a tool would have resulted in unpleasant consequences for me as a trainee at the German Riding School in Warendorf.

ACCUSTOMED TO FORCEFUL METHODS?

The view of things has changed a lot! With the horse world in general and the competition world specifically becoming more commercialized, it has become "normal" to use these methods. Regular use of these "training" reins has lead many officials to even consider including such "block and tackle" devices as tools in study material. Acceptance on the sport horse scene has grown so much that they aren't just used in training but have been around for a long time in the jumper warm-up areas at competitions. Horse people with experience know that a rider with the necessary feel, experience and ability doesn't need draw reins. The rider who uses them is not able to use them thoughtfully, and in such hands, draw reins can cause damage to the horse.

I would expect that those officials who are charged with ensuring horse welfare and fair judging would react against these devices rather than condoning their use.

Draw reins are absolutely unnecessary. Whoever forces a horse to lower his head in this way, injures the horse in the long run!

Recently, I was at a seminar in a neighboring European country. An international jumping rider presented his horse during the practical portion of the seminar with draw reins. It was a small, spirited horse. The rider complained that his horse was inclined to go very strongly forward—meaning he consistently ran away and was hard to ride turning to the left. The weekend before, the rider lost a 6,000 Euro prize because of failure to turn. I tried to explain to him that a horse couldn't be properly positioned or bent if he didn't have good balance and a swinging back. A leg mover held in a frame with draw reins

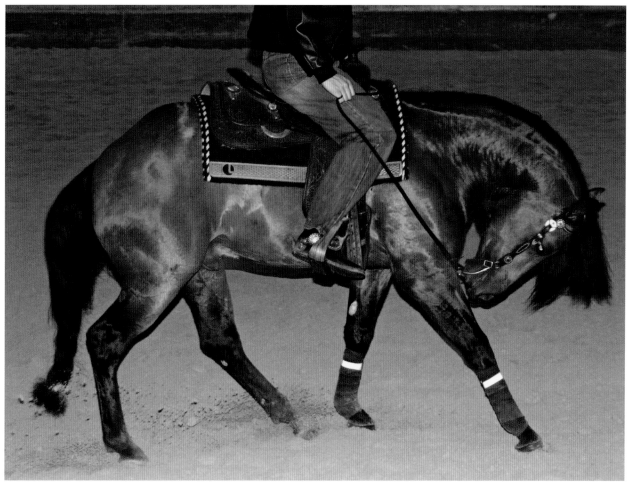

"Obedience" at any price? Western riding also uses questionable training methods that sometimes raise animal welfare concerns. Horsemanship and horse welfare are not always observed here.

will never live up to his potential, even in jumping, and will suffer physical as well as emotional damage.

Western sport

Although I can't describe myself as an insider on the Western riding scene, I know from my own observation that modern competitive Western sports, such as reining, sometimes involve methods of training and preparation that are excessively harsh to the horse.

Images seen in these Western events sometimes exceed the imagination of horse people from out-side this discipline. During important competitions and championships, incidents occur nightly that should arouse animal welfare concerns. I would like to emphatically encourage my veterinary colleagues who live in the land of origin of this previously wonderful sport to open your eyes and muster your courage to expose abuses. Only in this way can we work actively for the preservation of equestrian sports. We should not wait and watch until animal welfare organizations do this job for us!

Animal welfare concerns arise in all disciplines—with gaited horses, in dressage and jumping, and in Western sports.

PLEASURE RIDING AS A PROBLEM AREA

As discussed, horses participating in pleasure riding pursuits often hurry along out of balance. The situation is different for these horses: Forceful methods play a smaller role, and damage to the back, poll and legs usually occurs from causes unrelated to training techniques.

A pleasure horse without tension in the poll and back, one that moves in a natural horizontal balance, is often not straight but may be ridden nevertheless without health risks provided that there are signs of horizontal balance and the rider doesn't use forceful mechanical means to remove the natural crookedness. Under these assumptions, a pleasure horse often can serve a long time without damage even though he isn't exactly straight in the classical sense. If such a horse is trained in a measured way, movement disorders don't usually develop related to the riding techniques. If the horse doesn't have horizontal balance, he usually ends up with a board-hard, tight back, with all the negative ramifications that arise from not being balanced. However, even a pleasure horse that has "fallen apart" and is fully off the aids and moves without impulsion and without correct balance can carry his rider without damage far longer than a horse that moves with impulsion in negative tension!

This may be a reason for increasing interest and growth in the pleasure horse riding activities. (The term "pleasure or leisure rider" describes the rider who doesn't belong to a riding club and rides outside of organized competitive sport for her own private enjoyment—this is the largest group of riders.) The trend is favoring horses with shorter steps and less swinging movement (Iberian horses, Western horses, Icelandic horses, South American gaited horses). Because they move with little to no suspension, these horses can withstand poor riders better than can horses with natural impulsion and active movement. They accommodate the less experienced rider better because the horses are easier for the rider to sit.

The largest number of problem horses is found in the realm of the pleasure rider!

Define minimal requirements

Minimally required balance and a "minimal training goal" still need to be defined for pleasure riders to make it worthwhile and achievable as well as relevant to the needs of the horse.

In my view, national organizations, breed and pleasure riding associations have the responsibility to actively institute such training since many leisure riders will not reach the level of the Classical Dressage Training Scale. Goals must be defined that will satisfy animal welfare groups yet are achievable for a motivated hobby rider. It isn't enough to show them the Training Scale. In the name of animal welfare, it is important to encourage socially desirable riding habits. Consistent competition judging and correctly trained trainers and instructors at all levels help influence the desire for pleasure riders to develop a relaxed pleasure horse that is fun to ride.

I believe that as quickly as possible, we should stop the "competition train" that is rushing at full steam in the wrong direction, and thereby send it in the right direction. The sport of dressage should set a good example as it has done in the past. Such a shift could, however, result in innumerable trainer "gurus" losing their popularity.

A very well balanced pleasure horse under a rider who sits well—almost a perfect picture!

XX.

HYPOTHESIS

"Occupational" Illness—
Suspensory Injury

SICK AND INJURED DUE TO FORCEFUL RIDING

We have looked at rein lameness using the knowledge preserved by authors from the last couple of centuries and an understanding of today's principles of biomechanics. It is clear that lameness is found regularly for which there is no structural damage to tendons and support structures. Movement disorders can be caused directly by negative tension in the trunk of the horse.

A further question arises that considers the large number of lame horses with structural (organic) injury: What is the relationship between forceful training methods and the tissue damage seen in current lameness problems that are frequently diagnosed and treated?

In some areas, our current knowledge is sufficient to formulate key hypotheses, which may reveal a connection. Naturally, critics of these hypotheses request scientific proof—that is certainly correct and understandable. Nevertheless, the experienced horseman and rider may have a suspicion that training techniques could be related to certain injuries.

I propose a hypothetical correlation as an example: "Suspensory injuries are an occupational illness in young, big-moving horses and are caused by the horses being ridden consistently in tension."

TENSE TRUNK MUSCULATURE AND ITS CONSEQUENCES

In chapter VIII, "Balance: The Most Important Criterion," and in chapter XIV, "Collection: Shifting Horizontal Balance," I took a close look at the concepts of the back mover and flexion in the hindquarters. A critical indicator of a correctly trained horse is a back that is supple, carried, positively tense, but relatively relaxed. The back as the center of movement enables the horse to have a spring mechanism through all his joints when he puts the foot of the hind leg on the ground and accepts the weight of the body, and when he lifts the foot up again.

The back-mover's spring in the haunches adjusts passively according to the size of the gait and the state of training as he takes on weight with muscle development. This spring mechanism acts a little like a shock absorber in the hind leg (see chapter XI, "Impulsion"). Naturally, this effect requires strong, passive holding power by the hind leg extensors. If

these extensor muscles are strong enough to meet this demand, then this spring mechanism provides effective protection. The horse carries himself and his rider in a favorably tense muscle sling (Stefan Stammer, *Reiter Journal*, January 2011, Verlag Matthaes Medien, Stuttgart).

A similar spring effect exists in the area of the shoulder girdle in a horse that is carrying himself. The trunk and chest are suspended between the shoulder blades primarily by muscles. If these muscles are *positively tense*, meaning the horse rises to a certain degree between the shoulder blades, then there is a spring apparatus similar to that of the hind legs, which is likewise protective. A horse that is "pulled together" sinks in the back behind the withers and is carried by connective tissue (see reference to writings by Stefan Stammer, above).

"Backward riding" affects the hind spring just as

negatively. In leg movers or overstretched back movers, this negative chain of influence works as follows: The horse that moves with a tight or hollow back no longer has this spring mechanism (passive sinking of all the joints of the hind legs) due to blockage in the center of movement (the back) and the propagation of that resistance (fascia connection) over the croup to the stifles. The stifle no longer bends passively as weight is taken on.

All the joints dependent on the muscles of the trunk and upper hind leg are stiffened and passively fixed, with most of the spring now fixed. Only the coffin joint, which is the joint least dependent on these same muscles, can be passively flexed and yield at every step. The spring has, so to speak, only one last spring "winding," which can effectively sink and yield. The anatomical facts definitively show that the natural angle of the pastern joint is essentially carried by the suspensory ligament and the associated flexor tendon apparatus. These structures are overloaded and often injured due to an almost constant load in an incorrectly balanced horse.

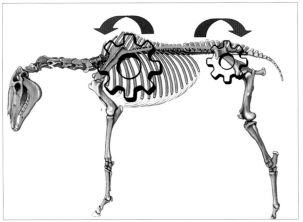

The biomechanical importance of neck and croup.

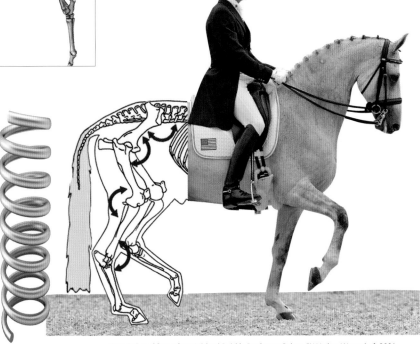

The spring mechanism of the haunches functions only in back movers. A horse with "disrupted" balance wears out his body.

© Variation of figure from Michael Strick's *Denksport Reiten*, FN Verlag, Warendorf, 2001

"Using" a horse with a tight back for an extended period of time will sooner or later lead to an overload of the suspensory apparatus. This depends on static loading of the whole leg through volume of the gait, length of time in the gait and the degree of negative tension.

From my point of view, this explains the growing number of suspensory injuries of the front and hind legs. Of course, there are numerous other musculo-skeletal problems that can be linked to forceful training methods. An intense scientific investigation into this relationship could help protect the horses in the wonderful "sport" of dressage. In this way, it would be possible to support and improve the practical application of classical, historically proven training methods.

Classical Riding theory is "applied animal welfare"!

A "blocked" back and the resultant loss of flex in the haunches selectively destroys the suspensory apparatus.

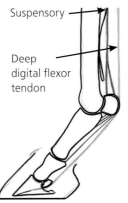

Suspensory

Deep digital flexor tendon

XXI.

INITIAL STEPS
Retraining Poorly Ridden Horses

BALANCE DISRUPTION CAUSED BY TRAINING ERRORS

Bad or incorrect training methods leave their traces. Retraining a poorly ridden horse can take weeks, months or longer. As long as a horse isn't physically damaged or isn't too old and badly balanced, almost every horse can be corrected.

Many competition horses, riding horses and pleasure horses have not been correctly trained. Small disruptions of balance that don't create significant tension in the horse's body are not necessarily damaging and subsequently pose little problem for the horse. Pronounced disturbances will almost always lead to health problems!

As a veterinarian interested in orthopedics and as a *Pferdewirt* with a major in riding, I am regularly confronted in my daily work and in lameness exams with statements like these:

- "My horse doesn't go on the bit. He is stiff in the poll. I can't flex him to the left or turn him. To the right, he won't go forward."

- "My horse rolls his neck too deeply. I can't keep his nose in front of the vertical. He always runs away with me, he doesn't stay calm. I can't sit in the saddle to effectively drive with my seat aids."

- "My horse is so crooked that I can't keep him on the track. He always falls on the outside shoulder in turns."

- "My horse is not controllable. He runs away. At the canter he sometimes bucks. I don't trust cantering him any more."

Quiet walk work is a regular part of good retraining. This horse still has too narrow a poll angle.

- "My horse is so lazy and I can't get him to move forward."
- "My horse rears when I try to back him."
- "My horse has been lame for a long time, especially in one direction, yet my vet can't find anything."
- "My horse has become dangerous. He bucks and rears constantly. I am afraid to ride him."
- "My horse has become so stiff it isn't any fun to ride him any more."

A large number of riders are struggling with problems like these. They are very often on their own without professional help, and sometimes are riding dangerous horses. The principles of Classical Riding theory provide the answers. They must only be appropriately applied.

In previous chapters, it was established that the back of the horse plays one, if not the decisive role in the training of a horse. Put another way:

When you have significant difficulties in training, the condition or sensitivity of the horse's back is usually the main problem!

There are three balance disorders that explain just about all of the listed training and riding issues: *leg movers, hyperflexed back movers* and *the horse that has fallen apart.*

The balanced back has positive tension, is actively carried by the musculature, and is relatively relaxed in every situation. Deviating from this state, there are back positions that make it impossible for the horse to move freely from negative tension.

The back mover is a balanced horse in the sense of Classical Riding theory (B.H. von Holleuffer, *Die Bearbeitung des Reit- und Kutschpferdes zwischen den Pilaren* [Training the riding and driving horse between the pillars], Olms Press, Hildesheim, Zürich, New York, 1896). Only one position of the vertebral column of the horse's trunk allows all the back muscles to work with dynamic suppleness to characterize the back mover. There is a distinct relationship between the position of the back, the position of the neck, and later the position of the pelvis (croup), which the rider influences with her aids, such as the hands, the seat (quality, weight) and the leg. The quality of the seat has an enormous and direct influence on the suppleness of the horse's back.

The most frequent balance disruptions are characterized by:
1. The correctly positioned, but tense back (stiff back).
2. The back that is lost downward (hollow back, leg mover).
3. The back that is lost upward (hyperflexed back mover).
4. The collapsed, hollowed back (the horse that has fallen apart).

In all these disturbances of balance, the back musculature no longer can fulfill its natural job as the center of movement. A citation from Udo Bürger remarks on this subject:

"In summary: the long back muscle is a true muscle of movement. It is active in forward movement and in establishing a secure carriage in movement, but was not meant to carry the rider's weight. The back is connected with the forehand through the broad back muscles and with the hindquarters through the large croup muscles. In this way, it is plugged into the rhythm of the movement and cannot be isolated."

Udo Bürger, *The Way to Perfect Horsemanship*, Trafalgar Square Books, North Pomfret, Vermont, 2012

With all horses in retraining, it is more or less a job of getting the back into position and getting it to work again. The long back muscles of movement must become supple, powerful and elastic again.

XXII.
INITIAL STEPS IN RETRAINING
Part One: The Tense Horse

DEFICITS IN BASIC TRAINING

Physical and psychological tension in the rider always leads to tension in the horse. Suppleness and "throughness" cannot be forced.

A horse with tense back muscles, even though he carries his back in a correct position, can show all sorts of symptoms. A few stand out. Depending on the type of horse, he may "pull against the hand," his neck may curl up behind the vertical, or he is lazy, not wanting to go forward. It is common for the nervous, tense horse to nearly "explode" when the rider barely touches him with her leg. The tense horse kicks out at his rider's leg, rears or runs backward. Such horses are often dangerous and must only be retrained by experienced trainers equipped to do so! Often these horses are declared unrideable. Many end up at the slaughterhouse or are euthanized.

The modern sport horse most frequently reacts by "bolting." A horse is by nature a flight animal that immediately tightens the trunk musculature and runs when he senses danger.

The causes of this tension are usually easy to identify. Today's highly talented, young horse has been bred to round his neck after the first or second ride.

This "over-rounding" replaces "going against the bit" as a defensive reaction: A modern young horse reacts in this way in the neck with the slightest defensive tension in the back, usually when first mounted. The extent of this cramping of the back depends on the rider's skill, experience, weight and ability to feel. Negative tension in the back often leads to curling of the neck, particularly in modern horses. It is noteworthy to repeat the passage from Paul Stecken that was mentioned earlier. A few years ago, he asked in one of my seminars:

"How would you explain to our young people that they should not accept the 'wonderful' necks that today's young horses demonstrate at the beginning of their training?"

As explained in the introduction (see p. 10), this question focuses on a profound truth. The high rideability of the modern riding horse can be problematic for training.

Subjectively, this horse's "round" neck is seen as beautiful and desirable. Many incorrectly believe that the horse is "on the bit" from the start. The silhouette of his frame looks like that of a well-trained horse. Most people don't realize that this subjective beauty of the frame is a deception. If this neck position is accepted by the rider and the neck isn't quickly relaxed into the position that is natural for the age of the horse, the horse will end up with tension in the poll and back. A young horse needs several months and often even one-and-a-half or two years to be secure in natural balance.

A higher and rounder neck position is necessary for collection. But this always depends on the ability of the horse to sit down and use his haunches. When this happens, the center of movement in the back remains supple (see chapter XVII, p. 144). A relatively elevated neck is the result of correct training, never negative tension of the back or excessive hand action.

Horses that go a long time in such an imbalance can show many of the symptoms described on p. 181. The extent of the rider's mechanical influence is therefore critical. If the rider tries to collect such a horse by shoving him together, resistance often develops. Contact issues also develop, like being behind the bit, against the hand, or resisting any correct contact. Many symptoms ultimately lead to a "fight" between rider and horse.

Additionally, the horse's natural crookedness is usually exaggerated, leading to all the attendant problems as previously discussed. These horses "hop" around in a disunited canter, not able to position or bend, have tongue and contact issues such as being "behind the bit," and rear when being turned to the stiff side.

Furthermore, it is not possible to collect such a horse. In competitons, even in middle to upper level dressage tests, tense and "show" trots are as commonly seen as a piaffe that is nothing more than stiff "stamping feet in place." In the turns and curved lines of young-horse tests, rhythm irregularities abound, ranging from slight to distinct, and all are a foreboding of rein lameness. In the Grand Prix tests, uneven steps are common in the extensions and especially in the passage, where

A tense driving seat always leads to a tense horse.

they are visible as "swaying steps"—that is, one short, one long.

The anatomy of a horse also plays a role here. These problems occur more often in horses with short and powerful backs. While a short back is stronger and more able to carry than a longer back, it is more difficult to loosen and supple.

Such difficulties can also be caused by a saddle that is too long: Larger riders (more prevalent than ever) need room on a horse's back. A saddle should sit only over the thoracic region of the back and not extend into the loins. It is in this thoracic region that the back musculature is well supported by a mobile underlay: the ribs. To the rear, the thorax attaches to the lumbar vertebral column, with its stiff, immobile,

hands-length, transverse spinous processes that stick out sideways, surrounded by muscles. An overly long saddle or one that is placed too far back tends to compress muscles over these unyielding transverse processes. The cramping that results can be responsible for all the symptoms described at the beginning of this chapter. The reactions triggered by an improperly fitted or placed saddle may occur only on one side of the horse with differing gait patterns when the horse is going in a different direction.

The back of the horse becomes tense on one side when the rider sits on that seat bone—on curved lines, this is usually the *inside* seat bone. The hind leg on the same side is restricted in stepping under due to the fascial attachments. The corresponding

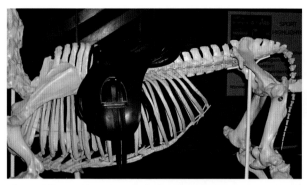

The saddle position should always sit over the thorax. A load on the transverse processes of the lumbar vertebral column leads to back tension.

hind leg steps distinctly shorter, as a rule. This leads to a reciprocal movement disorder according to the direction in which the horse is being ridden. Rein lameness may be triggered by a saddle that doesn't fit or is incorrectly placed. However, the movement of the shoulder blade should not be restricted.

A saddle should be placed as far forward as possible.

CORRECTING BALANCE IN THE FORWARD SEAT

With tight-backed horses, training problems must be addressed by correcting the balance of the horse.

The horse must be ridden rhythmically forward with a supple seat, until he opens his neck and steps into both reins. You must be able to drive with an effective but relaxed seat. It is important during re-training that the stirrup length is adjusted so that your knee has a clear angle, enabling you to achieve a light seat when necessary. Excessively long stirrups make it impossible to retrain a tense horse that runs through your aids.

I am often confronted with horses that have become unrideable and dangerous to some degree. When I first sit on them, I feel like I'm on a cannonball right before being shot off. In extreme cases, which unfortunately occur more often than you might think, there is only one way to loosen the unbelievable back tension. The recipe reads: a light seat, with a lot of sensitivity in the seat, carefulness with the legs and cautious forward riding. If the horse tends to curl his head and neck in, it is important to consistently and carefully keep his head up and to cautiously start driving more from the seat aids.

The first steps can really be dangerous. When "forward" is first achieved, the greatest danger is past. But the back takes a long time and the rider must be extremely careful. The clear goal is: poll up, neck long and nose in front. Not until the horse happily rides *forward* can you even think about stretching *forward-downward*.

The forward seat in trot and canter is a wonderful means of helping a tense horse to swing. It should be used when there is an indication of defensive tension in the back or as a short relaxation phase after work.

In difficult cases, such as retraining, the horse should be longed before riding. I have had the best experience with the longeing cavesson. The following procedure has proven itself: After an appropriate warm up at the walk and trot, an energetic forward canter is very effective. After that, continue with calm longeing, or start under-saddle work.

When establishing contact with open poll and neck angles (see p. 186), it is especially important to be careful your back is not tense. The rider's seat must be very soft to avoid triggering tension that may have been caused originally by the rider's seat or weight. It is recommended that heavy riders frequently use the forward or "young horse" seat.

On the subject of starting young horses and re-training adult horses, Gustav von Dreyhausen stated:

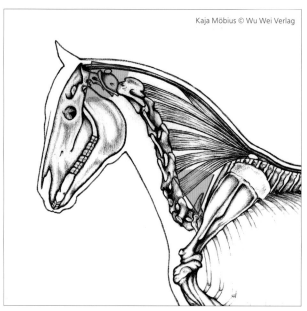

Kaja Möbius © Wu Wei Verlag

Shaded are the poll and neck angles of the vertebral column of the head and the neck.

"Horses with a weak, sensitive back and weak hind legs often rush out of discomfort and pain The rider must shift his weight on such a horse a little over his shoulders, standing in the stirrups in extreme cases to make it easier for the horse to move, until stretching and relaxing quiet the gait and the horse's back lifts up, allowing a better seat."

Gustav von Dreyhausen, *Grundzüge der Reitkunst* [Basic course in horsemanship], first publication 1951, new edition Olms Press, Zürich, Hildesheim, New York, 1983, p 42

Gustav von Dreyhausen also sees the necessity of riding in the forward seat on horses with weak, sensitive backs. He writes:

"A primary requirement of the trot is regularity. The horse must be calm to achieve this. The trot work must continue until pent-up energy and anxiety are released. The rider goes forward with his weight to match the more forward center of gravity of the horse in order to not stress the back and hindquarters, but rather to relax them. When necessary, the rider should stand lightly in the stirrups and use the knees to balance more forward."

Von Dreyhausen discusses two core messages: First, the significance of moving quietly and rhythmically, and second, the importance of being very careful with the haunches and back in a young or tense horse. In both I see the kernels of good retraining. The forward seat is also important with von Dreyhausen!

The correction of poorly ridden horses should only be done by truly qualified, experienced riders with the necessary equipment (helmet and back protector) because very dangerous situations can arise.

INITIAL WALK PHASE WITH STRETCHING

Every training session should begin with a long walk phase, where the reins are let out and taken up repeatedly, so said Martin Plewa, *Reitmeister*, at a seminar in 2010. I have tested it extensively, and found this repeated stretching to be very effective for the initial positioning and suppleness of the horse's back. Going forward in this way enables the horse to more quickly lengthen his neck, which is necessary for the back to relax and to establish balance. An initial good contact can also be developed in this way. The first, and perhaps most important goal, is to relax the horse, after which the objective is to find the rhythm and drive.

Very tense horses should be taken for a fresh, forward canter in the light seat after the walking phase to best resolve the worst of the tension. The neck should be left as long as possible.

Stretching at the walk is very valuable not just to reestablish balance when retraining the poorly ridden horse, but, as a general rule, for well-ridden horses, as well.

LONGEING WITH A CAVESSON

It is sensible to combine work under saddle with longe work, especially with young horses or when retraining older horses that have become dangerous. In my experience, longeing with a bare cavesson without a surcingle and side reins works best.

After a sufficiently long initial warm-up phase in walk and trot, an energetic forward canter in both directions is most effective. The horse is able to carry his neck freely, which helps to relax the back and enlivens the hindquarters. After that, calmly bring the horse in on a smaller circle in a very quiet tempo using the longeing cavesson to achieve a forward-downward stretch of the neck, meaning a stretch of the topline. This is achieved through "giving" on the longe. The horse's back relaxes proportionately. By pointing the longe whip at the horse's shoulder, he'll stay out on the circle. Horses prepared in this way have an easier time releasing resistance and working with the rider when under saddle. (Longeing with the cavesson is explained very well by Gabrielle

Rachen-Schöneich and Klaus Schöneich in *Straightening the Crooked Horse*, which was published in English by Trafalgar Square Books, North Pomfret, Vermont, in 2007.) Once most of the tension has been released, one of the most important goals for the under-saddle work is to develop a trot with a steady rhythm.

When the negative tension issues are mostly resolved and the rider can begin to drive with seat aids, then the Training Scale provides the guidelines for further training.

When longeing with the cavesson, whether under saddle or in hand, quiet stepping-over exercises and leg-yields are good for loosening as supplements to consistent "forward." It can be very helpful to use these exercises after a sufficient warm up and after the forward work that is appropriate for the age of the horse. From my experience, this process makes rebalancing of any horse undergoing retraining much easier, assuming it is done correctly. For older

A young riding horse with little back tension. He is not yet balanced and doesn't flex at the poll.

horses with a tight back, the additional work of correct shoulder-in at the trot and later at the canter is essential! As soon as this exercise can be ridden from a supple seat with correct carriage and bend by the horse, most of the retraining is done.

THE PSYCHOLOGY OF A HORSE IN RETRAINING

Finally, I would like to briefly address the psychological aspect of a tense horse in retraining. Horses tight in the back are usually very anxious, easily spooked and nervous! Since ancient times, man has known that there is a very close relationship between the *physiology* (back tension) of a flight animal such as a horse and the *psychology* (becoming nervous, running away).

Body tension in a flight animal in preparation for flight develops in a fraction of a second after he senses danger. All of his senses are sharpened, the body tenses like a bow before an arrow is shot. As the center of movement, the back is the most important part of the body.

Looked at the other way around, when poor riding causes the horse's body to tighten, the flight animal will always respond with psychological tension. The horse has all his senses oriented externally, away from the rider. He only needs the smallest reason for flight readiness to turn into actual flight. The nervous tension in the horse grows as the physical tension increases in rider and horse. The rider must have a supple seat and an even, calm demeanor to be able to retrain a tense, nervous horse. An emotionally excited, fearful or maybe even angry and impatient rider has no chance. She will only ruin the horse more, and put herself in danger!

Horses frequently don't accept the rider's leg and even strike against it. This will be addressed later in chapter XXIV "The Hyperflexed Back Mover" (p. 198).

RECOMMENDATIONS FOR RETRAINING

In summary, retrain the tense horse as follows:

➲ Without concern for the horse's frame (long neck, nose out in front), relax and calm him through free "forward" riding with a supple, light seat. Find the rhythm that is correct for the individual horse.

➲ Start driving with the seat aids, riding the horse from back to front to the hand. Don't ride "backward." Maintain a supple seat!

➲ Develop the horse's stretching—use correct "forward-downward" riding.

➲ Utilize diagonal aids such as stepping-over exercises and leg-yields from a soft seat, as slowly as possible.

➲ Develop the shoulder-in at walk, trot and canter.

➲ Keep the Training Scale in mind.

XXIII.

INITIAL STEPS IN RETRAINING

Part Two: The Leg Mover

THE HORSE WITH A LOW BACK POSITION

Expressive, but not correctly collected: A hollow back, high croup with the hind legs strung out, both typical characteristics of a leg mover.

With the term "leg mover," Bernhard Hugo von Holleuffer refers to the horse that moves "without the back" in his book *Die Bearbeitung des Reit- und Kutschpferdes zwischen den Pilaren* [Training the riding and driving horse between the pillars] (Olms Press, Hildesheim, Zürich, New York, 1999). Von Holleuffer uses the term "back mover" to indicate the correctly balanced horse. These terms found their way back into our lexicon about 10 years ago.

Leg mover describes a horse that has lost his back along the way in training. The main indicator of a leg mover is a hollow back position, which has a huge effect on the gait and the psychology of the horse. Anatomically, the leg mover differs in that he has a *longer*, maybe even a *long* back. Frequently, this is combined with a weak lumbar area.

The hollow back position is often the result of being elevated artificially and too early by the rider. The practice of accepting an early rounding of the neck with high artifical elevation while the long back is weak is what typically leads to leg movers. Horses predestined to be leg movers are those that have powerful necks, a poll that rounds very easily but doesn't really yield, in combination with a long and weak back. A poor anatomical transition through the loins in the lumbar area is especially problematic. Negative tension in the back muscles causing hollowing always occurs when such a back is loaded with a rider's weight. Absolute head-and-neck elevation, as well as going behind the bit, are further negative consequences.

Natural crookedness is a problem particularly in horses with a hollow back topline. Going to the right, a horse that is *hollow* going in that direction ends up pushing heavily with his hindquarters and not going forward well while also strongly resisting flexing and bending to the left. Remember: Only a horizontally balanced horse can be vertically balanced.

A leg mover can never be straightened!

Depending on the rider's feel and the quality of her seat, these horses will begin to run against the hand and their movement becomes hectic: The "poll angle" keeps getting smaller, or the horse fights against rounding the poll. There are some leg movers that, thanks to riders with skill and a sensitive seat, have been brought along to the highest levels of training exercises and successfully started in competition. However, even though these horses do not "run away" they will not be sensitive to the rider's seat aids. The key clue is the horse's hind legs that are lagging (strung out) behind and not fully active, especially during extensions. This imbalance is the result of receiving incorrect basic work as a young horse, which led to psychological and physical disorders, and secondary injury, for example, suspensory damage. The most important indications of this sort of balance disruption are: unwillingness to perform correct transitions; persistent and extreme crookedness; dragging hindquarters (especially when ridden with a stiff driving seat), as well as frequently extravagant motion of the front legs, such as "show" passage-like movements ("hovering") in the trot. Nevertheless, these incorrect mechanics of movement often deceive some judges, with the horse's performance awarded with high scores.

RHYTHMICALLY FORWARD

The first and most critical goal is to "establish horizontal balance." The neck must be long and lower, with the poll remaining as the highest point. The nose must be brought in front of the vertical. The most important effect of this posture is the lifting of the back. This balance correction works only with consistent forward riding, with the intent to bring the nose in front of the vertical. Initially, it may be necessary, especially at the canter, to simply ride fast in order to open a stiff or blocked horse and to motivate him to move forward. A brisk, forward canter should be followed by a specific, calm rhythm at the trot. *Riding forward* has nothing to do with speed; I am using the phrase to refer to the development of rhythmical "forward movement."

Depending on the anatomy of the horse, the ideal neck position is about horizontal. The poll should always be the highest point. Many horses react very well to an energetic forward canter in the light seat. Remember, check your stirrup length! Encourage the horse to "chew" the reins out of the hand at the canter. Basically, a true forward-downward stretch is only possible when three elements are achieved: The horse is driven in rhythm; the horse accepts the bit with the nose in front of the vertical; and he chews with a closed mouth. It is critically important to first establish *forward* with open poll and neck angles while the horse seeks the hand in a natural neck position, for only then can the rider correctly ride the stretch forward and downward. A correct stretch is an important goal in training for every horse, especially for horses that have "lost their back."

ACTIVATE THE HIND LEG

When retraining leg movers and dressage horses trained with forceful methods, there is usually a further difficulty to address: These horses have been elevated in a large, artificial trot without using their back, and the back is now under force and tension. There are many different terms that can be used for this pattern of movement in the trot: circus trot, show trot, or competition trot. All these terms mean that the horse trots with an exaggerated suspension phase with distinctly slow ground coverage. Because the hind leg activity is considerably reduced, a horse moving this way is referred to as "slow behind." The stepping arc of the hindquarters is flat and short.

False impulsion and artificial suspension come from a stiff back, not an active hind leg. The suspended leg pair in trot is distinctly disassociated (see my book *Tug of War*, Trafalgar Square Books, North Pomfret, Vermont, 2007). The hind cannon bone is no longer parallel to the diagonal front lower leg. The ground coverage of such horses is distinctly reduced; even in extensions, you have the impression of the horse stepping "on the spot."

A leg mover, at this moment in trot.

A back mover, at the same moment.

Correcting such a "destroyed" trot is usually very difficult—depending on the degree of damage done and the time span. In extreme cases, the retraining of older horses that have been ridden a long time in such an artificial suspension is difficult or no longer possible or reasonable because the back of these horses doesn't work anymore. Even the walk and the canter are changed, with the walk tending to a pace. The canter is dragging and/or slow almost always with an incorrect footfall—often in four-beat rhythm.

For horses not yet too old or those that haven't been moving long in this false balance, it is important to first energize the activity of the hind end with an eager forward ride and the horse extending his neck. This begins to relieve the back tension and cramping. The slower hover trot must not be accepted! It is hard to sit to the trot on a tight back so sitting trot shouldn't be done until the horse "carries" his back again, works supplely, and is eager to rediscover joy in movement.

LONGER NECK AND LATERAL MOVEMENT

It is especially important during retraining to value a lengthened neck. Longitudinal flexion created mechanically with backward hands leads to false balance with slow and dragging movement. When the horse goes sufficiently and consistently forward and has accepted the bit, the correct positioning of the back can be supported through quietly ridden stepping-over exercises and leg-yields. In my practical work, this sideways work has been very useful for adult horses in retraining.

The position of the nose is absolutely unimportant except that such a horse should never go with the neck curled in or behind the vertical. Moreover,

you should put great value on achieving the ability to step over with the lightest possible aids. The greatest effect is achieved when the exercises are ridden with a calm and supple seat. The greatest "suppling" effect of the back is achieved when these sideways movements are performed as slowly as possible.

As soon as a leg mover has found his rhythm, balanced his back and accepted the driving aids without hover steps, the way is clear for further work according to the Training Scale. Great value must be placed on correctly stretching forward and downward in all gaits.

CROSS-COUNTRY WORK

For all types of horses in retraining, it is valuable to regularly ride outside. Climbing hills and going over small jumps, together with brisk forward riding, improves eagerness and willingness by the horse to step to the rider's hand. Regular cross-country riding provides every horse with a motivating change in training.

The retraining (or training) of horses that have a naturally high neck set, a low topline, and a very weak hind end is difficult. It's a big challenge to bring such a horse into correct balance with the horse "carrying" himself. All the previously discussed training content is of great importance if you are to achieve a long-lasting rebalancing. (Unfortunately, Friesian and Iberian horses belong to this group. If you accept the natural high elevation at the beginning, then it is, in my vew, impossible to bring them into a balance that conforms to the guidelines.)

Cross-country work (riding outside the ring) should be fun for both horse and rider.

RECOMMENDATIONS FOR RETRAINING

In summary, the keys to retraining a leg mover are as follows:

- ➲ The horse must learn to go forward actively and without tensing the back.
- ➲ It is preferable to begin with a fresh forward canter in a light seat, and brisk, active trot work without pushing the horse beyond his comfortable tempo.
- ➲ Maintain a longer horizontal neck with the poll as the highest point and the nose in front of the vertical.
- ➲ Find the individual horse's rhythm at the trot.
- ➲ Begin driving with a supple seat.
- ➲ Avoid all tension in the seat.
- ➲ Ride the horse cross-country on a regular and frequent basis.
- ➲ Follow the principles of the Training Scale.

XXIV.

INITIAL STEPS IN RETRAINING

Part Three: The Hyperflexed Back Mover

THE HORSE WITH A "PUSHED UP" BACK

This overarched back is caused by an extremely low and deep-to-the-chest, forced head positioning (see photo on p. 198), or painful, self-protective tension in the horse's back (above).

Ahead-neck position that is much too deep is indicative of a horse that has "lost" his back, so to speak, *upward*: It becomes too high and thereby tense. This posture is what is meant by the *over-stretched* or *hyperflexed back mover.*

The huge progress in breeding of the last decades has improved the rideability of horses so that young horses often start rounding the neck when first mounted. The short, round neck results from defensive tension in the back: Young horses push their back upward for their own protection against the weight of the rider.

I have already mentioned that this problem is something new in the last few decades, and is "self-protective" behavior. Every horse needs his neck long during the initial ground work phase and in the first training phases, in order to prevent damaging and unbearable back tension.

A young horse that curls his neck inward must be ridden rhythmically forward with relatively short stirrups and a light, forward seat.

Consistent forward riding will open the neck angle, and encourage acceptance of the bit. As a result, the previously raised back should drop and relax. When the rider can start driving sensitively with her seat, improvement begins to be achieved.

Today, it is not uncommon to see numerous horses purposefully trained with an extremely deep, round neck position as a means of gymnasticizing the horse.

"ROLLKUR" AND HYPERFLEXION

The term "Rollkur" has been in modern usage since the late 1970s. It was used by a German riding sport magazine as a headline to an article by Professor Heinz Meyer on the subject of "deep head-neck position." This word embodied a manner of riding with an extremely deep head-neck position with the nose curled toward the chest.

In 2006, a group of highly successful Rollkur "supporters" wanted the term changed to "hyperflexion." At a meeting in 2010 in Lausanne, such aggressive training methods were officially disapproved. This resolution did not just refer to hyperflexion, but also to every form of mechanized, forced head positioning. Deep positioning without physical power and force was recommended by the Dutch participants and referred to as the *LDR Method* (low, deep and round). This is a term that, while accepted, had no basis in logic. So, the FEI referred to this concept as "long, deep and round," which at least made a little sense and was agreed upon with animal welfare in mind. A deep although not forced neck position assumed by the horse was not viewed as counter to animal welfare whereas forced longitudinal flexion—regardless of how high or deep—was regarded as unacceptable. The 2010 resolution accounted for the quality of training practices rather than limiting the time a horse is forced into longitudinal flexion. The revised wording, adopted by the FEI, included a

Forced longitudinal flexion of the horse is, in my view, a result of incorrect training of today's highly rideable young horses. This mechanized method of training leads to early injury.

depiction of the positions that are acceptable on the grounds of animal welfare in accordance with the

resolution. This 2010 decision is a first step in the right direction, with yet a long way to go.

LEARNED HELPLESSNESS

A mechanical, extremely deep longitudinal flexion—regardless of whether it is done with or without draw reins—is the worst possible thing for the back and balance of the horse. Most modern sport horses forced to move in such a posture start to run. They attempt to escape from the rider's weight on their tight back much as a flight animal would with a predator on his neck. However, it is best if the horse is connected to the rider through an active, driving seat that influences and controls the horse. This stops the horse from running off.

When a horse suffers from an excessively tight back, the only way to stop him may be with strong use of the reins or by moving him as safely as possible toward an external object, like a wall. The emergency situation that requires stopping the fleeing horse by any means often leads to renewed and stronger use of the reins, with the horse's head ending up on his chest. Physical power by the rider and exhaustion by the horse eventually lead to the horse becoming accustomed to this forced position.

The term "learned helplessness" was adopted from experts in behavioral research. They found that the flight reflex gradually decreases as the horse becomes more habituated—eventually he surrenders and gives up. But harmony and the relationship between horse and rider don't stand in the center of the endeavor, only submission and servitude.

It is striking that when compared to far less well trained pleasure horses, the horses at the highest levels have to be prepared for competition through hours of riding. Multiple hour-long exhaustive riding procedures are common on the international sport scene, and are damaging to the horse. Too many horses "disappear" after a short appearance on the sport stage and are never seen again. Any horse presented at the highest levels of competition should only need a short and calm warm-up phase.

As I explain below, this curled-in neck and head-on-the-chest position leads to high tension emanating from the bit in the mouth to the back of the stifle.

EXTREME DISRUPTION OF BALANCE AND THE FLIGHT REFLEX

The entire topline of a horse in forced longitudinal flexion is overstretched; the back is lifted too high, locked and tense. The attachment from the back ligament to the sacrum "pulls up" the sacrum, which overstretches the LS joint. Such incorrectly balanced horses develop a flat croup line through the constant pull on the rear attachment of the neck-back ligament.

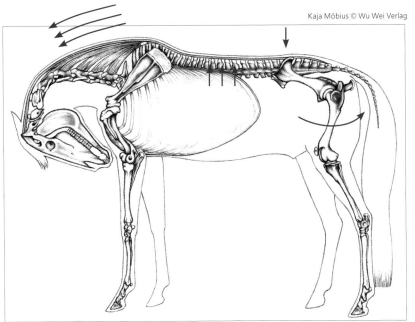

Kaja Möbius © Wu Wei Verlag

Horses with a neck that has been rounded by force always have a tight, straight back, a hyperflexed lumbo-sacral joint (LS; straight croup), hind legs that sprawl out behind, and stiff haunches.

This pulling up of the sacrum, the bony foundation of the pelvis, raises the entire pelvis caudally (toward the rear), thereby increasing tension on the gluteal muscles. The long gluteal muscles attach in the area of the back of the stifle. Subsequently, the stifle is pulled back due to increased pull from this muscle group; with the haunches stretched in place, so to speak. This poses an extreme disruption to the horse's balance, leading to the hind legs not being able to be brought forward naturally under his body in the forward swing-phase. During the support-phase, the same effect occurs and the stifle joint can't spring forward at the moment the horse weights the corresponding leg. High negative tension in the upper muscle chain hinders the bending of the haunches. A horse tensed and positioned by force in this way can never be collected.

Psychologically, the horse responds to such back tension by "running away" from the rider's seat—the "flight effect" kicks in.

PSYCHOLOGICAL RELAXATION

As described in the last chapter, a primary step in retraining hyperflexed back movers is to encourage psychological relaxation and calm. A second retraining element is to reactivate the hind leg that has become sluggish and inactive. Both steps have the goal of reestablishing the balance and returning mobility to the back. This is frequently a big problem: How does the rider drive a horse from her seat

Left and below left: Two successful dressage horses showing imbalance the moment the pictures were taken. Compare the piaffe on the left with the horse shown below. Below: A well-balanced horse in good collection with correct flexing of the haunches.

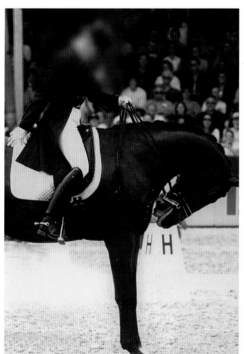

© Variation of a figure from Michael Strick's *Denksport Reiten*, FN Verlag, Warendorf, 2001

201

when the horse is already "running away" from her aids? The problem often gets so bad that the horse that has been mistreated in this way is considered unrideable. The horse has learned to use his board-like, "blocked" back as a weapon against the rider's weight. It could even be life-threatening to get on such a horse!

LONGEING WITH A CAVESSON

Longeing with a cavesson plays an indispensable role in defusing the initial flight reactions in horses that truly have become dangerous. The horse should be allowed to gallop forward energetically after an appropriate warm-up phase, and for as long as necessary until the initial and greatest tension is released. Going forward in this way may be necessary for a few days to as long as a few weeks! The rider should only mount the horse and begin work in the saddle once the horse tolerates her weight without any "defensive" tension appearing. It is at this point that the retraining process can be continued.

Rhythmical and lively forward work must be very consistent. The horse must be allowed to use his neck; value is placed on a long, almost horizontal neck. From a biomechanical point of view, the goal of training is the same as for other horses being re-trained: suppleness of the back. Energy in the hindquarters and suppleness of the long back muscles are synergistic. Rollkur (hyperflexed) horses are sometimes extremely tense, very fearful and often unpredictable, depending on the extent of the

Longeing in a cavesson is used to physically and mentally relax the tense horse.

physical and psychological damage. These horses are ones that may benefit well from regular cross-country riding (see p. 194).

A first stage goal is to reestablish natural balance, which is part of the first three steps of the Training Scale: Rhythm, Suppleness, Contact.

VERY DIFFICULT HORSES WITH A FLIGHT TENDENCY

Retraining a horse that has been mistreated in this way for a long time is often very difficult. In my experience, these are horses that will react to even a light seat with flight. They run randomly against the rider's hand and can only be stopped by rough action of the reins with no fulfillment of any elements of the Training Scale, which means there is no Rhythm.

There is another way forward with such horses. After an appropriately long walk phase (very long!) the experienced and softly seated rider allows the horse to trot while she tries to stay soft and light in short stirrups, and above all, find a very calm tempo. The tempo should resemble a Western jog. It is especially important to sit lightly and steadily and to try to lengthen the horse's neck. At first, the horse may attempt to curl his neck in as an evasion, move with a quasi leg-yield—an undefined sideways motion. I work such horses in this quiet tempo on curved lines and sit very quietly, almost passively, until I sense that the horse is beginning to stay with me: Wait for your horse! I use these moments to lighten my seat and then to sit down again. If the horse stays with me

When retraining is dangerous because the horse manifests self-protective mechanisms like rearing or bucking, longeing with a cavesson is a good starting point to remove, or at least lessen, his defensiveness.

and accepts sensitive driving in a forward seat, we have come a long way. I remember a mare that took three months to relax!

To be able to correct such a horse, a rider needs experience, inner calm and above all, endless patience.

At the beginning, I never rode this mare two days in a row in order to avoid her getting a muscle cramp that could become an "enemy" to progress. Additionally, she was in the pasture all day with the herd.

RESISTANCE AGAINST THE RIDER'S LEG

A horse with a tense back, whether due to active hands (hyperflexion) or through curling the neck in on his own, frequently exhibits a further symptom: not accepting the rider's leg. The pattern runs from resistance to the leg, mostly on the horse's stiff side, and being dull to the leg on the hollow side, to massive attacks: Such horses can kick out against the rider's leg or energetically back up as soon as the rider attempts to use it. When the strongest movement muscle of the back (the long back muscle) is tense, then the corresponding antagonist (above all, the external oblique abdominal muscle) reacts the same way: A tense back results in a tense abdomen. According to the temperament of the horse and the degree of his tension, there will be varying degrees of resistance to the leg.

Reestablishing natural balance is the essence of retraining. The horse must "get his neck back"—that is, he must learn how to stretch to the bit and to accept the bit farther forward. The horse with a short, curved neck poses a problem that is best corrected by a sensitive and experienced rider. She must be good at the light seat in trot and canter and be versed in careful and slowly developed forward riding. Be careful! These horses frequently—and happily—buck at the canter not because they are being bad but instead, it's a sign of beginning suppleness.

When such a horse has found his balance and relaxed his back, it is generally easy to get him accustomed to the leg aids.

THE INTERPLAY OF THE AIDS

On this subject, I'll touch briefly on the basics of giving the aids. The Classical Training philosophy builds on a feeling that communicates the difference between *driving* and *holding* aids. The better the horse is trained, the more important the rider's seat. When this goal of influencing the horse via the rider's seat is achieved, rein and leg aids move more to a supporting role, becoming lighter and lighter

until finally, they function simply as organizers. At the same time, coordination of seat, leg and rein aids becomes more demanding. To ride a halt on a horse with a yielding poll requires the coordination of all forms of influence!

A separation of the aids, as in leg without hand and hand without leg, only makes sense with young horses and horses in retraining.

A driving aid is not likely to be successful when coupled with a holding or taking rein in a horse with a tight poll and back. In this case, it makes sense to separate these aids. A horse in correct balance, without poll resistance or back tension, should be worked with finely tuned coordination of the driving and holding aids.

A strict separation of the aids is found only in training philosophies that are not based on a horse with a "carried" and supple back. This is acceptable when the horse is in a different balance, namely moving with a deep, loose back and lightly hanging reins without impulsion from the hindquarters (*Lègéreté*). As soon as the upper muscle chain (rider hand → chewing musculature → poll → neck's topline → back → croup → buttock muscles) is positively tensed through a correct contact, the horse is "through" and accepts the interplay of the aids. Horses that require a separation of the aids are not back movers in the sense of the Classical Training philosophy!

RECOMMENDATIONS FOR RETRAINING

To summarize, the following can be recommended for retraining the hyperflexed back mover:

◉ Be careful when riding an extremely tense horse. Hyperflexed back movers are often unpredictable. They are physically and psychologically extremely tense!

◉ An extremely tight back can be loosened up quite well through expert longeing in a cavesson.

◉ It is very important to have a long neck with the poll being the highest point. Horses must be lifted up if the poll sinks too low.

◉ Riding forward in a regular rhythm is key. You must be able to drive with an active, supple seat.

◉ Correct driving from a sensitive calf and an encouraging seat staying supple activates a lazy hind end. (Be careful since a stiff seat blocks the back—so, no "braced" seat!) Incorrect driving is when the rider stiffens and braces her back.

◉ Find the horse's unique and individual rhythm.

◉ When possible, ride regularly out in the country, up and down hills and at an eager forward canter, always being cautious about your safety.

◉ Mobility and suppleness of the horse's back determine when the Training Scale work can begin.

XXV.
INITIAL STEPS IN RETRAINING
Part Four: The Horse That Has Fallen Apart

THE LEG MOVER CAUSED BY INSUFFICIENT POSITIVE TENSION

A unique form of disturbed balance that results in "leg moving" is seen regularly in pleasure horses that aren't trained or ridden by knowledgeable people. However, these horses become leg movers passively: When burdened with a poor sitting rider who is often too heavy as well, the horse can "fall apart," that is, he comes completely off the aids. The horse lacks the basic balance and positive muscle tension in his back, which are necessary to support the load. And because his back is too heavily loaded, it gives way and hollows.

THE TRAINING LEVEL OF THE PLEASURE RIDER

The pleasure rider includes professional horse people who have trained to the highest level and have come close to the ideal of classical teachings. However, a larger proportion of pleasure riders are people who have no or very little training about horses and aren't interested in training. A third group of pleasure riders are dedicated to special horse breeds and are dedicated to the associated manner of riding. There are educated and interested horse people among the representatives of all breeds and

Two relaxed and content ponies in balance.

the associated culture and ways of riding. Due to this diversity, overseeing the quality of training and riding is more difficult. It is also getting more difficult to define breed-specific standards of quality. Individualists are overtaking the field. The span runs from the South American gaited horse to the cold-blood to the various Western breeds. The diversity in this group provides a varied mixture of breeds and ways of riding. I see in this a great enrichment of the horse world on one hand, and a great challenge for the associations and their officials on the other.

A large group of pleasure riders have not been attracted to the training methods and opportunities of national or breed associations and teaching institutions. Riding is limited frequently to "going forward on a horse" and the classic riding teachings and knowledge about caring, feeding, and saddle fit come up short. A horse moving with a saddle that doesn't fit under a poor sitting rider has difficulty finding his balance. Slowly over time, these horses may be damaged even though typically they aren't forced into incorrect positions. Points 1, 3 and 7 of the "Nine Ethical Principles of Horsemanship" (p. 9) state that the rider is responsible for the training and care of the horse, for the well-being of the horse. Saying "I didn't know that" doesn't count! On behalf of the horse, the rider is responsible for the training and care of her horse.

A pleasure horse that has fallen apart travels with a tight back.

BALANCE "DISRUPTED" BY THE RIDER'S LACK OF KNOWLEDGE

The horse that has fallen apart lugs his rider on a back that isn't getting any carrying help from positive tension in the neck and topline structures. The long back muscles that run horizontally try to lift the additional weight of the rider by tightening, and this tight back disturbs the natural motion and balance. After being ridden in this way for a while, most horses will let their back drop. Such improperly balanced horses end up with a tense poll, stiff back, hind legs that sprawl out behind, and they go on their forehand.

I find it extremely difficult to define a minimum training goal for pleasure riders, but it should be in accordance with animal welfare principles and the Ethical Principles (p. 9). At the same time, the bar shouldn't be so high that pleasure riders and competitors in broad public equestrian sports give up. The content of the Training Scale is not reachable nor a desirable goal for many riders although it may be possible to fulfill the initial three criteria of the Training Scale: Rhythm, Suppleness, and Contact.

MINIMAL REQUIREMENTS FOR PLEASURE RIDERS

In the ideal case, a pleasure rider would fulfill the first three points of the Training Scale. That in itself provides reasonably good training and establishes the basics for the seat and the rider's feel for movement.

I believe it is unrealistic to choose this as a starting point. Pleasure riders should, in my opinion, work to develop their own balance and a supple seat. The coordination of the aids need not be so developed that the rider can work his horse in different states of balance. He should strive, however, to maintain his horse in a natural balance. For that, he needs a supple and balanced seat and a light and sensitive contact on the reins. The rider should be able to control his horse in the three basic gaits and to not tense his horse's back. In so doing, he would achieve the three first points of the Training Scale, or come close to it.

OUTSIDE WORK IN A REGULAR FORWARD RHYTHM

Consistent trail riding forward with a regular rhythm plays the biggest role in retraining. The horse must rediscover his joy in moving. Back activity is strengthened by climbing hills and crossing small jumps. When joy in movement is reawakened, the next step is to quietly add in stepping-over exercises, for example, leg-yields at the walk to positively influence the horse's natural (basic) balance. Later, developing contact enables correct stretching. Retraining of these horses requires significant equestrian experience and should not be done by the rider who caused the faulty balance.

Classical Riding knowledge is active animal welfare!

XXVI.
FUNDAMENTALS
Thoughts on Retraining

CALM LATERAL WORK AT THE WALK AND LATER AT THE TROT

François Robichon de la Guérinière recommended the shoulder-in as the retraining exercise of choice.

Correctly executed lateral movement is very effective for retraining and generally doesn't require a great expenditure of energy, especially at the walk. There is more to say, however, to appropriately value the importance of this exercise and the importance of the rider holding her hand higher.

A few years ago, I became more conscious of the importance of calmly executed walk work through my experiences at the *Rosenhof* of Anja Beran in southern Germany. Iberian horses were regularly worked laterally at the walk. This is of great importance when developing suppleness, especially a horse in retraining. A variety of walking exercises, from simple stepping over on up to the lateral ex-

ercises, is of inestimable value for the retraining of poorly ridden horses.

De la Guérinière advises about the shoulder-in:

"I regard this exercise as the beginning and end of all training. It builds the horse throughout his body. It is true that every ruined horse becomes just as supple as previously, when one works a few days in shoulder-in."

Although his time frame is certainly very optimistic, de la Guérinière recognized the extraordinary rebalancing and "loosening" effect of lateral work on the back. In addition, there is a significant direct and indirect effect on the poll. Mouth activity begins, which contributes to suppleness of the poll.

More than 200 years later, Waldemar Seunig wrote about "chewing":

"A simple and unfailing method, when done right, of enlivening an apparently dead mouth and encouraging a resistant neck to stretch to the bit is the turn-on-the-forehand while moving. The hindquarters are pushed around the forehand, which makes a small circle. In contrast to a turn on the forehand on the spot where the inside front leg creeps back or stays planted, the whole horse goes in regular

steps in this loosening exercise, without being allowed to stop or lean. At any time, he is able to change from steps moving around two concentric circles to straight ahead."

Waldemar Seunig, *Marginalien zu Pferd und Reiter* [Marginalia to horse and rider],Wu Wei Verlag, Schondorf, 2011, p. 73

◆

Waldemar Seunig doesn't describe the biomechanical effect of this movement on the back of the horse. He certainly knows the effect, however. He talks about getting horses with resistant necks to stretch to the bit and chew. A horse with a blocked back, as described earlier, tends to move backward when asked to turn-on-the-forehand. Executing the turn while moving diminishes this tendency and significantly increases the benefit. Moreover, crossing of the front legs significantly loosens the shoulder region.

Restoring basic balance

Practically speaking there are many obvious benefits to asking for a turn-on-the-forehand. The horse begins to chew (see "Jaw-Mobilizing Effect of the Lower Muscle Chain," p. 153), which in turn leads to poll suppleness and rounding, or at least some improvement. It has been my experience that about 90 percent of horses have a tight back. Stepping over relaxes the back through the upper muscle chain, especially the lumbar portion of the long back muscles, and leads to the back lifting into the desired position. The rider suddenly feels movement in the previously "dead" back. In adult horses, a very effective stretch of the neck is almost always achieved through stepping over—this stretch lifts the back behind the withers and improves the balance. "Swinging," as described by von Holleuffer, requires lifting and balancing of the back; if successful, then rhythm, suppleness and contact all improve immediately, as does impulsion at the trot. A decisive step in the direction of basic balance is achieved!

Stepping-over exercises also lead to the horse tuning-in to the leg of the rider, and with steadily improved sensitivity. Tuning the horse to the subtlest leg aids is an important and critical goal—then the horse responds with the "breath of the trouser leg." After a few days of practical application (see de la Guérinière, p. 211), most horses move sideways when asked by a rider's supple seat; the lower leg plays only a very light monitoring role. In this way, the rider learns to apply the lightest aids and the horse learns to react to the lightest aids. A reflexive contraction of the "external oblique abdominal muscle" follows, which leads to a willing and quiet lateral stepping over or stepping under of the hind leg. Horse and rider both profit tremendously from this fine-tuning—each communicating with and understanding the other.

Sit supply and aid sensitively

Practically speaking, there are a few key prerequisites for success. The seat of the rider must be supple. Any initial resistance of the horse should be addressed with skillful and sensitive use of the whip aid and not with spurs. From the beginning, you must avoid sitting on the horse with squeezing legs. If the rider clamps the adductor muscles of the thigh, that tension is transmitted immediately to the body of the horse—the horse clamps, too. If the rider sits with a tight back on her horse, exactly the same thing occurs in the horse: The horse then feels "heavy."

The positive benefits mentioned above can only be achieved when the rider sits really supply and aids with feeling. Sometimes, with horses that have been badly ridden, that is not easy; nevertheless is essential! Successful retraining of a horse with these

In his book *Marginalien zu Pferd und Reiter* [Marginalia to horse and rider], Waldemar Seunig recommends lifting the inside hand while stepping over in the volte, (a small circle approximately 6 meters in diameter) in order to activate the mouth and to relax the poll.

exercises requires calmness, mental relaxation, and physical suppleness in the rider, and slow movements. The tighter and stiffer the back, poll and haunches, the more important it is to do this exercise slowly.

You may understand this from your own body with a muscle cramp—you can loosen it only through very slow movement. Mobility and promptness re-

quire supple muscles. Moving sideways quickly is not effective with a tense horse and can even be disadvantageous as the horse learns to run away from the rider's seat aids.

Waldemar Seunig describes the practical execution of stepping over and the special use of the inside hand:

◆

"The process is as follows: The horse in a snaffle bridle stands straight with no lateral bend. The horse is pushed by the right lower leg to the left in calm, regular steps. The rider's left leg guards against hurrying and drives quickly forward when the horse's forehand wants to stop. The right hand lifts with arm outstretched from the shoulder joint, toward the ears, without any pressure, while staying in light contact with the corner of the horse's lips.

213

The right rein is vertical. The left hand maintains its normal position. Ring and little fingers open softly and vibrate.

"The stimulus acting on the right side of the mouth is released as soon as the swallowing movement of the tongue leads to chewing. At the same time, the right hand is lowered back in place. The left leg that has up until now acted as a barrier to prevent the horse from speeding sideways, now wraps against the body of the horse with the same pressure as the right driving leg so that the horse now leaves the volte and moves straight forward. The rider gives the reins forward and praises the horse."

Waldemar Seunig, *Marginalien zu Pferd und Reiter* [Marginalia to horse and rider], Wu Wei Verlag, Schondorf, 2011, p. 73

IDEAL AND CORRECTING USE OF THE REINS

Seunig describes both the benefit of stepping over and the importance of the raised hand. He clearly says not to pull, rather only to feel the corner of the horse's mouth.

There is a key point of learning here regarding the correction position of a rider's hand:

"The hands are vertical with the thumbs on top, about four fingers apart from one another, and enclosing the horse's neck with the reins. They are held at a height that allows the lower arms and reins to form a straight line."

H.Dv. 12, New Edition, Wu Wei Verlag, Schondorf, 1997

This rein usage defines an ideal situation: a hand position that controls a balanced and "through" horse. While this ideal picture of a balanced horse is what many riders dream of, reality may look a little different—the majority of horses demonstrate problems with balance to varying degrees. As a result, there are almost always issues with bit contact. An overwhelming number of riders fight with horses going against the rein, behind the bit, or hanging on the reins. When the hand is held dogmatically in place, many riders start pulling with a deeply held hand. Very often we see riders at all levels and in all disciplines tending to pull the inside rein hand backward toward the thigh.

Every backward pull on the rein by the rider calls forth a counteracting pull by the horse against the rider's hand pressure. An attempt to mechanically force a head/neck position always leads to defensive tension in the horse. Every living creature reacts in this way. It is the kernel and essence of Classical Riding theory to achieve a beautiful external frame that reflects balance and harmony as the result of correct training. However, when this desirable frame becomes a prerequisite, rather than encouraging this

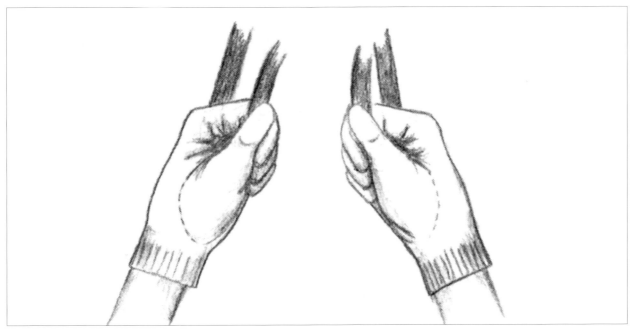

Correct hand position for a horse in balance with a yielding poll.

desirable frame through correct riding and exercises, a rider may be compelled to mechanically force the position. A deep and/or backward-pulling hand leads to a tense poll, which leads to a tense back, and then to stiff haunches. The horse is strengthened in his natural crookedness, and damage occurs to his natural gaits. In an extreme case, motion is disturbed and the horse develops rein lameness. Structural injuries and lameness issues are other consequences that may develop.

A dogmatically placed, immobile hand causes this vicious cycle. Every trainer wants a sensitive hand placed exactly between the supple horse's mouth and the elbow of the rider. Because large numbers of horses are in need of retraining, the rider must be advised on a reasonable procedure that enables horse and rider to find suppleness and harmony.

Experienced trainers know that every pull on the mouth of the horse results in not only increased tension in the horse, but it also frequently has a bad effect on the rider. Many riders sit with their whole body cramped as a result of persistent struggles with the horse's mouth. The rider's back tightens to resist being pulled forward by the horse's head. And, to avoid tipping forward in the saddle, the rider ends up clamping her thighs together as an anchor.

Clamping the thighs pulls the rider's legs up. As the rider clinches with the full of her legs, tension increases through the horse's whole body. Holding tight with the hands causes the rider's shoulders to tense. From that position, the elbows, wrists and hands cramp, lose feeling, become rigid and tend to orient backward in a non-ending cycle of tension. Scarcely anyone succeeds in breaking out of it without help. The objective is to re-orient the rider's entire riding focus on suppleness and sensitivity and to drive with an active seat in order to achieve harmony.

Chewing reflex from lifting of the rider's hand

In retraining a horse, the struggle is to avoid fighting

215

against massive stiffness in the horse's body. Loosening this tension requires an absolutely supple rider. With few exceptions, when retraining, the hand should never go below an imaginary line drawn from the rider's elbow to the horse's mouth. A hand sinking below this line pulls on the horse's mouth. Since most horses react reflexively to every backward pull with defensive tension, a deep hand position is to be avoided. To counteract this tendency, it is very effective to lift the hands (without pulling), especially on the inside rein. Waldemar Seunig describes that through an interplay of the aids, using the reins in this way releases a chewing reflex, encourages poll suppleness and as a result, poll rounding. That is the first prerequisite for good stretching. A common saying advises:

"A high hand rounds the necks; a low hand lengthens it."

If the hands are deep, they should give. The exception is when a horse that has his neck so extremely curled that he won't accept the bit with the methods described above. In such a case, it can be useful to lower the hands and passively wait for his counter-pull. When the counter-pull comes, allow it and follow it as the horse moves his head forward. Such measures are best executed by experienced and confident trainers.

Independent seat and subtle hand influence
It is especially important to sit really "independently": Only when hands are independent of the body can the rider react appropriately to every situation with her reins without causing tension in the horse's poll and neck. Within the framework of gymnasticiz-

ing the horse, there is one reaction that must be avoided, namely pulling backward on the reins so that the angle of the lower jaw becomes smaller, that is, mechanically forced longitudinal flexion. Such a use of the hand is only to be tolerated for a short time and only as a necessary educational method for a horse that is deadened to the feel of the rider's aids. A horse that leans on the bit and no longer reacts to several pulls on the reins must eventually be stopped sharply and mechanically. The goal of such a measure must always be to resensitize the horse's mouth. Such a correction is considered successful when the horse begins to respond to softer rein aids.

With the young horse, you should strive to develop balance systematically. Correct contact with an active mouth begins when the horse starts to find his rhythm and swing his back. If the rider carefully begins using her seat at this point, the horse will begin to chew. It doesn't make sense to get the horse to chew artificially through reflex. Waldemar Seunig writes:

"Experience shows that every attempt to create an active mouth is bad if it is before the horse is ready for it. The horse is prepared through months of gymnastic work that consists primarily of forward riding on straight lines with careful changes of tempo. Then progress can be realized by making the mouth more active through discreet influences of the hand. The course of dressage training accelerates. According to the principle of reciprocal influence of all the muscle groups in the moving horse, progress in training the mouth to soften improves suppleness of the body. We aren't talking about riding the head of

the horse or about the primary importance of the hand. On the contrary, the back and the leg are of primary importance. It is only being suggested that in the concert of aids there is a role to be played by a sensitive hand that 'shows the way.'"

Waldemar Seunig, *Marginalien zu Pferd und Reiter* [Marginalia to horse and rider], New Edition, Wu Wei Verlag, Schondorf, 2011

Seunig makes it clear that the seat of the rider is the foundation. A sensitive hand used with skill can have an important and positive effect.

The classical way of training is clearly defined and irrefutable as a positive influence. Nevertheless, I believe that an experienced and sensitive horseman can match her aids to circumstances as necessary. Why not softly stop an unbalanced and tense horse through light lifting of the outside rein when the "classical" half-halt would only cause stiffness and resistance in such a horse?

XXVII.

THE VETERINARIAN

Expertise and Pre-Purchase Exams

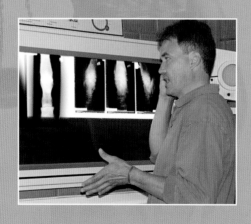

TRAINING AS A CRITERION OF VALUE

I have explored the importance of the quality of training to a horse's value in this book. Veterinarians are hired to determine a horse's state of health and to support an estimation of value. The vet's self-image and job depend on the condition of the horse being examined. Based on the importance of training to the presentation of the horse, the clinical picture and the value of a horse in a "pre-purchase exam" are not solely dependent on the horse's physical health. For example, "rein lameness" has no structural cause in the body of the horse. Consequently, the quality of a horse's training is a very decisive criterion of value.

Unfortunately, the quality of training is often assumed from the horse's list of competition successes. While there are excellent horse people in the competition world, it is noteworthy that we see very successful horses at the highest championship levels (Olympic Games, World Equestrian Games) who "disappear from the picture" after a relatively short time despite intensive medical and paramedical support! Many horses climb to the highest level of the sport in spite of poor and rough training methods. The price is very often mental and physical damage to these horses.

The higher the level of training a horse has reached, the higher the presumed financial value of the horse. It is easy to overlook that many horses may have been subjected to crude, forceful riding methods: Such horses show physical and mental damage that frequently is not visible even to the veterinarian and expert but which nevertheless can restrict rideability and usefulness. Tension that has long manifested in the poll and back of a horse can reduce the suitability of this animal to zero for an average rider. The well-trained horse distinguishes himself in that he can be ridden without a problem

by anyone. Frequently, a horse is declared unrideable because he was ruined through rough training. It is not uncommon to see the loss in the horse's value attributed to conditions that have little to no effect on performance, such as minor changes of the spinous processes as identified on radiographs.

A horse with a blemish-free back as identified on radiographs may respond poorly to a heavy or rough rider. The equestrian capabilities of a buyer play a very large role in the development of rideability issues and rein lameness. In my opinion, only extreme findings, as for example advanced bony changes of the spinous processes, lead to issues even with the best riders.

The examining veterinarian is generally not in a position to evaluate the quality and success of training in advance of the examination, or with what competency the horse will be ridden after the sale.

Even suspensory injuries, which have become an overly common diagnosis, are directly related to the quality of the training, as discussed in chapter XX (p. 172). A horse that has been forcefully compressed into a frame is under significantly greater risk of suffering such damage as compared to a classically and correctly trained horse. For example, many sales horses have been trained too quickly due to time pressures and sometimes they enter the sales barn with injuries. Here again, the role of the examining veterinarian is challenging at best since no expert is able to be clairvoyant!

An interested buyer should pay careful attention to how the seller interacts with and trains the horse. No matter whether the horse is being sold at auction or through a private enterprise, it is important to pay attention to whether or not the horse has been trained according to classical principles rather than having been compressed and squeezed into a frame. Forced training techniques lead to various problems: The horse is hard to ride and train, and perhaps has elevated health risks. Proactive animal welfare comes through Classical Riding theory that preserves rideable and healthy horses.

The Training Scale has an extreme value as a guideline for correct horse riding:

Rhythm—Suppleness—Contact—Impulsion—Straightness—Collection

XXVIII.

SUMMARY

A Review

BACK TO THE PROVEN PRINCIPLES OF TRAINING

The foundation of Classical Riding theory, which has been valid for about 100 years, has been discussed in detail. The central principles of this philosophy are not being lived up to consistently; this is evidenced by what is seen in many top national and international horses, as well as the broad mass of horses presented at regional and small competitions, shows and auctions. It has long been recognized that today's path is not correct for the horse. Instead, we should heed the advice: "Go back to the proven principles!" We run the risk of one day colliding with animal welfare groups. Such a development could damage all riders, even the riders who place great value on correct horse training. It is alarming that similar warnings were given more than 50 years ago. Erich Glahn wrote in reference to the Olympics of 1956 in Stockholm (The second Olympics after the Second World War):

"The horse moving from the back was denied. The path to leg movers and the 'mechanized horse' was taken. The aids that lead to back movers—supple seat, lower back, driving aids—were disregarded and the means of mechanizing were held high, as the typical leg movers were given the high prizes again, as in Helsinki in 1952."

Erich Glahn, *Reitkunst am Scheideweg* [Equitation at the crossroads], Erich Hoffmann Verlag, Heidenheim, 1956, p. 89

Glahn called emphatically for a return to the Classical Training principles:

"'Impulsion'—This was what Saumur and the true representatives of the great French dressage riders demanded first of all. They increased the demand to 'veritable impulsion,' meaning thoroughly forward impulsion through the poll, and found themselves in full agreement with the traditional German, Swedish, Dutch and Austrian-Hungarian concept of dressage, which has as the end goal, the pinnacle of the riding art: the back mover. This was preached by Steinbrecht and Seeger, Oskar Stensbeck and Meixner, Josipowitsch and Seunig, Westphalen and Walzer, Bürkner and Wätjen, G. Rau and Decarpentry."

Erich Glahn, *Reitkunst am Scheideweg* [Equitation at the crossroads], Erich Hoffmann Verlag, Heidenheim, 1956, p. 90

It is hard to understand how we can have the exact same development and the same problem before us almost 60 years after this publication. The difference lies merely in the consequences. Breeding has improved the horses, so the legs fly higher.

Technical perfection has improved and the leg mover has become the measure of all things. Logically the question is asked: How long can we keep going on this path? We have long lost the riding culture and loyalty to the concept of riding as an art.

For me, the same question has existed for years: "How is it that we read and teach one concept yet accept and honor exactly the opposite?" I know no answer to this question!

Heinz Meyer comments about the evolution of the dressage sport in the 1990s: He urgently discusses the status of hyperflexion/rollkur and references the publication, "The Nine Ethical Principles of Horsemanship" (p. 9):

---◆---

"Evil tongues say that such ethical principles have been recently proclaimed because reality is so far from the ideal. Even worse tongues represent the view that such principles have an alibi function, meaning that the organizations hide a bleak reality in many areas behind them and a limited ability to improve the situation."

Heinz Meyer, *Rollkur*, Wu Wei Verlag, Schondorf, 2008, p. 41

---◆---

In his extensive work, which is a standard treatise about derailed training methods, Heinz Meyer clearly outlines the contrast between the ideal that is enthusiastically announced and instructed, and the reality at competition grounds. Many people who care about the well-being of the horse regularly experience this unacceptable conflict at home. It seems logical that those who have the responsibility and authority should intervene, but when they do not, it may be because: a) There is a lack of knowledge or acceptance; or b) There is little interest.

Both answers throw a very negative shadow over the equestrian world. Our main protagonists, the horses, can't speak for themselves. On behalf of animal welfare, it would seem that riders, trainers, riding organizations, officials and judges have a duty to ensure that the rules are applied consistently and as specified. Economic concerns like sponsor money and television ratings also should have a strong role in standing behind the well-being of the horse.

Gustav von Dreyhausen writes about the riding and training system present after World War II:

---◆---

"If I have judged correctly, I would like to say that today's German art of riding lacks nothing more for perfection than to recognize and honor what is already begun, as well as to spread the practical application of the terms suppleness (without force according to Herrn von Heydebreck) plus impulsion. Perhaps in the past we adhered excessively to formalism. But, if this high state is achieved with the core (relaxed impulsion) then you can quietly make the claim to be in first place in international competition."

Gustav von Dreyhausen, *Grundzüge der Reitkunst* [Basic course of horsemanship], New Edition, Olms Press, Hildesheim, Zürich, New York, 1983, p. 25

---◆---

Despite the vaunted high quality of the German training philosophy, Gustav von Dreyhausen sensed a present and overvalued formalism. For him the root was in the past. He believes in a positive future on the basis of widely developed riding theory that only needed small improvements. He could not suspect that his warning marked the beginning of a dangerous and false evolution.

The question remains: Where has the highest value of Classical Training from the first half of the last century gone?

XXIX.

SCIENCE

Its Role and Limitations

METHODS OF PROOF ARE LACKING

I hear consistently from people that my theses are not proven scientifically. These are people who use more or less forceful training methods, have been rewarded by the established system, and who feel confirmed through habit and false examples or through success. They make assertions and stand against me with their own practices and experiences. They are right in one regard: my explanations are not scientifically established because the necessary methods of proof are still lacking.

Nevertheless I maintain that it could be proven today if science could support the correctness of the logic of Classical Riding theory. I give you the grounds for my view of things: Any "sport" that brings two living beings together and still takes up the flag of aesthetics and harmony can't so easily be scientifically and/or purely physically studied, analyzed and evaluated.

As has been discussed, riding, and especially dressage riding, is about harmony. But harmony can only exist when there is no mental and physical tension between the partners.

This fact makes it clear that an experienced rider doesn't need science to be able to differentiate good, from less good, from bad. A rider sits relaxed on the back of an unknown horse, feels the back with her seat, the trunk with her calves and the horse's mouth with sensitive hands and knows in seconds if the horse will be an unwilling partner that has been trained with force, or will be a compliant partner developed through Classical Training techniques.

Recently I heard a question posed by a top dressage athlete on the subject of training principles: "Where is it scientifically proven that tension is damaging?"

To me, this question is bizarre. On one hand, he agrees that the horses are tense. On the other hand, anyone who has experienced lower back pain understands the painful tension that results. Physicians, especially those involved with sports medicine, are able to answer this question, unambiguously. An entire profession of physiotherapists makes their living by loosening up painful tension!

Even if the scientific proof for my position is lacking, through knowledge of cell biology research, scientists in human medicine have proven how muscle cells function and how tension develops. Physicians agree that such muscular tension can cause damage to tendons, ligaments and joints in addition to creating limitations on muscular function and performance.

Tension is the enemy of every sport! Tension affects health and also adversely affects harmony and aesthetics in riding. Waldemar Seunig explains about the importance of developing a good seat:

---◆---

"These seat exercises free the beginner more and more from imbalances and are the best protection against enemy of the state number one: stiffness."

Waldemar Seunig, *Reitlehre von heute* [Riding lesson from today], Erich Hoffmann Verlag, Heidenheim, 1956, p. 82

---◆---

There is a long list of authors who have come to the same conclusions after many decades of their own experience. Rather than having to prove the value of classical philosophy after an illogically forced method has been introduced, the question should be phrased this way: "When will tension-laden, mechanized riding be outlawed as harmful to horses?"

Who asks for proof that a gymnast or a ballet dancer must be supple to remain healthy?

How can a rider or trainer believe that she can ride a harmonious test when it is built on forced training methods that force the horse's head down, stiffen his back, poll and haunches, and cause psychological stress?

The horse is a prey animal that needs to carry his ears and eyes high. A training philosophy that dia-metrically opposes the being of one of the two partners can never lead to harmony. Imagine a dance pair, where the leader wants to force harmony and suppleness using muscular strength against his partner and, when necessary, use devices to force an unnatural position!

Classical Riding theory and its biomechanical foundation need not be scientifically proven in an attempt to justify inappropriate behavior of today. History shows repeatedly and at regular intervals that the attempt to train horses through mechanical and forceful means invariably fails.

XXX.

RIDING CULTURES

Dialogue Instead of Exclusion

ACCEPTING DIFFERENT TRAINING GOALS

For many years, I have campaigned in my seminars for tolerance and acceptance of other riding cultures and training philosophies.

Like many of my contemporaries, I, too, grew up with the teachings and the philosophy of the German Equestrian Federation (FN), our oversight organization. I have learned the Training Scale and tried to apply it as well as possible. In recent years, it has become obvious to me that there is a growing group of riders and horse fans whose horses, although well ridden, look and move differently. They have little or no impulsion. The back does not swing although these horses are very nice to sit on. The concept of Contact doesn't exist in the same context as classical theory. Rhythm has little to no meaning. Natural crookedness is handled in a different way and horses are straightened through other means.

I emphasize that in well-ridden horses the balance points are *different*, not better or worse! This "other" I have discovered primarily in the worlds of Iberian, Western and gaited horse riding. Whoever has ridden these well-trained horses from other equestrian cultures can confirm that these training philosophies would easily pass an examination based on animal welfare and "ethical principles."

Nevertheless to this day, riding and horse training have been lumped together. The differences in the balance of horses and in the training goals with the backdrop of history are not appreciated. People talk *over* one another, not *with* one another. I challenge our associations to finally think about the differences and similarities between various equestrian cultures. I challenge the various worlds to recognize each other, to respect and at least to make the attempt to understand each other. In this way, there can be fruitful communication and learning from each other. An FEI dressage rider should have an idea about why an Iberian horse or a Western horse, having been trained according to those traditions, trots on the circle with head and neck extended. Why in this manner of riding it's about "shoulder control," whereas contact with the outside rein plays a subordinate role, if any. There are many highly interesting thoughts about training in the different cultures that could be useful to all riders if they would take the time to learn about and understand them.

From a wider vantage, a rider is better able to choose a path for her riding pursuits and her horse. It is counterproductive to mix the concepts relating to the balance of the horse! Certainly a rider may try interesting aspects from one riding culture and find out, for example, "It can be that light? Why have I had so much weight in the hands for so many years?"

It helps every rider's development when she looks into the training of other horse breeds and other riding cultures, both practically and theoretically. A balanced seat can be felt faster on a Western or Iberian horse than it can on a Warmblood full of impulsion. It can also be beneficial to sit on a horse that sensitively follows the seat and is ridden with the lightest leg and rein aids, like a well-trained Western horse. We should talk more and compare different riding cultural ideas with our own, and then try out new methods.

In reality, we regularly find people today who invent new riding theory, talk about it eloquently and see themelves as the hub of the universe. We don't need new riding theory, nor is there likely to be a new conclusive one. The anatomy of the horse was, is, and remains the same. Our riding rules are founded on the anatomy of the horse and the decades of experiences of excellent riders.

Along the way I would like to stimulate consideration about the regional, historically evolved and differing riding cultures. The "omnipotent" dominance of modern competitive sport, which is now oriented toward the "spectacle," cannot leave other mature training philosophies in its wake and erase innumerable regional and extra-regional, traditional riding cultures. Different breeds were bred for specialized purposes and have been ridden differently for centuries. For example, such horses may move in what might be considered an incorrect, tense medium trot when compared to Classical Riding theory. National and breed associations should encourage respect and retention of regional training philosophies. Riding and horse training is not solely about a 20- by 40- (or 20- by 60-) meter arena and competitions, but rather is also about the preservation of many different cultures.

Tear down dogmatic walls

Recognition of the diversity of breeds and culturally defined training could awaken a wonderful dialogue that tears down walls of dogma to advance the concept of lightness to which everyone strives.

The FEI should assure that Article 401 of its own rules doesn't just sit on paper. Moreover, a world federation with the importance of the FEI should be conscious of the fact that examples created by today's media have a big influence on all horse nations. We need examples that express the classical principles and show young people a path that has the horse and his welfare as the central focus of all the effort!

I wish our officials great courage, a sure hand and a sound feel for the steering of the "most beautiful sport in the world" into the future.

Heartfelt Thanks!

I thank my endlessly energetic German publisher, Isabella Sonntag, and her team. You are truly a fantastic team, capable of effectively motivating your authors, even with intensive support in emergencies! Thank you for your work. Thanks to Sandra Bürgel for her assistance in compiling the "dedication list." Sabine Neumann helped me substantially with the development of the text, especially the introductory chapter. All the statistics came from her research. Her thoughts inspired further analysis and observations. It was very helpful that she is an experienced rider. Many thanks for your motivated work, dear Sabine! Not least, thanks to my riding graphic artist Christine Orterer for her tireless commitment. She worked on our project despite the hay harvest and kept me busy in picture selection. Thank you for your commitment!

Finally, a special thanks goes to my wife, Johanna. I'm sure most readers can imagine how much time and energy was needed for the development of a reference book. For an endlessly long time, I had to pore over the literature, think it through and test it in actual practice. The "two finger writing system" is also not the fastest. Finally, there were days, weeks and months of work, which weren't especially easy for a practitioner like me. In short, the family, this time more than before, had to deal with a member that was always reading, writing, searching desperately for a literature citation and was often nervous, tired or grumpy. Most of this load was carried by my wife, Johanna. In the heat of the final phase, she spent many hours with me at the computer, selecting photos. Dear Johanna, I thank you from the bottom of my heart for your patience and support! You were and are the best partner and "manager" that I could ever wish for! Hopefully you know that you will need a lot of energy for the next projects!

Many thanks,
Euer Gerd

Trafalgar Square Books would like to thank translator Coralie Hughes and editor Dr. Nancy Loving for their efforts in the production of the English edition of this book.

BASIC RULES OF CONDUCT IN HORSE SPORT

Rule 1: Riding must be distinguished by respectful interaction between participants. All equestrian athletes deserve the same respect and esteem regardless of their level of instruction, athletic success, and material wealth; regardless of their style of riding; and regardless of their preferred breed of horse.

Rule 2: Every equestrian should be confronted in a fair and constructive manner by a riding friend or associate when there are apparent deficiencies in the equestrian's instruction and/or his/her interaction with his/her horse runs counter to the "Ethical Principles of Horsemanship" (see p. 9).

Rule 3: Competitive success, or lack thereof, depends on the rider's qualities. The ability to look at one's performance objectively and (self-) critically is more noble and effective then assessing the horse's abilities as the source of deficiency.

Rule 4: The trainer/instructor must be technically grounded in pedagogically impeccable theory. He must promote personality development in the riding student entrusted to him, including autonomous and socially acceptable behavior. He must always set an example in his own commitment to horsemanship and reject illegal and/or cruel performance-enhancing methods.

Rule 5: The riding student treats his/her riding teacher with the same respect that he/she expects to receive. Open discussion regarding fears and expectations is more proactive than silent struggle and/or emotional outbursts.

Rule 6: Parents of young riders should encourage their children while still ensuring expectations are in line with reality.

Rule 7: When boarding or training in a full-care facility, the rider entrusts his/her horse to the barn manager and barn staff, and expects good treatment and care that meets the needs of the horse. Service rendered by barn staff should be recognized and appreciated. Occasional mistakes should be reasonably discussed and resolved.

Rule 8: The competition judge must score a performance without prejudice on the basis of his/her technical training and should never be suspected of bias.

Continued on page 232

Rule 9:	The competitor must accept the judgment of the judge in the evaluation of his/her ride. When an evaluation is not understood, a clarifying conversation with the judge is the only fair resort. Public controversy disqualifies the rider and goes against the basic rules of sport.
Rule 10:	Breeders and horse dealers must follow the laws governing the horse trade and match the horse's level of training and the expected use of the horse with the appropriate buyer.
Rule 11:	Sport officials must be conscious of their special responsibility to the sport and the horses. Officials are not just responsible for the orderly conduct of business at a riding facility, association, or competition; they are also representatives of and spokespeople for the interests of equestrian athletes, trainers, and breeders, in politics, agriculture, and business.
Rule 12:	Every equestrian athlete is the beneficiary of the available structures and opportunities within his/her sport. All those who work voluntarily or full-time for the long-term benefit of horse sports deserve recognition and support.

INDEX